The Search for the Secure Base

In recent decades, attachment theory has gained widespread interest and acceptance. However, the relevance of attachment theory to clinical practice has never been clear. With *The Search for the Secure Base*, attachment becomes for the first time a therapeutic modality in its own right.

The Search for the Secure Base introduces an exciting new attachment paradigm in psychotherapy with adults, describing the principles and practice of attachment-informed therapy in a way that will be useful to beginners and experienced therapists alike. Based on the scientific foundations of attachment theory and research, Jeremy Holmes identifies the areas within which attachment-informed therapy operates, including secure base, exploration and pleasure, anger and protest, and loss. Therapeutic techniques include providing a secure base, methods of listening and responding, facilitation of emergent meaning, and reflexive practice. Jeremy Holmes uses a wide range of clinical and literary examples to illustrate these techniques, and discusses topics such as basic fault, the intergenerational transmission of attachment insecurity and working with traumatized and abused clients. Viewing attachment-based therapy as a variant of object relations, the book argues strongly for a rapprochement between psychoanalysis and attachment theory.

The Search for the Secure Base will be welcomed by practitioners and trainees in Psychotherapy, Psychoanalysis, Psychiatry, Psychology, Counselling, Social Work and Nursing.

Jeremy Holmes is Consultant Psychotherapist in North Devon and Senior Lecturer in Psychotherapy in the University of Exeter. He is current chair of the psychotherapy faculty of the Royal College of Psychiatrists. He is the author of over 100 papers and book chapters as well as 12 books, including the acclaimed *John Bowlby and Attachment Theory* and *Introduction to Psychoanalysis*, with Anthony Bateman.

The Search for the Secure Base

Attachment theory and psychotherapy

Jeremy Holmes

First published 2001 by Brunner-Routledge
27 Church Road, Hove, East Sussex BN3 2FA

Simultaneously published in the USA and Canada
by Taylor & Francis Inc
325 Chestnut Street, 8th Floor, Philadelphia, PA 19106

Brunner-Routledge is an imprint of the Taylor & Francis Group

© 2001 Jeremy Holmes

Reprinted 2002

Typeset in Sabon by RefineCatch Limited, Bungay, Suffolk
Printed and bound in Great Britain by Biddles Ltd, Guildford and
King's Lynn
Cover design by Jim Wilkie

British Library Cataloguing-in-Publication Data
A catalogue record for this book is available from the British Library

Library of Congress Cataloging-in-Publication Data
Holmes, Jeremy.
The search for the secure base : attachment theory and
psychotherapy / Jeremy Holmes
p.   cm.
Includes bibliographical references and index.
ISBN 1-58391-151-0 — ISBN 1-58391-152-9 (pbk.)
Psychotherapy.   4. Psychotherapist and patient.   5. Object
relations (Psychoanalysis)   I. Title.
RC455.4.A84 H657   2000
616.89'14 – dc21   00-054664

ISBN 1-58391-151-0 (hbk)
ISBN 1-58391-152-9 (pbk)

For Martha

Contents

Illustrations

Figures

Tables

Preface

Finding a title for a book is rather like naming a baby. After the evanescent pleasures of conception, there follows a long period of gestation, usually a mixture of excited anticipation, some discomfort and eventual hard labour. Then the moment comes when a name becomes a necessity. I first thought, provocatively, of 'Why I am not a Psychoanalyst', but soon rejected it – the book assumes common ground between attachment theory and psychoanalysis, not an implied fight. Next I considered 'Thinking about Listening'. The ability to listen and think at the same time is clearly what psychotherapists do; attachment theory understands that process, since secure attachment arises out of the ability of parents to see the child as a thinking being in its own right, and to think about themselves as care-givers and their impact on their dependents. One of the key hypotheses of this book is that what good therapists do with their patients is analogous to what successful parents do with their children. So 'Thinking about Listening' was right in principle, but as a phrase somehow seemed too bland and unfocused. Finally, when I settled on 'The Search for . . .', I was torn between '*a* Secure Base' and '*the* Secure Base'. The difference may seem minuscule but the latter implies a universal psychic entity comparable to 'the good breast' or 'the holy grail', whereas the former suggests a more historically immediate struggle for consensus in the psychological sciences. In the end, I opted for *the* as conferring greater authority on the secure base concept, but both senses are implicit in the book.

There has been an explosion of interest in the ideas and research findings that collectively comprise contemporary attachment theory over the past decade. The culmination of this research aspect is Cassidy and Shaver's (1999) magnificent compilation. Attachment ideas have perhaps been slower to percolate through to clinicians, especially those working with adults, but here too the field has changed, and these days attachment seems to be on everyone's lips. My own perspective is unashamedly clinical, this being my third attempt at writing a book about attachment in the past 10 years. I started with a biography and exposition of the ideas of John Bowlby who, with Mary Ainsworth, was the originator of attachment theory

(Holmes 1993). This was followed by a collection of essays linked by the attempt to show how attachment theory, whose main clinical applications had been to work with children and families, could inform and guide the practice of psychotherapy with adults, mainly in psychiatric settings (Holmes 1996). The present volume is in a sense a continuation of that project, but here I try to grapple more intensely with the connections and separations between psychoanalysis and attachment theory, and develop the theme of narrative as a bridging concept that brings together clinical practice, attachment research and the psychoanalytic tradition.

One of the paradoxes of psychology and psychotherapy is that although the seminal ideas in the field generally aspire to universality, more than other branches of science they often reflect both the personality of their inventors and the *Zeitgeist* within which they were working – reassuring perhaps for those who believe in counter-transference. Certainly, my own combination of avoidance and ambivalence has meant that I have oscillated in my relationship to psychoanalysis ever since it swam into my ken, being both deeply attracted by it and suspicious of its insights and mysteries. Attachment theory is where I seem to have found a home, a theory that was, at least in its origins, itself ambivalent in its relationship to psychoanalysis. But I am by nature an integrator, a quality that no doubt, to some extent, reflects a certain cowardice and inability to own healthy aggression, but also has virtues when no single undisputed psychological paradigm reigns supreme. What I write is necessarily coloured not just by personal strengths and weaknesses, but the necessarily integrative context in which I work as a consultant psychiatrist in psychotherapy, primarily in the National Health Service.

In trying to assess the relative contributions of psychoanalysis and attachment theory, I adopt an integrationist perspective, hoping that each discipline can helpfully illuminate the other. Attachment theory puts the search for security above all other psychological motivators, and posits the attachment bond as the starting point for survival, a precondition for all meaningful human interactions. Psychoanalysis starts from desire, rather than safety. For Freud, what binds us to the object is not the need for protection but libido, the gratification that comes from the satisfaction of oral need. This polarization is reduced once an object relations rather than a classical psychoanalytic viewpoint is adopted. Bowlby (1988) insisted that attachment theory was no more than a scientifically based variant of object relations theory, and Fairbairn's (1952) famous statement 'sex is a signpost to the object' is a similarly convergent concept.

Both attachment theory and psychoanalysis can be described as binary theories. Love and hate, eros and thanatos, the life instinct and the death instinct, splitting and integration, are the polarities with which psychoanalysis works. The equivalent polarities for attachment theory are approach and avoidance, security and insecurity, attachment and loss.

Bowlby (1988) contrasts proximity-seeking with flight when the individual perceives or fears danger, which, in normal circumstances, would be flight to the secure base. Severe pathology arises when the individual is confronted with danger but has no sense of a secure base to which to turn – or, even worse, if the supposedly secure base is itself the source of threat. Unprovoked aggression, directed towards the self or others, may arise out of the overwhelming anxiety provoked by this unresolvable dilemma (Fisher-Mamblona 2000). Other aspects of aggression may be part of normal exploratory, foraging or territorial drives, and may also be a means of maintaining a secure bond. In psychoanalysis, the counterpart of libido is the death instinct and its manifestations in such emotions as envy, rage and perversity. A secure psychology needs to be able to draw on all these ideas, and more.

Clarity of vision is essential in any psychological theory, especially those that inform psychotherapy. Psychotherapy research suggests that therapists with clear models get better outcomes than those whose theoretical underpinning is less focused. But both psychoanalysis and attachment theory can run the risk of reductionism, in the sense of seeing all pyschological phenomena as manifestations of one or other aspect of their theory. In addition, both have implicit moral overtones, which can likewise be a strength or a weakness. Attachment theory contrasts secure and insecure attachment and sees the former as a desirable state to aim for in psychotherapy. In contrast to those who are insecurely attached, or have disorganized patterns, securely attached people are more likely to regard others as sentient beings and so to develop compassion and considerateness in their relationships. Similarly, Kleinian psychoanalysis tries to foster a move towards depressive position thinking in which self and other are seen as whole objects, mixtures of good and bad, in contrast with the paranoid-schizoid position, which relies on splitting and projection and, therefore, distorts reality in maladaptive ways.

These sophisticated psychological versions of what it is to live a good life can themselves become clichés, in which their subtley and complexity is denied. The various patterns of insecure attachment often co-exist with security and there may be oscillations between them, just as the tension between depressive position and paranoid-schizoid position is never fully resolved. Here the two theories come together not only as developmental models, but also as moral maps. Having a secure base will foster depressive position thinking and, conversely, the capacity to relate to whole objects will facilitate the achievement of secure base in relationships.

This brings us to the third strand of this book: the link between attachment and narrative. F.R. Leavis (1975) described the novel as a 'moral tale', and the stories that our patients tell us reveal not just attachment patterns and the balance between depressive position and paranoid thinking, but also a moral universe of meanings and attributions which we must enter if an attachment bond, or therapeutic alliance, is to develop. Psychological life is embodied in stories, and that is where psychotherapists start from, helping patients to begin to tell their story, to make sense of the stories they are caught up in, and to break free from the distorted stories which may have been imposed upon them or which they may have learned to tell themselves.

This emphasis on stories is a reminder that this is the work of a clinician rather than a theorist or researcher. I see myself primarily as a host and catalyst, inviting patients and colleagues into a space where creative thinking can begin to occur. A catalyst, literally, is something that brings reactants into close enough proximity so that they can begin to interact. A book such as this is also catalytic in the sense of hosting other people's ideas, research findings and life stories in the hope that the reader, as guest, will gain some enjoyment and understanding from them. In a similar vein, this work could not have happened without a network of relationships and attachments in which I am sometimes host, sometimes guest.

I end then by acknowledging many debts of gratitude. First and foremost, as always, to my family, and especially Ros and Josh, who provide the secure base without which any exploration and discovery is compromised by anxiety and thus unenjoyable. Next, I am deeply grateful to my patients, not just for providing me with a fascinating and rewarding job, but also, ironically, for helping me, through their pain, to know myself better. I hope they will not object to the case histories in this book, which are both true and false – I have tried to invent, change and make anonymous clinical material in such a way that it remains faithful to life, while at the same time maintaining confidentiality. For those who have explicitly given permission for me to tell their stories, I am especially grateful. Next, I thank my colleagues, friends and family, to whom many of the ideas in this book will appear familiar, arising as they did out of conversations, e-mail correspondence, supervisions and seminars with, among others, Nic Sarra, Anthony Bateman, Ros Holmes, Lorne Loxtercamp, Judy Malone, Chris Evans, Glenn Roberts, Peter Fonagy, Anna Harrison-Hall, Howard Steele, Sebastian Kraemer, Adelheid Muller, Arietta Slade and Robert and Lorraine Tollemache. Finally, I must thank those who have invited or encouraged me to share my ideas at various conferences and seminars, especially Peter Hoey, Jon Monson, Tony Bates, Charlie Hampson and Ian McIlwain. I seem to be a member of that species which needs an external stimulus to think and work. Nothing concentrates the mind more than the knowledge that one has to give a lecture at a defined point in the not-too-distant future. This book is the distillation of that combination of fear and exhilaration. I hope the reader will find it an interesting and serviceable brew.

Chapter 1

The psychological immune system

An extended analogy

Modern medicine began with Jenner's discovery of vaccination against smallpox. The notion of disease agents and the body's defences against them – the science of immunology – remains a central medical paradigm, even if it is now recognized that disease also arises when defences themselves become disordered and that illness can come from within the body as well as from without.

Defence and the integrity of the individual organism are central to physical health. Attachment theory takes as its starting point a comparable need for psychological security, and sees much psychological ill-health as resulting from compromised safety systems. For Bowlby (1988), the key to psychological security is the attachment bond. The vulnerable newborn infant on the ancestral savannah needed to ensure proximity to care-givers if he was to be safe from predation. The mother–infant attachment responses (i.e. distress calls and proximity-seeking) keep him safe from macro-predation and help regulate his emotional states, just as the antibody-rich colostrum she provides keeps micro-organisms at bay.

For Winnicott (1965), famously, 'there is no such thing as an infant, only mother and infant together'. Our physical and psychological security depends utterly on our connections with other people. To paraphrase Auden (1962), we must attach to one another or die. What has changed is that threat comes now not so much from competing species as from our own kind – the Stranger – and, as the idea of the Oedipus complex encapsulates so clearly, from the fact that those we love are also potential competitors and rivals. Relational competence in adult life starts from attachment patterns in childhood. In Chapter 3, I look in detail at how stress and trauma in childhood have long-term effects on an adult's relational competence, including ability to parent – a finding that applies to primates generally and not just to our own species (Rosenblum et al. 1994). Chapter 7 shows how attachment patterns provide a psychosocial mechanism for inter-generational transmission.

Affects and their disorders are central to many psychological illnesses and each can be seen in terms of attachment. The psychological immune system is mediated via *affect*. Our feelings alert us to whether we or our loved ones are safe or in danger. As Bowlby (1988) remarked, falling in love essentially means the formation of an attachment bond, whether between two adults or between parent and child. Sadness and sometimes depression result if an attachment bond is severed, anger and anxiety if it is under threat. Mania is a triumphant and delusional sense that attachment bonds can be dispensed with altogether or effortlessly formed. Excessive fears of attack underlie many phobias, and threats to status within the group play a significant part in the onset and maintenance of depression. Borderline personality disorder can be usefully seen as a disorder of the regulation of affect in which, for example, minor threats to a tenuous attachment bond are experienced as devastating and disequilibrating.

Self-esteem and security are intimately linked. We feel good about our-selves to the extent that we feel part of a network of family and friends and valued within that network. With the backing of such a group we feel we 'cannot fail'. As we go about our business – which is, for the most part, relational – we are constantly appraising situations and our part within them. The capacity to negotiate and think about relationships – whether affiliative or aversive – increases the chances of maintaining individuals' integrity and security and of optimizing their 'resource-holding potential' (Gilbert 1997). But just as the immune system may react excessively to threat in allergic conditions like asthma, or against the self in autoimmune diseases, so this appraisal mechanism may be faulty, especially if attachment bonds are weak. Negative thoughts, such as thinking of potential dangers to the self in new situations, are necessary if we are to evaluate possible threats from those we encounter. Like the phagocytosis of potentially cancerous cells by lymphocytes, these fears are normally disposed of by the 'psycho-logical immune system' and banished to unconsciousness. If we have good self-esteem, based on secure attachment, we know we will be all right. But without a secure base, they may persist. Then minor setbacks may come to look like disasters; the world becomes threatening; the mental pain associ-ated with loss of status, rather than acting as a spur to the formation of new bonds, may gain a life of its own and feel overwhelming.

A key concept in immunology is that of self–other recognition and its breakdown in disease. Failure of the normal differentiation of self and other is central to psychotic illness. In paranoia, sufferers may attribute to reality malevolent intentions that properly belong to the self. In schizophrenia, the normal labelling system by which we distinguish our own thoughts and feelings from external perceptions is compromised. As a result, sufferers feel naked and exposed – defenceless – and may react with extreme terror, withdrawal or occasionally violent counter-attack.

In autoimmune disorders, sufferers attack their own tissues as though they were intruders. A similar process is at work in the self-denigration and intrusive unwanted thoughts of depression, which are the target of much of cognitive behaviour therapy. Excessive immune responses are seen in atopic conditions like asthma; anxiety disorders and ambivalent attachment have comparable features. Sometimes an appropriate immune response fails to a occur at all; the analogue here is with those emotionally promiscuous individuals often suffering from borderline disorders, who are unable to protect themselves from emotional abuse.

Psychoanalysis has long recognized the existence of 'defence mechanisms', first systematically explored and classified by Anna Freud (1936; Valliant 1993). In classical psychoanalysis, defences are both necessary – it is useful not to be aware of potentially disruptive erotic and aggressive feelings – and an encumbrance – the effort of removing such thoughts from awareness restricts and compromises loving and self-assertive possibilities. Freud's resolution of this was to argue that, 'where id is there ego shall be'; in other words, self-knowledge is the highest good, but feelings have to be seen for what they are, not acted on. An attachment version of this would argue that understanding affect and imagination – our own and those of others' – are essential to survival if we are to negotiate the vagaries of interpersonal life. The capacity to reflect on one's story is a feature of secure attachment in which people find a middle path between being overwhelmed with emotion in ambivalent attachment and the switched-offness of the avoidant position.

An attachment perspective on defence emphasizes the inter- rather than the intra-personal aspect. Defence mechanisms describe particular patterns of intimate relationship. A securely attached individual can draw on the support of others (via the 'secure base') when needed and can talk coherently and with appropriate affect about psychological pain and difficulty (Hesse 1999). If the 'immunity' afforded by the protective other is suboptimal, a compromise will be reached in which the individual sacrifices some aspects of psychic life in return for a modicum of security. The avoidant strategy means staying near to a protective other, but not too near for fear of rejection or aggression – here a measure of intimacy is sacrificed in which affect is 'deactivated' (see Mallinckrodt 2000). The ambivalent individual has been subjected to inconsistent responses when distressed, and so clings to the care-giver even when no danger is present. Here there is a 'hyperactivation' of attachment responses and exploration and autonomy are jettisoned in return for security.

Disorganized attachments are associated with traumatic care-giving. Trauma overwhelms and disrupts the psychological immune system altogether. Disorganized responses and narratives lack any clear coherent strategy for self-protection. They are likely to arise when a care-giver is him or herself the source of threat, an extreme example of which is seen in child abuse. This sets up the typical approach–avoidance oscillation seen in borderline disorders. Less dangerous versions arise when the care-giver has herself been traumatized, and seems unable therefore to cope with infant distress. In both cases, the child may resort to extreme defensive measures to maintain some sort of internal coherence: splitting, dissociation, role reversal and excessive controllingness.

Immunology uses a variety of methods to boost or, occasionally, to dampen the individual's defence mechanisms. Therapy itself can be seen as a sort of 'passive immunization' in which the temporary presence of the therapist provides a measure of protection. This is especially relevant to the companionable interaction (Heard and Lake 1986) of supportive psychotherapy, and in behaviour therapy where the therapist explicitly takes the position of the secure base to help patients face their fears. A basic assumption is that self-awareness is inherently protective. The more we can use our imagination to know ourselves and others better, the more adept we are likely to be at negotiating the interpersonal world we inhabit (Humphrey 1984). A key aim of much psychotherapy, whether dynamic or cognitive, is to enhance consciousness of our own mental life – 'narrative competence' is a psychological equivalent of immunological competence (Holmes 1992). In the latter, around the moment of birth, the body 'knows' itself and so can distinguish between its own antigenic structures and those of potential pathogens. Similarly, coming to know oneself psychologically, and to distinguish between one's own feelings and those of others and, ultimately, to understand the representational nature of thinking itself (cf. Fonagy 1997), is a key to psychological survival.

Therapists aim to create some of the parameters of secure base in their dealings with patients: consistency, reliability, responsiveness, non-possessive-warmth, firm boundaries. This, it is hoped, becomes internalized as a 'place' in the psyche to which the patient can turn when troubled, even after therapy has come to an end. Fonagy (1991) and Meins (1999) argue that a key feature of the parents of securely attached children is their 'mind-mindedness' or reflexive function, the ability to empathize with their children and to see them as separate beings with feelings of their own. Mind-mindedness is also a crucial therapeutic skill.

What is the 'mechanism' underlying this empathic responsiveness? The immune system works on an evolutionary principle of natural selection. There is a huge variety of T-lymphocytes, each with different receptors on its surface. When a new antigen is encountered, those immune cells with complementary configurations are 'selected' so they proliferate and are able to mount a full-blown immune response the next time that antigen is met. Empathy depends perhaps on an analogous mechanism. As care-givers, to put ourselves in the other's shoes, we take a small fragment of our own experience and amplify it so that it fits with that of the person in our charge. In this way, our own experience as receivers of care is used when we become care-givers ourselves. Just as a tropical diseases expert needs to be immunized against the organisms she is likely to encounter, so personal therapy for therapists can be seen as an immunization process, not just to protect them and their patients from themselves, but also to extend the range of experience that therapists can then draw on in working with clients.

A final theme in this extended analogy concerns the issue of conscious and unconscious awareness of psychological immune mechanisms. Most of the time, we are no more aware of the part played by the need for security in our everyday life than we are of the workings of our lymphocytes. A 5-year-old who has hurt his knee at school may put a brave face on it until the moment when his parents come to collect him, when he will suddenly burst into tears (see Chapter 3). He has not consciously been waiting for their arrival, but the attachment response can only be activated when the secure base is present. Our security measures are biologically programmed and do not necessarily need to reach consciousness to be activated. In addition, however, there may be an element of active repression. It has been suggested that feelings of dependency and vulnerability are best kept from conscious awareness, since others are a potential source of danger, and even to be aware of weakness may be to reveal it (Nesse 1990). At times it pays us to be unaware of our vulnerability, however much our thoughts and behaviour may be influenced by it.

There is a link here with the rise of individualism and with it the expansion of therapy as a cultural presence. In traditional societies, the secure base is provided by the family and tribal group, with a hierarchy of available care-givers (Van Ijzendoorn and Sagi 1999), although, interestingly, the mother is almost always at the top of the ladder. So long as he is within the bosom of the group, the individual feels safe. Threat is generally located without and illness is attributed to jealousy and witchcraft emanating from an external source, although occasionally angry ancestors are also held responsible (i.e. from within the group).

As this traditional pattern has been superseded by the nuclear and the subnuclear family, so individualism, anomie and alienation become the themes of modern psychological life. To the extent it is not available outside, a secure base has to be constructed within the self. Psychotherapy is needed to facilitate that precarious process. The neo-Kleinian perspective on Oedipus sees gain in being able to stand outside situations – freedom of thought is the prize that compensates for loss of exclusive possession of mother (Britton 1999). Similarly, an 'internal secure base' (i.e. a representation or 'working model' of security) provides freedom of movement, both literally and emotionally, that was not perhaps available in traditional societies. But without a well-functioning psychological immune system, the path of freedom leads to chaos and failure. We accept that universal immunization is necessary for the physical health of our children. Bowlby (1988) insisted that fostering psychological security is an equally important aspect of public health. This book is motivated by a similar attempt to argue the case for psychological stability and security through psychotherapy, other treatment methods in psychiatry, and in society generally.

Chapter 2

The six domains of attachment theory

As a therapeutic modality, attachment theory has had a long gestation, partly because of its ambivalent relationship with psychoanalysis, which, with ethology, was one of its principal forebears. This has been as much a strength as a weakness. Half a century of research now underpins attachment approaches to therapy, and practitioners can feel confident that their interventions are based on evidence rather than unsubstantiated authority or persuasion. The aim of this chapter is to summarize the contribution of attachment ideas to psychotherapeutic practice. Implicit is the view that general or 'non-specific' factors are equally as important in producing good therapy outcomes as the specific features often claimed by 'brand-named' therapies to be the secret of their success. Patients seeking therapy are typically torn between the need for secure attachment and a terror of intimacy. Like Fisher-Mamblona's (2000) goose Feli, they fear aloneness but, at the same time, are terrified of getting close. They want to run away, but have no secure base to run *to*. For people to form a trusting relationship – an external secure base – and then to internalize it so that they feel secure in themselves is a developmental as well as a cognitive process and, inevitably, takes time.

Van Ijzendoorm and Sagi (1999) usefully summarize the findings of attachment theory under four main headings:

- *The universality hypothesis.* In all known cultures, human infants become attached to one or more specific care-givers.
- *The normativity hypothesis.* About 70 per cent of infants become securely attached; the remainder are insecurely attached. There are three main categories of insecure attachment: avoidant, ambivalent and disorganized. Securely attached infants settle more easily in response to stress. Thus, secure attachment is both numerically and physiologically normal.
- *The sensitivity hypothesis.* Attachment security is dependent on sensitive and responsive care-giving.
- *The competence hypothesis.* Differences in attachment security lead to differences in social competence; securely attached children are more

likely to relate successfully to peers and teachers and are less likely to be bullied or to bully.

To these we can add three further hypotheses:

- *The continuity hypothesis* (see p. 28). Attachment patterns in childhood have far-reaching effects on relationship skills and their mental representations in adult life.
- *The mentalization hypothesis*. Secure attachment is based on, and leads to, the capacity for reflection on the states of mind of self and others (Fonagy 1991; Meins 1999).
- *The narrative competence hypothesis*. Secure attachment in childhood is reflected in adult life by the ways in which people talk about their lives, their past and in particular their relationships and associated mental pain (Holmes 1992). Table 2.1 summarizes the connections and continuities between childhood attachment patterns as measured in the Strange Situation and adult narrative competence as revealed in the Adult Attachment Interview (Hesse 1999).

Based on these hypotheses, attachment theory provides a set of linked overarching concepts that embrace many aspects of psychotherapeutic practice. Six main attachment domains can be delineated, each of which can be applied to individuals, couples and families. These comprise secure base, exploration and play, protest and assertiveness, loss, internal working models, and reflective capacity.

The six domains

Domain 1: Secure base

The first, and most important, domain is that of the secure base (SB). 'Secure base' originally referred to the care-giver to whom the child turns when distressed. That secure base may provide secure or insecure attachment depending on circumstances. Thus, confusingly, a secure base may provide an *in*secure attachment experience. The point here is that, without *some* sort of secure base, survival is impossible.

The early attachment thinkers tended to see the secure base in behavioural terms, referring to the care-giver to whom the infant visibly turns when threatened or ill, and who is able, to a greater or lesser extent, to provide the essential protection needed if the infant is to survive. This concept seemed to have limited application to adults until it was realized that the secure base can be seen not just as an external figure, but also as a *representation* of security within the individual psyche.

The original care-giver/child secure base experience can be thought of as

Table 2.1 Adult Attachment Interview classifications and corresponding patterns of infant strange situation behaviour

Adult state of mind with respect to attachment	*Infant strange situation behaviour*
Secure/autonomous (F) Coherent, collaborative discourse. Valuing of attachment, but seems objective regarding any particular event or relationship. Description and evaluation of attachment-related experiences is consistent, whether experiences are favourable or unfavourable. Discourse does not notably violate any of Grice's maxims	**Secure (B)** Explores room and toys with interest in pre-separation episodes. Shows signs of missing parent during separation, often crying by the second separation. Obvious preference for parent over stranger. Greets parent actively, usually initiating physical contact. Usually some contact maintained by second reunion, but then settles and returns to play
Dismissing (Ds) Not coherent. Dismissing of attachment-related experiences and relationships. Normalizing ('excellent, very normal mother'), with generalized representations of history unsupported or actively contradicted by episodes recounted, thus violating Grice's maxim of quality. Transcripts also tend to be excessively brief, violating the maxim of quantity	**Avoidant (A)** Fails to cry on separation from parent. Actively avoids and ignores parent on reunion (i.e. by moving away, turning away or leaning out of arms when picked up). Little or no proximity or contact-seeking, no distress and no anger. Response to parent appears unemotional. Focuses on toys or environment throughout procedure
Preoccupied (E) Not coherent. Preoccupied with or by past attachment relationships or experiences, speaker appears angry, passive or fearful. Sentences often long, grammatically entangled, or filled with vague usages ('dadadada', 'and that'), thus violating Grice's maxims of manner and relevance. Transcripts often excessively long, violating the maxim of quantity	**Resistant or ambivalent (C)** May be wary or distressed even before separation, with little exploration. Preoccupied with parent throughout procedure; may appear angry or passive. Fails to settle and take comfort in parent on reunion, and usually continues to focus on parent and cry. Fails to return to exploration after reunion
Unresolved/disorganized (U) During discussions of loss or abuse, individual shows striking lapse in the monitoring of reasoning or discourse. For example, individual may briefly indicate a belief that a dead person is still alive in the physical sense, or that this person was killed by a childhood thought. Individual may lapse into prolonged silence or eulogistic speech. The speaker will ordinarily otherwise fit Ds, E or F categories	**Disorganized /disoriented (D)** The infant displays disorganized and/or disoriented behaviours in the parent's presence, suggesting a temporary collapse of behavioural strategy. For example, the infant may freeze with a trance-like expression, hands in air; may rise at parent's entrance, then fall prone and huddled on the floor; or may cling while crying hard and leaning away with gaze averted. Infant will ordinarily otherwise fit A, B or C categories

Sources: Adapted from Hesse (1999).

Notes: Descriptions of the adult attachment classification system are summarized from Main *et al.* (1985) and from Main and Goldwyn (1984a, 1998a). Descriptions of infant A, B and C categories are summarized from Ainsworth *et al.* (1978) and the description of the infant D category is summarized from Main and Solomon (1990). Data from Main (1996).

comprising: (1) a set of behaviours activated by threat; (2) a response to those behaviours by the care-giver; and (3) a psychophysiological state that is the end result of those behaviours. Care-giver responses associated with secure attachment include responsiveness, sensitivity, consistency, reliability, attunement, the capacity to absorb protest and 'mind-mindedness', the ability to see the distressed child as an autonomous and sentient being with feelings and projects of his or her own. The psychophysiological state includes such physiological elements as relaxedness, warmth, closeness, feeling soothed, satiation, a full stomach, steady breathing, reduced pulse rate, calmness and a psychological component with thoughts such as 'all's well with the world', 'everything will be alright', that where there was chaos and confusion there is now order, and that everything is 'under control'.

Adults, however seemingly autonomous, as well as making physical contact with loved ones at times of stress, also have an *internal* SB zone – which can also be conceptualized as a schema or object relationship – to which they turn when needed, especially as part of affect regulation. Activating internal SB may come about through comforting thoughts or images and/or behaviours including resorting to self-soothing resources, such as hot baths, bed, favourite foods, music, books or TV programmes, duvets and alcohol. A measure of security must be achieved whatever the cost: psychological survival requires some kind of SB experience, compromised though this may be by the limitations of the care-giver's capacity to give and the recipient's capacity to elicit appropriate care. The internal representation of the secure base can be activated by different parts of the SB cycle – that is presumably why the softness and warmth of baths and bed produce the desired states of calmness.

Pathological variants of SB behaviour include binge eating or starvation, substance abuse, compulsive masturbation or deliberate self-harm. How can apparently self-injurious behaviours produce security? They recreate some element of SB cycle described above and this, in turn, has a soothing function, however self-destructively it has been achieved. For example, escalating chaos followed by relief is characteristic of self-harming episodes in people suffering from borderline personality disorder. Many will describe a temporary feeling of peace and calm when they see blood flow after self-cutting, or when they lie down after taking excessive tablets, or the nurturance they feel following a stomach wash-out. In the starvation behaviour of anorexia, the sufferer struggles with the longing for food – a SB element – and, paradoxically, by temporarily mastering her desire to eat produces comfort: she is not at the mercy of a need for a secure base over which she has no control. The ingredients of these behaviours are also to be found in unhappy couples, for example those for whom sex is only possible after a major row.

The Strange Situation and Adult Attachment Interview delineate insecure patterns of the secure base. Although as used in research both are categorical measures, it is possible to imagine two separate axes: one a horizontal bipolar continuum from dismissing/avoidant through secure attachment to preoccupied/ambivalent, and the other a vertical unipolar axis running from coherent/autonomous to incoherent/disorganized (Figure 2.1). These can be related to what I have called the triangle of attachment (see Figure 2.2; Holmes 1996). Insecure variants are essentially trade-offs. The avoidant individual stays close enough to a rejecting care-giver to get a measure of protection, but not so close as to feel the full pain of rejection. Ambivalent people cling to their care-givers so that they are less at the mercy of their inconsistency. Neither perhaps achieves the full SB state of security and so a sacrifice has to be made. In infants, exploratory play is inhibited; in adult avoidants, intimacy is compromised, while the preoccupied restrict their autonomy in the service of security.

In both variants of insecure attachment, self-esteem is precarious. In ambivalent attachment, it is dependent on the proximity and positive regard of the clung-to attachment figure; if they are lost or critical, ambivalent individuals will suffer. In the avoidant pattern, self-esteem is short-circuited within the self; external validation has little impact, and the avoidant person does his best to be in control and to keep intimacy at bay as it threatens this self-contained system of maintaining self-esteem. At best he can only feel good about himself when giving to others. The secure individual has a balanced self-esteem system that is open to external validation, but not completely dependent on it; a reciprocal relationship, in which giving and getting both play a part, and is sought as the most reliable source of good feelings about the self.

Disorganization and incoherence are so disruptive of the care-giving environment that people will go to great lengths to create some sort of order, however problematic and sub-optimal those efforts may be. For example, there may be attempts at control via obsessionality (as in the anorexia cycle described above); by a switch from responsive to an aggressive and coercive form of care-giving or care-eliciting; by the use of dissociative strategies in which overall chaos is reduced by splitting; by delusional attempts to impose

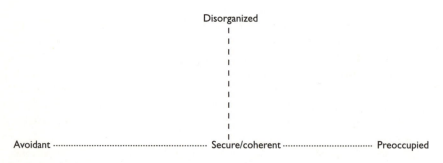

Figure 2.1 Dimensions of secure and insecure attachment

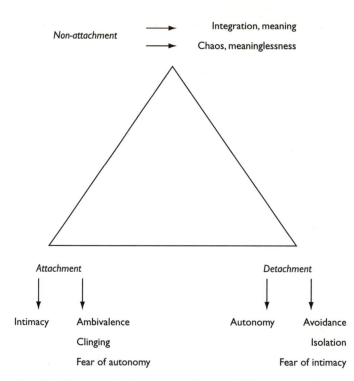

Figure 2.2 The triangle of attachment (Holmes 1996)

coherence from within in the face of either physiological disorganization (i.e. 'genetic' schizophrenia), or environmental confusion (i.e. communication deviance in the family); or through the predictability of clinging to a sick role.

Secure and insecure variants of SB phenomena are to be found within adult relationships. In couples, each adult acts as the secure base for the other, and each brings his or her own internal SB representation and expectation – with varying inbuilt insecurity – into the couple relationship. If the partnership is stable, then out of these representations a 'third element' can be forged, which provides far greater security than either member of the couple can achieve on their own – the relationship itself and the pattern of mutual expectations that implies.

Seeing a relationship as separate from each of its component parts is a point of contact between the psychoanalytic and the attachment perspective. Intimate relationship in adults offers the possibility of moving from a two-person, pre-Oedipal position to a three-person, Oedipal constellation. From a neo-Kleinian perspective, the Oedipal situation is seen as a developmental step where, if the child can tolerate the separateness of the parental couple and the loss of exclusive possession of mother that implies, he or she gains a decentred perspective and a freedom of thought essential for interpersonal success (Britton 1998). The attachment analogue of this process is the establishment of a secure base *representation* – and especially representation in language – so that the child no longer is wholly dependent on the physical presence of the care-giver but can be comforted by the thought of 'mum-and-dad', or 'home'. This, in turn, depends on the care-giver's ability to represent her child's representations; to see the child as a separate and sentient being (Fonagy 1999a). Similarly, healthy functioning in couples depends on the capacity to see and think and talk about their relationship as an entity in its own right, separate from the two individuals who comprise it (see Domain 6 below).

Domain 2: Exploration and enjoyment

Companionable interaction and the capacity for mutual pleasure, whether playful, sexual or intellectual, is central to secure base capacity. Attachment theory postulates that there is a reciprocal relationship between secure base behaviour and exploration. When people feel threatened, they will seek out their secure base and, for the moment, fun and play will be correspondingly inhibited. Anxiety is the enemy of enjoyment. Attachment does not exclude other motivational forces or aspects of relationship, but is a precondition before they can be activated. Insecure children find it difficult to play. Similarly, in adult life, if one member of a couple does not feel secure – for example, worrying that her partner will abandon her at any minute – it is unlikely that she will be able to enjoy their sexual relationship. Helping couples to grasp this very simple concept is often a gateway to understanding sexual difficulties, or their inability to profit from the 'quality time' so beloved of agony aunts and informal advice-givers.

In general, Bowlby (1988) had little to say about sex; perhaps he was keen to emphasize 'his' instinct, as opposed to that of psychoanalysis. There is now a large literature on adult relationships and the ways in which they are shaped by different attachment patterns (Cassidy and Shaver 1999). People may avoid emotional closeness in sex as in all relationships, or may attempt to 'short-cut' to the physiological aspects of secure base while splitting off the emotional and psychological aspects. 'Compulsive' sex may be a manifestation of ambivalent attachment, a form of clinging in which the primary aim is physical proximity rather than pleasure or procreation. A successful sexual relationship involves a number of features relevant to attachment: mutual emotional attunement, the capacity to contain and not feel overwhelmed by mounting excitement, overcoming fear of transgression while retaining repect for boundaries, the capacity to regress and re-integrate, and the ability to separate and cope with loss, secure in the knowledge that a sexual couple as an internal representation will survive.

Domain 3: Protest and anger

Rows with a partner, violence and rage are common reasons for people seeking help, especially men. From an attachment perspective, anger is triggered when there is a threat of separation and, in what is essentially a negative reinforcement schedule, has the function of ensuring that the attachment bond remains intact. A child who runs across a dangerous road is chastised by the care-giving parent to keep him by her side in future.

The role of anger as an attachment regulator can be seen in many different ways in adult relationships. If one member of a couple threatens it by having an affair, this will straightforwardly evoke rage in the betrayed one, as their security and self-esteem is so bound up with their partner. More subtly, anger is often provoked when one member of a couple fails to be considerate or to take into account the other's point of view. As we have seen, a crucial component of the secure base is 'mind-mindedness', the capacity to see the other as having a psychological perspective and feelings of his or her own. 'Inconsiderateness' ignores the other's feelings and so threatens this aspect of the secure base, thus triggering protest in an attempt to re-establish it.

Assertiveness training helps people to escape from the traps of passive submission or uncontrollable rage, and to use anger effectively to restore attachment bonds and to maintain the secure base. Good self-esteem is bound up with secure attachment. For example, relationships, whether within families or between patients and therapists, consist of a series of intimate moments and separations, interspersed with 'ruptures' in communication. People with good self-esteem are usually good at 'rupture repair': they are confident that closeness can be restored, just as the secure infant in the Strange Situation expects that his protest will be heard, his distress will be dealt with and he will be able to return to exploratory play.

Another attachment perspective on anger views unexplained outbursts of rage as a form of 'displacement activity' triggered when an individual is torn between the need for a secure base and the fear of achieving one (Fisher-Mamblona 2000). For example, a spouse might suddenly attack his partner on discovering that she is having an affair. Here the threat to the relationship would activate attachment behaviour, but conflict is exacerbated because the potential secure base is also a source of threat. In this state of unbearable conflict, rage provides some sort of outlet and may possibly help the individual clarify what his real needs are.

Domain 4: Loss

For Bowlby (1988), loss or threatened loss was central to much psychological distress. He viewed the capacity to cope with loss as a key component of psychological maturity. The paradox of intimacy from an attachment perspective is that it can only be achieved if its members can negotiate separateness more or less successfully. For Francis Bacon, a spouse and children were 'hostages to fortune'. To have something is to run the risk of losing it. Taking *this* path means that one cannot take *that* one. In adult relationships, each member brings with him or her a history of separations and losses and of a more or less secure internal secure base which will colour their relationship. One reason why the death of a child is so devastating for couples, and divorce rates are so high after such a tragedy, is that each is so grief-stricken that neither can provide the comfort of a secure base for the other.

Working through past losses is an essential part of attachment-informed therapy. 'Working through' – a glib term for an often unbearably painful process – can only happen because of the possibility of 'representation'; the lost loved one cannot be recovered in the external world, but can be 'reinstated' (to use a Kleinian term) in the inner world of the bereaved. If the therapist can provide a temporary secure base, then the anger and despair associated with bereavement can be negotiated towards at least partial acceptance.

Domain 5: Internal working models

It is impossible to practise an atheoretical psychotherapy. Any attempt to help people in psychological distress will be underpinned by a set of implicit or explicit models about the structure of the mind, the nature of thought, characteristics of intimate relationships, and so on. Different approaches use different languages and it is often hard to distinguish between points of overlap and real differences. For example, the notion of internal representation is described psychoanalytically in terms of an inner world populated with internal objects and the relationships between them. Cognitive therapy focuses on schemata, fundamental and relatively immutable assumptions about the self and its relationships. Systemic therapists have become interested in 'event scripts', sequences of behaviour of self in relation to others that are laid down in childhood and give colour and shape to subsequent relationships. Bowlby's (1988) version was the notion of 'internal working models', a phrase chosen deliberately as an 'action language' that would capture the Piagetian 'scientist-practitioner' process by which children construe their world (Bretherton 1999).

Bowlby (1988) wrote of 'defensive exclusion' to describe the ways in which unwanted painful feelings and thoughts are kept out of awareness, and the consequent restrictions to internal working models, and therefore adaptability, which that entails. Internal working model is a more 'cognitive' construct than the psychoanalytic internal world, which consists of affective schemas associated with significant others. The distinction between implicit and explicit memory can perhaps help overcome the cognitive/affective gap (Schacter 1992). Implicit or procedural memories are those that are laid down in the early years of life and consist of the 'ways in which things are done' (i.e. patterns of relationship), including, for example, parental responses to infant distress, which are stored within the child's mind and which will influence subsequent relationships even if there is no explicit awareness of their role. Explicit or episodic memories are the specific events and self–other behaviours that comprise people's memory-store.

In adult life, each member of a couple brings to it a complex set of working models, schemata, scripts and/or object relationships. Couples are attracted to one another if there is some kind of 'fit' between their own inner world and that of the other. Each must consciously or unconsciously know the steps of the other's dance. The more intimate they are able to be with one another, the more their own inner world will be exposed. Areas of pain and vulnerability will inevitably come into play. Thus, paradoxically, a certain maturity is needed – confidence in the coherence and survivability of the self – for the child-like regression that is inherent in intimacy to take place successfully.

The three main variants of insecure attachment provide a useful framework for thinking about the vicissitudes of this process. The avoidant individual sacrifices intimacy for an exaggerated form of autonomy, while the ambivalent person gives up autonomy for the sake of a dependent form of intimacy (Holmes 1996). Each will seek out a partner who can tolerate the pattern dictated by their internal working models, but each is also unhappy with the restrictions it brings, so every relationship also contains the hope that old patterns will be transcended. Individuals and couples need to come to understand how the 'trigger' points in their relationships – for rows, disappointment or misery – arise at these nodal connections between one person's set of painful assumptions and the other's.

Trauma destroys part of the security regulating system altogether (Garland 1998). If internal working models are partially inactivated, such people become 'immunologically incompetent'. They over-react to minor stimuli reminiscent of the traumatic event, no longer confident that their secure base will protect them, or they fail to react at all to threat and so become embroiled in more and more risky situations. Internal working models are not just restricted but have lacunae, for example in the area of sex or physical violence. People with disorganized attachments, typified in patients suffering with borderline personality disorder, find it hard to provide a consistent relationship pattern for their partners to adapt to, and, except when partners are excessively avoidant, tend to have radically unstable relationships.

Domain 6: Reflexive function and narrative competence

A key finding in the attachment literature is the relationship between 'reflexive function' as revealed in the Adult Attachment Interview – the capacity to talk cogently and coherently about oneself and one's difficulties – and security of attachment (see Chapter 3). The importance of this for psychotherapy is self-evident: psychotherapy is essentially a narrative process in which therapist and patient together develop a dialogue both about the patient's life and the nature of the therapist–patient relationship itself. Therapy is an *in vivo* experience in which the patient learns to become self-reflexive. This is exploited in particluar by the transference-based approaches. When representations can be made explicit in language, they are available for metacognition, or 'thinking about thinking', and so modification. This is the cognitive aspect of the neo-Kleinian conceptualization of the Oedipal situation already referred to.

In summary, attachment theory has a number of features which comprise its unique contribution to psychotherapeutic practice:

- With its ability to move from external observable behaviours to mental representations, attachment theory is able to integrate psychodynamic, cognitive and behavioural perspectives.
- Attachment theory provides a coherent theory of the patient–therapist relationship, seeing it as informed primarily by the patient's need to seek out and find a secure base figure. The attachment model of a responsive care-giver who is likely to promote secure attachment corresponds with that of the good therapist: sensitive, responsive, consistent, reliable and psychologically minded.
- Attachment theory provides, via the Adult Attachment Interview, a theoretical underpinning for the story-telling, story-listening and story-understanding that form the heart of psychotherapy sessions.
- The classification of secure, avoidant, ambivalent and disorganized attachments provides an important evidence-based nosology for psychotherapeutic formulation.
- The notion of the secure base enables some of the apparently self-defeating behaviours found in psychiatric patients, especially those suffering from borderline personality disorder, to be understood, thus informing treatment approaches.

Attachment in practice

The application of these themes to therapeutic work forms the central preoccupation of this book. They form the theoretical background to an attachment-based approach to psychotherapy. But what does it mean to work with attachment in practice? The reader will find in the Appendix details of a Brief Attachment-Based Intervention (BABI) based on the six domains described in this chapter, devised by the author and currently being pioneered in the setting in which I work. At the time of writing, it is in the pilot stage and has not been validated or subjected to controlled evaluation.

There are many case histories in this book, which represent the fruits of psychotherapeutic work informed by attachment over the past 20 years, long preceding this more explicit model. Working from an attachment perspective emphasizes several key aspects of day-to-day practice. None of these are peculiar to attachment approaches, but taken together they form a consistent integrative stance that is characteristic of attachment-based interventions, whether brief or prolonged.

1 *Attunement.* Empathic responsiveness to the patient and one's own emotional state, or 'attunement', is an essential part of any therapeutic intervention. Listening to patients' feelings and, simultaneously, to one's own feelings as they arise in an encounter is essential. Trying to put oneself in an other's shoes and, when necessary, using one's own feelings as a guide to theirs are part of this process.

2 *Emotional proximity.* A secure base in adult life arises out of emotional proximity – rather than, as in childhood, physical closeness – to an understanding and protective care-giver. The arousal of affect, whether sadness and tears, anger or fear, in sessions is a crucial means by which emotional proximity is achieved and arises out of the therapist's efforts at attunement.

3 *Forming and maintaining the therapeutic alliance.* The first task of any therapy is to create a working alliance, in which the patient feels committed to the therapy and has confidence that the therapist can help. Different attachment styles will require different strategies here. The avoidant patient will be wary, and the therapist must respect this caution and allow the patient gradually to feel safe in sessions and to 'come in' at her own pace. The ambivalent patient may mask her anxiety by a too-ready acceptance that therapy is valuable, and may need to be helped to find her own investment in it, for instance by being asked to think carefully about entering therapy before committing herself. The disorganized patient lacks a consistent attachment strategy and may oscillate, miss early sessions, drop out, etc. This must be tolerated and if necessary, the therapist must approach the patient by writing, telephoning or even occasionally visiting until, for instance, the borderline patient is ready to enter treatment. Once formed, the alliance will at times be subject to strains and fracture. 'Alliance rupture repair' is another crucial therapeutic task: without the alliance there can be no secure base, and without secure base there will be no exploration.

4 *Challenge.* Within the context of a secure base, the therapist's task is to challenge habitual assumptions and relationship patterns and create sufficient turbulence for new structures to emerge. Interpretation, confrontation and clarification are all technical means to achieve this end.

5 *Balance.* The aim of attachment-based therapy is always to bring patients into a balanced position *vis-à-vis* themselves and the world. In relation to the therapist, they must neither be too close nor too far; they must be able both to laugh at and take themselves seriously; they must be neither too fearful nor too bold; and so on. The therapist achieves

this balance in different ways with different aspects of attachment style. The avoidant patient is helped to get closer emotionally and to be more open to his feelings; ambivalent patients to get a distance on themselves and to see their feelings in perspective; the disorganized patient to find coherence. It is as though patient and therapist are on a see-saw and, once firmly, safely and trustingly established there, the therapist will always move patients in the opposite direction to the one they habitually take.

6   *The therapist's freedom of movement.* Another helpful metaphor is that of the boxing ring. The ring itself with its containing ropes represents the secure base of the therapy itself – the regularity of time and place and consistency of therapist behaviour. Within the ring, the therapist must always have freedom of movement, never allowing himself to be 'boxed in' or cornered by the patient. The insecure patient wants to hold onto the therapist, to know where he is at all times and to control him. This is typical of insecure attachment patterns, especially ambivalent strategies. The therapist's aim is to help the patient to trust himself, to know that security can only arise from the realization that there is no absolute security, and that being able to choose is what makes for freedom, not clinging on either to oneself or another. Thus the patient who asks, for example, 'Do you like me?' or 'Do you believe in God?' feels that security will flow from a definite answer to her question. The technically correct response is not 'yes' or 'no' as that would be to box oneself in, but rather, for example, to explore why the question is so important to the patient. As recorded by several distinguished therapists (e.g. Symington and Symington 1996), sometimes extreme measures are needed – jokes, outbursts of controlled anger or even shouting – if the therapist is to release himself from being trapped in this way and regain the centre ground within the therapeutic ring.

7   *Negative capability.* This is Keats' well-known prescription for approaching poetry – the capacity to tolerate uncertainty and doubt and to 'stay with' the material. Often one does not know what is going on with a patient. The therapist needs to be able to tolerate that state, secure in the knowledge that meaning will eventually emerge. Sometimes this can be used consciously as the 'Colombo principle' (Margison 2001), after the American TV detective who feigns confusion to trap his quarry. Saying, necessarily with a grain of truth, 'I don't quite understand what you mean by that . . . ' in a humble and apparently simple-minded way can help the patient to feel more secure, thoughtful, powerful and in control, as the care-giver asks the care-seeker for help.

8   *The thinking mind.* Finally, and perhaps most importantly, the therapist has to communicate to the patient that she is *there*, using his mind to think about what is going on in the patient's mind, trying to understand, and contain his mental representation of her feelings, to put them into

words, and that this is part of a coherent care-giving strategy. Ultimately, emotional security comes from the experience of being understood in this way. This will inevitably involve struggle. Patients are often trying *not* to think about their pain, or to project it into others who will act on it rather that re-present it to them. To be thought about is both relieving and terrifying. The therapist has to be able doggedly to carry on with the thinking task without persecuting the patient with his thoughts. Thus at times he is a quiet presence, at others actively engaging the patient in debate about the nature of the patient's own thoughts.

Clearly, many, or all, of these strategies form the bread-and-butter of psychoanalytic psychotherapy, enhanced with the 'jam' (in the sense of something both enriching and bonding) of an attachment perspective. The next chapter explores in more detail the complex interaction between psychoanalytic ideas and those of attachment theory, and argues for narrative as a linking concept between them.

Chapter 3

Attachment theory and psychoanalysis
Finding a common language

When Oedipus met Laius at the crossroads, it was a battle to the death, with implications not just for the politics of Thebes but, thanks to Freud, for the subsequent history of psychology. According to the literary critic Harold Bloom (1997: 5), 'strong poets misread one another, so as to clear imaginative space for themselves' – Oedipus had to get Laius out of the way before he could progress. Bloom's views on the 'anxiety of influence' in literature, a basically Freudian idea, apply equally to psychoanalysis. For Bloom, weak talents merely idealize their illustrious predecessors, while major figures attempt both to assimilate their forerunners and find their own unique voice. In doing so, they necessarily distort, devalue or diminish the heroes who are both a source of inspiration and a curse. For Bloom, Shakespeare is the one exception, an untouchable colossus who stands over the entire Western literary cannon. Freud is psychoanalysis's Shakespeare. Bowlby was undoubtedly in Bloomian terms a 'strong poet', although his main feud was not with Freud, but with Klein and her followers. His misreading and dismissal of Kleinian psychoanalysis (Holmes 1993), with its inevitable backlash – in his case repression for two decades of his entire oeuvre within the psychoanalytic literature – was both necessary and disastrous.

My argument in this chapter is that the time for *rapprochement* is long overdue. Attachment theory, with its strong scientific roots, has never been a 'school', and has not felt the need to stick to the Bowlbian letter. At the same time, psychoanalysis has begun to open out to the wider world of psychotherapy generally, as well as neurobiology and contemporary philosophy – partly because, centurion at last, it has come of age and feels more at ease with itself, and partly out of an urgent need to escape from intellectual isolation.

As with any well-resolved conflict, each side can legitimately claim victory. Bowlby was critical of the psychoanalysis of his day for its reliance on authority rather than evidence, its insistence on the primacy of phantasy over real trauma in the aetiology of neurosis, and the limitations of an intrapsychic as opposed to an interpersonal perspective on relationships. Today we can point to the strength of empirical research in psychoanalysis

(Fonagy 1999), the acknowledgement by psychoanalytic writers of the centrality of abuse and trauma, especially in the origins of borderline pathology (Garland 1998), and to the flourishing interpersonal school that has arisen out of the work of Winnicott and Sullivan (Mitchell 1998). Equally, when it comes to clinical work, attachment theory has always accepted that it is essentially a variant of object relations theory, and recognized that the account of external behaviours with which it originally concerned itself needed to be complemented by experiential description of their correlates in the inner world – in Main's (1995: 410) evocative phrase, by a 'move to the level of representation'. What is *felt* is not an attachment bond – still less one that is, say, anxious, avoidant or ambivalent – but a self, problematic or otherwise, in relation to an other, whether it be mother, lover or therapist.

I am arguing that the anxiety of influence is well and truly over and that psychoanalysis and attachment theory can begin to allow each to affect the other with less defensive projection and splitting.

Neurobiology and psychoanalytic psychotherapy

Bowlby always insisted that psychotherapy was no less 'biological' than pharmacological approaches to psychiatry. Our capacity to form relationships has been shaped by evolution and is mediated by the physical and biochemical architecture of the brain. For both political and clinical reasons, psychotherapists ignore biology at their peril. Politically, the power of science in society (not to mention the influence of pharmaceutical companies within medicine) is so strong that any psychological discipline needs to be able to contend in that arena. Freud had no difficulty in acknowledging the contribution of what he called 'constitutional factors' in neurosis. If, as seems likely (see below), trauma and ineffective parenting in infancy have structural effects on the brain, which in turn affect physiological responses to stress in later life, psychotherapists need to take that into account in their work. Similarly, we need to know to what extent psychotherapy can reverse or mitigate adverse physiological responses and whether *that* manifests itself in altered brain function. What follows is not a systematic review of the neurobiology of relationships, but highlights some themes germane to the central argument of this book.

In interuterine life, infant physiology and that of the mother are intimately connected. There is a tendency to assume that this state of affairs comes to an abrupt end at the moment of birth, and that from then on the mother–infant relationship is mainly psychological. Hofer (1995) studied the physiology of newborn rat pups as they nest with their mothers. He found a complex relationship between various aspects of the interrelationship and the physiology of the growing pup. The pup's activity and mobility are regulated by the warmth and smell of the mother, growth hormone secretion by her touch, heart rate by the amount of intra-gastric milk, and sleep rate by the periodicity with with the milk is delivered. Thus the mother contributes to the infant's physiological homeostatic mechanisms and regulatory systems long after birth.

These studies illuminate one of the arguments between attachment theorists and psychoanalysts, the former emphasizing the ways in which mother and infant actively relate to one another from the moment of birth, while Mahler's (Mahler *et al*. 1975) influential account preserves Freud's 'egg' model and assumes a rather undifferentiated symbiosis in the first few months of life. Hofer's work suggests that both sides are right – there *is* physiological symbiosis, but it arises *out of* the relationship. One cannot be certain about the clinical significance of this, but it is tempting to speculate that affect dysregulation in borderline personality disorder has its origins in disturbances of the early mother–infant psychophysiological regulatory system, partly due to temperament, but also perhaps due in part to maternal stress or depression and concomitant disorganized attachment in her infant.

The idea that early disturbance of the mother–infant relationship can have lasting effects on physiological responses in adult life is supported by the work by Rosenblum and Coplan (Rosenblum *et al*. 1994) using bonnet macaque monkeys. Harlow's classical surrogate mother studies (Harlow and Bowlby were close friends and much influenced by one another) used extreme conditions of deprivation, quite unlike those normally encountered even in the most dysfunctional families. Coplan and colleagues have created a more life-like analogue of families in difficulty, in which the mothers are exposed to a 'variable foraging condition', in which they have to spend quite a lot of time and energy getting food during their offspring's infancy. These mothers are more anxious and less responsive to their infants than comparable mothers in a 'low foraging demand' condition. The infants were then allowed to grow up and, as young adults, compared in their physiological responses to the anxiety-provoking agents yohimbine (noradrenergic) and mCPP (serotonergic). Those with 'variable foraging condition' mothers showed markedly abnormal responses, showing hyper-reactivity to yohimbine and hyporesponsivity to mCPP. The authors concluded that 'early events may alter the neurodevelopment of systems central to the expression of adult anxiety disorders' (Rosenblum *et al*. 1994: 226).

These studies suggest that what we call an 'attachment bond' is a complex psychophysiological state. Bowlby saw how the whole-organism methodology of ethology could help put psychoanalytic ideas on a sound scientific footing, in contrast to the limitations of stimulus–response behaviourism of his day. We are now beginning to go beyond that and to link ethological observation with neurochemistry and brain architecture, clinically as well as experimentally. We can now look directly at the impact of psychotherapy on the brain. In a single case design, Viinnamaki *et al*. (1998) used single photon emission tomography (SPET) to compare two young men with depression and borderline personality disorder, one treated with a year of dynamic psychotherapy and one not. Initial SPET imaging in both individuals showed reduced serotonin uptake in the medial prefrontal area compared with 10 healthy controls. After a year of therapy, the treated patient's SPET pattern had reverted to normal, whereas that of the untreated patient remained the same. This is particularly interesting in the light of a neuroimaging study by Teasdale *et al.* (1999), who suggested that the medial prefrontal cortex is important in the processing of affect-related meanings.

Alan Schore (1997), who is both a brain researcher and psychoanalyst, depicts intense mother–infant interchange, based predominantly around the visual systems, but also touch and vocalization, in which the right brains of each are in a state of constant unconscious communication. In this 'buzzing booming world' (as William James described it), the infant learns both the pleasures of social intercourse and how to manage its disruptions. Visual interactions release endogenous opiates in the infant, and the mother is attentive in her attempts to help the child learn affect regulation and to repair the inevitable discontinuities of attachment that arise in everyday life.

This link between meanings and biology also emerges from Insel's (1997) work on the neurobiological mechanisms underlying attachment itself. In his studies of monogamous prairie voles, Insel found that partner preference following mating could be blocked in males by vasopressin antagonists and in females by oxytocin antagonists. He suggested that these peptides are released during mating (as they are during human mating) and act to cement a specific pair bond, in contrast to the related but promiscuous montaine voles. Here perhaps we find confirmation of Fairbairn's (1952) famous statement that 'sex is a signpost to the object', and the identification of a possible molecular basis underlying the formation of an attachment bond. We can also speculate that the quasi-addictive quality of perverse self-soothing behaviours, such as cutting in borderline patients, might be mediated in a similar way – if endogenous opiates or peptides are released, then such pathological behaviours will also be self-reinforcing. The argument here is that when faced with stress an individual seeks out a secure base; the bonding process releases endogenous opiates which makes the individual relax and feel safe. Such apparently perverse acts as self-cutting may short-cut this process and produce the physiological secure base state, using the body rather than another as the means to achieve this. This biological argument is not incompatible with psychological explanations, such as Fonagy's (1997) idea that, in insecure and especially disorganized attachment, the body becomes a vehicle for an introjected 'alien' other from and with which the individual can neither peaceably separate nor harmoniously co-exist.

Neo-Darwinism

Mitchell (1998) made an important distinction between what he called 'Freud's Darwin' and 'Bowlby's Darwin'. As befitted his nineteenth-century origins, Freud concentrated on the Darwinian message about the influence of man's phylogenetic heritage: how 'primitive forces' lay behind the veneer of civilization. Bowlby's Darwin, by contrast, is concerned with adaptation and survival. In the 'environment of evolutionary adaptation', where infants are exposed to predators and the only guarantee of security is the bond to a parent, there would be strong selective pressure towards attachment behaviours, and hence it is legitimate to see attachment as a drive, 'hard-wired' (as the metaphor goes) into the nervous system.

This divergence around Darwin points to important differences between attachment and psychoanalytic perspectives on the nature of the unconscious and psychological defences. In the Freudian unconscious self-centredness, sexuality and aggression are actively held at bay – out of awareness – by defence mechanisms such as repression and splitting. Similarly, attchment theory postulates that our thoughts and actions are shaped by forces over which we have little control and which we are often unaware, but there is no war in the mind here. Attachment behaviours are no more or less unconscious than are, say, our digestive processes. As already suggested, the child who hurts himself at school, protests little at the time and then bursts into tears when he is collected by his mother at the end of the day, is not so much repressing and then giving vent to his Oedipal rage at being excluded by his parents, but simply behaving according to the silent dictates of the attachment imperative – when faced with threat or illness, seek out and cling to a secure base attachment figure until comforted, before resuming autonomous exploration and play.

We might term these two senses of the unconscious the 'automatic' and the 'active' unconscious. Indeed, it is possible to imagine a hierarchy of 'unconsciousnesses' starting with the physiological unconscious; moving to the behavioural unconscious implicit in attachment theory; through Freud's preconscious, which is akin to that postulated by cognitive behaviour therapy, in which automatic thoughts determine feelings and actions without our being aware of them; and, finally, to the classical Freudian unconscious in which disturbing thoughts are actively kept out of awareness by mechanisms like repression and splitting. Clearly, the automatic unconscious and active unconscious are not mutually exclusive. An insecure child with an avoidant attachment style might, on meeting his mother after school, long to cry and cling to her, but have learned from experience that such behaviours are more likely to lead to angry rebuffs ('what a silly fuss about a minute graze!'), and so hover silently nearer to her than usual, without making his feelings explicit either to himself or her. Here we *can* postulate an active suppression of attachment needs and of any anger there might be about these not being met, akin to the Freudian notion of repression. The child might be struggling with feelings of shame at his 'babyish' wish to be comforted, which, in turn, would feed into low self-esteem, narcissism and, via identification with the aggressor, the need to attack others more vulnerable than himself – avoidant children tend to be bullies (Main 1995).

The key point about defences from an attachment perspective is that they are interpersonal strategies for dealing with suboptimal environments. Their aim is not so much to preserve the integrity of the individual when faced with conflicting inner drives, but to maintain attachments in the face of relational forces threatening to disrupt them. The body is the intermediate zone between the mind and the Other. Dimacio (1994) argues that we think with our bodies, and attachment theory suggests that the way in which we experience our bodies (e.g. feelings of tension or panic on separation, for example) is relational in origin. Bodies and their attachments ensure that minds are inescapably social.

This links with attempts by Slavin and Kriegman (1992), Chisholm (1996), Nesse (1990) and others to bring neo-Darwinian ideas to bear on psychoanalysis. Adaptations leading to increased fitness are always compromises: trade-offs, for example, between choosing to colonize an inclement environment with few competitors and a more fertile one where competition is more intense.

As in humans, adaptation in social animals is as much to the interpersonal environment as it is to the physical and here, too, compromise is essential. In human society, we are both competitors for resources *and* mutually dependent for our survival. Nesse (1990) questions the adaptive significance of repression – surely the more we know ourselves, the better able we are to succeed in cooperation or even in gaining an advantage over our fellow humans. He suggests, however, that we underestimate the role played by deceit in social relations. The hurt child with a stressed rebuffing mother is more likely to get at least some crumbs of nurturance if he persuades her that he is not going to bleed her dry with his demands. Nesse suggests that he may be more likely to achieve this if he deceives *himself* (i.e. represses his neediness and rage) as well as her.

How do we square this rather cynical view with the psychoanalytic valuation of self-knowledge and attempts to lessen the power of defences? There are two answers to this. First, the weaker one's position, the more the need for deception – of self and others. From an evolutionary perspective, after the first few weeks of life, there is a potential conflict between the needs of the mother and those of the child. The child wants as much as he can get – love, attention, food, protection – from the mother. She needs her child to survive, but she also wants to produce more children and, for that to happen, she will turn her attention to her partner and to any further children that result. It is therefore in the child's interests to repress Oedipal wishes for exclusive possession of his mother and fear and resentment of his father – to deceive both himself and others for the sake of family stability. At this stage, repression is adaptive. As the child grows in strength and his dependence lessens, his fitness may depend more on his ability to understand himself – to have a 'mind of his own' (Caper 1999) – and to be able to tolerate the separateness of others and the fact that their interests and his may diverge.

A second point concerns the difference between short-term and long-term reproductive strategies. In adverse conditions, parents may 'decide' that their best hope is to maximize their numbers of offspring, in the hope that at least some may survive, choosing quantity rather than quality (Table 3.1).

Here, the child's ability to deceive may be crucial to survival. The avoidant child keeps near enough to a rejecting parent to remain in touch and therefore achieve some measure of protection, but not so close as to provoke overt rejection. The ambivalent, clinging child senses the inability of the parent to provide secure consistent long-term support, and so clings on in the hope of extracting as much nurturance as he can in as short a time as possible. Neither strategy is 'maladaptive' given the circumstances they face. What we call 'repression' and 'insecure attachment' are ways of coping with suboptimal environments. As with the offspring of variable foraging condition monkey mothers mentioned earlier, insecurely attached children will be handicapped when it comes to handling their emotions as adults, and hence may have diminished reproductive competence, but at least they have survived. Undoing repression and splitting, or learning secure rather than insecure attachment patterns, will only be adaptive when environmental conditions become favourable.

All this may seem somewhat speculative and theoretical, but it has

Table 3.1 A model depicting how the three main patterns of attachment organization might result from the interaction between parents' reproductive strategies and children's developmental (i.e. incipient reproductive) strategies

Attachment classification	Parental reproductive strategy	Child developmental (i.e. incipent reproductive) strategy
Insecure avoidant	• Short-term • Unwilling to invest • High mating effort • Dismissing, rejecting of child	• Maximize short-term survival • Avoid rejecting, potentially infanticidal parent
Secure	• Long-term • Able and willing to invest • High parenting effort • Unconditionally accepting, sensitive, responsive to child	• Maximize long-term learning, quality of development • Maintain investment from 'rich' parent
Insecure anxious, ambivalent	• Short-term • Unable to invest • Parenting effort with inadequate resources • Inconsistent, preoccupied but not rejecting of child	• Maximize short-term maturation, 'quantity' of development • Maintain investment from 'poor' parent

significant clinical implications. We tolerate the manipulativeness of children and even find it endearing, but when our 'borderline' patients try to manipulate us – deceiving themselves and us – we respond angrily with rejection, thereby perpetuating the vicious cycle. With the help of psychotherapy, we may be able to help them move from insecure to more secure patterns of attachment, and to become more self-aware and less reliant on repression and splitting. But this is only likely to succeed if they are able to find a stable environment, one in which long-term strategies of nurturance become adaptive. There is an important link here between social psychiatry and psychotherapy. Therapeutic communities, which are needed for very damaged severe personality disordered patients, try to provide just such an environment (Campling and Haigh 1999).

In summary, for Freud, intrapsychic conflict is between a 'primitive' Darwinian id, a harsh superego and an ego doing its best to mediate between them. Bowlby's neo-Darwinism is much closer to contemporary psychoanalytic concerns. Here conflict is between the narcissism of an organism determined to maximize evolutionary fitness in the short term, and the long-term need for collaboration, which means the ability to put purely selfish aims to one side when necessary and to value relatedness. Being able to understand another's point of view is an essential part of this process, as is the ability to see oneself and one's desires from the outside. Psychotherapy can play a vital part in fostering those abilities.

Categorical versus narrative approaches in psychiatry and psychotherapy

Mary Main's development of the Adult Attachment Interview (AAI) is perhaps the single most significant factor in attachment theory's current revival and popularity in psychotherapeutic circles (Main and Goldwyn 1995). The AAI is comparable to a psychotherapy assessment interview aiming, in Main's words, to 'surprise the unconscious' into yielding up its secrets. The key innovation in Main's approach is that she looks at the style and form of the linguistic responses of the respondents, rather than concentrating on content. It is the *way* in which individuals respond to questions about trauma, parental relationships and losses that counts, not the trauma itself.

In coming to a formulation at the end of an assessment interview, a mature clinician will be as influenced by the style with which the patient tells his story as she will to the story itself, and will pay close attention to her own emotional responses to the pulls and pushes of the patient's psyche. The AAI allows for this kind of sophistication, yet apparently produces stable and reliable categories that can be used for research purposes and which can guide clinical practice.

Although attachment theory's three main categories of insecure attachment – avoidant-dismissive, ambivalent-enmeshed and disorganized-incoherent

– have research validity, we should be cautious about assuming that attachment categories map easily onto clinical phenomena. Many of the patients seen in clinical practice show both avoidant and ambivalent patterns at different times and in different circumstances. Nevertheless, much that is fascinating and useful has come out of this classification. I will mention a few highlights.

1   *Inter-generational transmission.* First, we are beginning to understand the mechanisms of inter-generation transmission of psychological health or vulnerability – psychotherapy's answer to the genome project (see Chapter 7). Pregnant mothers rated as insecure on the AAI tend to have infants who will be similarly classified in the Strange Situation Test at one year, while secure parents tend to produce secure infants (Fonagy *et al.* 1995); this has been replicated several times. Thinking about possible mechanisms by which this could happen leads to another important finding.

2   *Reflexive function.* Fonagy (who with his colleagues has been in the forefront of the rapprochement between attachment theory and psychoanalysis; Fonagy 1999a; Fonagy 2001; Fonagy and Target 2000) has identified 'reflexive function' – a version of the psychoanalytic notion of insight – as the key feature of secure narratives on the AAI. The ability to think and talk about past pain is a protective factor leading to secure attachment, no matter how traumatic a childhood may have been. This inspiring finding is in itself an endorsement of psychotherapy, one of whose main functions, it can be argued, is to enhance reflexive function.

3   *Developmental pathways.* Classifying infants' attachment status and then following them up, the longest period thus far being about 18 years, has confirmed one of the basic assumptions of psychoanalysis: the continuity between relationship patterns in early childhood and those of later life. Depending on attachment status, children behave consistently at school entry, at 10 years and when they are asked to participate in an AAI interview in their teens (Main 1995). Secure children are more outgoing, more likely to be able to ask teachers for help and to be more popular than their insecure counterparts. Avoidant children tend to be bullies, while ambivalent children are frequently victims. In the former, coercion is used to maintain contact with the other; in the latter, it is victimhood. These continuities extend backwards into the first year of life and relate to parental handling in that period. Children whose parents are responsive, sensitive and attuned are more likely to be securely attached; those with brusque rejecting parents are more likely to be avoidant, those with inconsistent parents to be ambivalent and those with parents who themselves have experienced major trauma to be disorganized. Attachment styles seem to represent stable developmental pathways in which particular patterns of security or insecurity evoke

care-giving responses that perpetuate those patterns and in which particular care-giving behaviours are consistent across the life cycle and so
tend to reinforce pre-existing relationship styles. That is not to say that
movement from, say, insecure to secure pathways cannot occur – for
example, when depressed mothers receive psychotherapy or when they
form good relationships with new partners.

4   *Normal and abnormal development.* A key difference from some
schools of psychoanalytic thinking is the sharp differentiation that
attachment theory makes between normal and abnormal – or secure and
insecure – developmental pathways, which appear to diverge from the
early weeks of life. There is a tendency in some psychoanalytic writing
to see 'primitive mental mechanisms' as a normal feature of infancy, to
be overcome, to a greater or lesser extent, as development proceeds, and
often leaving a residual 'psychotic core' to the personality. This viewpoint is captured in the aphorism 'we are born mad, achieve sanity, and
die', covering as it does early psychotic mechanisms, the hard-won
depressive position and, finally, the necessary acceptance of loss.
Research influenced by attachment theory suggests that this model
should not be taken as a blueprint for psychological development generally. For example Mahler's (Mahler *et al.* 1975) well-known developmental 'sub-stage' of rapprochement, where a curious toddler appears
to lose confidence in the world and cling to mother, may represent a
version of insecure attachment rather than a normal developmental
phase – which is not to say that insecure attachment must always be
thought of as meaningfully 'abnormal'.

5   *The origins of a sense of self.* Bowlby (1988) was keen to emphasize the
continuity of attachment needs throughout the life cycle; for him,
attachment was intrinsic to human nature, not some childish propensity
to be outgrown with maturity. There is no doubt that the attachment
dynamic continues throughout life and that, in an 'automatic
unconscious' way described above, adults seek out their secure base,
turning to attachment figures at times of threat, stress or illness – and
hospitals can often become surrogates in this process. If, however, non-
clinical samples of adults are asked to describe their secure base, as
outlined in Chapter 2, in addition to mentioning partners, pets, family
and close friends, and quasi-transitional object-type resources such as
hot baths, duvets, photograph albums, being in touch with nature,
favourite books and music, they will also describe the reassurance of a
sense of self – of knowing who one is, where one came from and where
one is going to.

Attachment-influenced infant observation can help delineate the origins of
a sense of self that complements psychoanalytic views. For Trevarthen
(1984), 'primary inter-subjectivity' refers to the mother's capacity to identify

with her infant; this capacity to have one's needs and emotions responded to helps with the process of knowing who eventually one is. As Fonagy has pointed out, this ability depends in turn on the mother being able to know who *she* is. Stern's (1985) notion of attunement, especially 'cross-modal attunement', in which the parent picks up and reflects back the infant's self-generated rhythms, is for him a basic nucleus of the child's sense of self.

In Winnicott's (1967) famous formulation, the *mother's face* is the mirror in which the infant first begins to recognize himself. Gergely and Watson's (1996) studies of mother–infant interaction extend this insight by showing how, in short, clearly defined interactive episodes, the mother engages the infant in mirroring play. She does this in two main ways: first by 'marking', a form of exaggeration in which the mother amplifies normal facial expressions and vocalizations, thereby separating them off from her own everyday facial expressions; and, second, by 'contingency', a rigorous setting of herself aside so that she only imitates or follows the baby's lead, rather than (in these brief mirroring episodes) initiating or imposing her own feelings.

These observations suggest how a sense of self arises out of an interpersonal context, and might provide a secure base at times of need. It also suggests how an *insecure* sense of self might arise if the mother is unable to bracket off her own feelings and so fail to provide the marking and contingency required. If she is depressed or troubled by her own uncontained feelings, she may impose these feelings, or be unresponsive, so that what the child 'sees' in the face-mirror is either blankness or his mother's sadness, which, in turn, may set up insecure models of attachment. The avoidant individual has a split off self, unavailable for processing or comfort. The ambivalent individual has a deficient sense of self and has to cling to another person to know who he or she is. The role-reversal and compulsive caring associated with disorganized attachment (Main 1995) may have their origins in this extreme sensitivity to the mother's moods that occurs when the mirroring relationship is distorted or reversed. This theme is discussed in more detail in Chapter 7.

We can further speculate that the ground rules of psychotherapeutic technique – marked boundaries between therapy and 'normal life', i.e. 'on the couch' and 'off the couch' behaviours – and the capacity to follow the patient's lead rather than imposing one's own agenda, are analogues of the mirroring process and suggest ways in which therapy can enhance a sense of self in its subjects. All this may take place at an unconscious or certainly non-verbal level. Beebe and Lachman (1988: 19) emphasize 'the analyst's and patient's mutually regulated interactions of affect, mood, arousal and rhythm. Nonverbal interactions at the microlevel of rhythm matching, modulation of vocal contour, pausing, postural matching and gaze regulation are usually not given adequate recognition in the treatment process'.

But mirroring alone is not enough for successful therapy. Dozier *et al* (1994) administered the AAI both to clients and their therapists. They found that insecure clinicians tended to *reinforce* their clients' insecure attachment styles, whereas secure clinicians were more likely to *redress* their difficulties. Enmeshed clients were seen by insecure clinicians as more needy and requiring greater clinical input than their avoidant counterparts, while secure clinicians had the opposite perception. Conversely, secure clinicians saw avoidant clients as needing greater input, while insecure clinicians tended to reinforce their avoidance. Here the AAI is used as a reliable measure of counter-transference and suggests that the processes leading to security in therapy are meaningfully analogous to those found in infancy. Interestingly, a similar conclusion emerged from a totally different type of study, looking at therapists' and patients' facial expressions in relation to outcome in brief therapy (Merten *et al.* 1996). Good outcomes were correlated with 'complementary' facial expressions (e.g. therapist remaining serious when the patient appeared light-hearted), while bad outcomes went with 'reciprocal' (i.e. matching) patterns of facial affectivity. This suggests, in addition to 'mirroring', a balancing response – in which the therapist is able to identify split off or repressed aspect of the patients' inner world – is equally important in producing successful outcomes.

Diagnostic categories in clinical practice

The distinctions between avoidant, ambivalent and incoherent patterns of insecure attachment are not in themselves new. They map comfortably onto broad-brush psychoanalytic formulations of schizoid, hysterical and borderline pathology. Attachment theory' research base in developmental psychopathology has been able to establish the robustness of these categories as descriptions of real phenomena in a variety of populations across different cultures (Van Ijzendoorm *et al.* 1995).

But how useful are these classifications in clinical practice? Clearly, they are of some value. For example, Hobson *et al.* (1998) has shown that 'borderline' patients referred for psychotherapy are much more likely to be rated as disorganized on the AAI than are patients with depressive disorders. Fonagy *et al.* (1995) suggested that avoidance predicts better outcome in response to psychoanalytic psychotherapy than ambivalence. This can be understood in terms of Stiles and co-workers' (1990) 'assimilation model' (discussed in Chapter 5) in which identification of warded-off feelings is a key task for psychoanalytic as opposed to cognitive therapies. Avoidant people deny or 'deactivate' feelings, and can be helped to get in touch with them via psychoanalytic approaches; ambivalent patients 'hyperactivate' attachment strategies and this tendency may be exacerbated by unskilful psychoanalytic therapy. It may be clinically preferable to view avoidance and ambivalence as dimensions rather than discrete categories (Brennan *et al.*

1998) (see Figure 2.1). Thus studies of patients with eating disorders show a mixture of ambivalent avoidant patterns, with no clear links between bulimia as opposed to anorexia and any one attachment category. Most clinicians can probably identify aspects of all three patterns of attachment in many of their patients.

This suggests a fundamental divergence between the way in which categorization is used in research and clinical work, a contrast between evidence-based and narrative-based approaches in medicine (Roberts and Holmes 1998). As I argue in Chapter 8, psychotherapy is quintessentially a narrative discipline in which categories act not as researchable discrete entities, but more as heuristic prototypes that enable the clinician to penetrate further into the individual story. Terms like 'obsessionality', 'psychotic thinking', 'splitting', 'avoidance', 'good breast' or even 'mother' and 'father', and in the terminology of this book, 'secure base', are used loosely to designate ideal types that help us to think about any particular patient. Classification of attachment styles by contrast is based on standard scientific methods of reliability and validity.

Britton (1999) argues from a psychoanalytic perspective that 'we should refer to syndromes, as psychoanalysts, on the basis of the characteristic experience they have and engender in analysis, rather on the basis of their symptoms or psychiatric nosology'. Discussing Freud's Anna O, he goes on to say 'it is characteristic of hysteria that the primal scene is idealised and erotic and sometimes one of a romantic union in death'. He argues that, in the origins of hysteria, the mother–infant relationship is not 'privileged' and, therefore, feelings of 'castration' and the 'death' of one's own sexuality are fundamental, leading to a compensatory romanticization of the parental couple. Britton's complex ideas seem far removed from attachment categories, but nevertheless links can be made. Insecure attachment arises out of an 'unprivileged' mother–infant relationship. The rebuffed avoidant infant, or the inconsistently attended to ambivalent infant, may well feel shame and confusion about their 'unmet greed' (L. Loxtercamp, personal communication), feelings that could be summarized as 'castration'. Idealization emerges in avoidant narratives in which a childhood may be described as 'brilliant', 'perfect' or 'normal', but without elaboration or accuracy. Separation and loss feel like deaths to the ambivalent clinging individual.

Attachment theory and psychoanalysis complement each other here. Attachment theory remains wedded to evidence – to measurable behaviours, whether they be ways of responding to questions on the AAI or to separation in the Strange Situation. Attachment theory shows how meanings, in the sense of narrative patterns, arise out of childhood behaviours and parental handling. When the parent goes out of the room in the Strange Situation Test for 3 minutes, this has an impact on both the automatic and active unconscious of the infant. It activates attachment behaviours – protest, distress, anxiety – *and* has an 'Oedipal' meaning, evoking all the fear and phantasies the child may have about his parents' relationship and what goes on when he is excluded. Psychoanalysis is concerned primarily with meanings and with data that are essentially subjective. In both attachment theory and psychoanalysis, there is an oscillation between the 'data' – the observable behaviour of the patient, or the responses of the analyst's counter-transferential 'instrument' – and a theoretical superstructure that informs clinical intervention. Just as Britton's (1999) use of Kleinian ideas like projective identification and depressive position extend Freud's under-standing of Anna O, so attachment theory can help clarify and guide therapists in the complexity of their interactions with their patients, as I shall illustrate in the following chapter.

Conclusions

Mary Ainsworth (1989) identified attunement, sensitivity and responsive-ness as the hallmarks of parents who are able to provide secure attachment for their children. But attachment theory is as much to do with breakdown and loss as it is about attachment. The key feature of the Strange Situation is the response of parent and child to a brief separation. Parents able to pro-vide secure attachment are those who can, in Bion's (1962) terminology, contain and metabolize negative emotions – their children's unhappiness and protest about the separation. Parents of insecure children tend to retali-ate, ignore or be overwhelmed by their own and their children's pain at parting.

Similarly, therapy influenced by attachment theory is not, as Bowlby (1988) sometimes implied, merely a matter of providing a secure base for the patient. It is about empathy and responsiveness, but it is also about the separateness of the therapist – his capacity to have a 'mind of his own' (Caper 1999) – and the ways in which patients cope with the rhythm of attachment and parting that is integral to the therapeutic relationship. At the heart of attachment research is the Strange Situation, which briefly upsets and stresses the infant, observing the interactive pattern of parent and child around rupture and repair of the attachment bond. Alliance rupture and repair are as much a part of the work of psychotherapy as are key changes and harmonic tension and its resolution in music. Only in the context of an object found, lost and refound can a patient begin to develop autonomy – a sense of self to which he can turn in times of stress. This is the external and visible sign of an inner world characterized by depressive position thinking and the resolution of the Oedipus complex.

This chapter began with Bloom's (1997) description of the strong poet, for whom the archetype is Milton, and his protagonist in *Paradise Lost*, Satan. In Bloom's perspective, Satan starts with loss, with the fall: 'There and then, in this bad, he finds his good; he chooses the heroic, to know damnation and to explore the limits of the possible within it' (Bloom 1997:

21). This is reminiscent of Freud's famous epigraph from Virgil for *The Interpretation of Dreams* ('If I cannot bend the heavens, then I will arouse Hell'). The strong poet is one who can descend into hell, who does not fear death and who is therefore able to come to terms with loss. All of which, it seems to me, was true of Bowlby in his ability to learn from, but not cling slavishly to, psychoanalysis.

So, if attachment theory has a significant contribution to contemporary psychoanalysis, it may be to help it to accept the death of its founder. As Lear (1998: 31–2), writing about attacks on Freud, put it:

> Freud *is* dead. He died in 1939, after an extraordinarily productive and creative life. Beneath the continued attacks on him, ironically, lies an unwillingness to let him go. It is Freud who taught us that only after we accept the actual death of an important person in our lives can we begin to mourn. Only then can he or she take on full symbolic life for us. Obsessing about Freud *the man* is a way of keeping Freud *the meaning* at bay.

Bowlby can help us let Freud go. Freud is dead; long live psychoanalysis – and the new paradigms which, with the help of attachment theory, child development studies, neurobiology, linguistics and neo-Darwinism, it can help to forge. But let us now turn away from these grandiloquent themes to the bread and butter of clinical work.

Chapter 4

Attachment in clinical practice

Borderline patients and the hospital

In this chapter, I look at some clinical material from an attachment perspective. My first illustration will be very familiar to those who work in general psychiatric settings. The relationship between borderline patients and psychiatric services are frequently problematic. These patients present for emergency help in states of distress, often at unsocial hours, and are admitted to the ward by worried and inexperienced junior doctors. The nursing staff frequently feel furious, exasperated and put upon. Ineffective 'contracts' are imposed on the patients, who are often then discharged precipitously after some episode of disturbed behaviour, only to begin the cycle again within a short time. Alternatively, patients who have been coping at home may begin to regress in the hospital setting, with threats of suicide or helplessness making it apparently impossible for them to be discharged, leading them to outstay their welcome.

We know that most patients with severe personality disorder show insecure patterns of attachment on the Adult Attachment Interview (AAI). Their relationships are characterized by frequent crises and they are intolerant of being alone. Once they have made contact with medical services, the hospital becomes a secure base to which they will, following attachment principles, turn at times of distress (which are frequent, given their stormy relationships and difficulties with self-soothing). However, the hospital often acts – or is induced to act – like a typical insecurity-reinforcing parent. The patient may be rebuffed (avoidant pattern) or, alternately, given excessive attention and then ignored (ambivalent pattern). As a result, the patient is in a constant state of frustrated attachment, either hovering in the vicinity of the hospital, without being able to make use of it, or clinging to it, in mortal fear of being ejected or rejected. The more these behaviours occur, the more they evoke rebuffing or inconsistent responses from the staff, leading to a vicious circle of escalating frustration. Whatever happens, the assuagement of attachment needs, which requires a mixture of firmness and warmth, is infrequently attained. This is not surprising, because allowing the patient to stay in hospital for a while – offering them a secure base – is counterintuitive, in that it might seem to reinforce rather than restrict the patient's dependency, especially when hospital beds are in short supply. But, just as it has been shown that offering a cup of tea and a bun to frequently attending homeless tramps in a casualty department, instead of summarily ejecting them, can actually reduce recidivism, letting borderline patients know that a secure-making attachment experience is available when needed can similarly and paradoxically reduce the length of stay in hospital. One week of a good experience is worth 2 months of frustration and eventual ejection. One of our very disturbed borderline patients has reduced her annual nights in hospital dramatically simply by being given control of admission herself with instant access to the ward. She is permitted to come in two nights a month (but no more) whenever she feels she needs to. What is important about this is not the specific arrangements of a contract, but the fact that a 'listening mind' is there to contain and respond to the patient's distress, secure in the sense that it is neither rejecting nor manipulable.

Listening strategies

The capacity for acute and sensitive listening is a crucial ingredient of successful psychotherapy. Much contemporary psychoanalytic writing concentrates on the therapist's ability to attend to (or 'listen to') her own emotional responses to the patient – to identify and understand the 'pull' exerted by the patient's unconscious on her own and, in her interpretations and responses, strike a balance between empathy and detachment that will, via resolution of Oedipal and depressive anxieties, help in the patient's process of individuation (Caper 1999). But, as we listen to ourselves, we are of course also listening to the patient – the therapist's role is that of an accompanist to the patient's solo efforts.

Here attachment thinking can make a clinical contribution that complements standard psychoanalytic technique. As Slade (1999) puts it, 'it is possible to develop an ear for attachment themes, as well as for attachment patterns, without necessarily falling prey to overly simplistic ways of thinking that – valuable as they may be in research – are indeed too narrow for the clinical situation'. The AAI takes narrative style and translates it into attachment patterns. In the clinical setting, the patient's narrative style – in particular, her tone of voice – provides a similar clue to the state of their object relations. Tone of voice, together with facial and bodily expression, is what the patient brings into the room – an invaluable clue to the transferential attachment pattern.

A story of two telephone calls

What follows is an account of two sessions, each of which centred around a telephone call. Telephone conversations are literally disembodied – a relationship mediated by vocal means alone and, as with the patient on the couch, thereby more likely to be under the sway of phantasy compared with face-to-face interaction.

Kate: avoidance in therapy

Patients with avoidant styles characteristically have harsh unmodulated voice timbres, often at variance with an imploring or pleading look in their eyes. Kate, who was childless and in her mid-forties, had been married three times and sought help with the unremitting depression that seemed to follow the inevitable breaks of her relationships. A successful solicitor, she had an older brother whom she was convinced was her parents' favourite. Her parents had married in their late thirties, her father a charming but alcoholic covert homosexual and her mother, a former golf champion, a brusque woman who had little time for any signs of unhappiness or weakness in her offspring. After a few months of therapy, she met a new man and, when the inevitable attachment crisis occurred – he failed to turn up when she was expecting him – instead of her usual strategy of 'getting her retaliation in first' (i.e. rejecting before she herself was rejected) and then plunging into depression, she was able to hold on long enough to her anger and panic to tell him about how she felt and, when he seemed to understand, this led to a deepening of their relationship.

In therapy she dreaded the silent start to sessions and would talk about her longing for a man who would just do things *for* her – wash her car or repair her washing machine – rather than having to do everything for herself. This is typical of the avoidant patient, beneath whose apparent self-sufficiency is a deep need to be looked after. Her harsh voice and black-and-white views made sessions at times intimidating for the therapist. In one she talked about a girlfriend who was living abroad. She was fed up, she said, with this woman, who never answered letters and who expected her, Kate, to do all the work in the relationship (yet more transferential complaints, I thought). The friend had rung during the week to apologize for not being in touch, but Kate had felt so furious that she had simply told her what a useless friend she was and put the telephone down.

All this was told in a harsh, blaming, self-justifying tone of voice which the therapist found intensely painful. He felt forced into one of two uncomfortable positions, either to agree how hard done by she was or to challenge her for being so rejecting, thinking to himself 'You complain about your loneliness but what can you expect if you treat your so-called friends like that'. He tried to find a third way by commenting on how sad and lonely she must have felt when she hung up, and to make links both with feelings of utter misery when she was sent away to boarding school at the age of eight and to an upcoming break in therapy. With tears in her eyes, and now in a much softer than normal tone of voice, she volunteered how she just could not tolerate the bleak feelings of emptiness stirred up in her by rejection, and that to be angry and rejecting herself was the only way she knew how to cope with them, even though she realized how she was reinforcing her isolation by doing so.

Later (see Chapter 8) we shall see how therapeutic interventions with avoidant patients involve *breaking* open the self-contained narratives with which they protect themselves from feelings of insecure attachment. For a moment, Kate stood outside her story of 'hard-done-byness' and was able to reflect on it. She could see her attachment *at the level of representation* – how her controllingness, combined with denial of need, was what led her to sabotage relationships. She could momentarily grasp the repressed feelings of rage and abandonment that lay beneath her righteous indignation towards her friend. At this point, she mused sadly about how she had lost the ability to cry, even at her father's funeral, and how she envied those who could do so.

The attachment concept of 'avoidance' here helped to formulate the patient's difficulty. The avoidant person has to walk a tightrope between fear of intimacy and fear of aloneness; anger is often a pardoxical attempt to stay in touch with the object without destroying or being destroyed by it.

Oliver: ambivalent attachment styles in therapy

If the tone of voice of avoidant people tends to be harsh and unmodulated, that of the ambivalently attached is often monotonous and rambling. The therapist wonders when the patient is going to come to the point and finds it hard to facilitate genuine dialogue. Oliver, married with a teenage son, was a struggling land-agent in his mid-forties suffering from major depressive disorder for which he had been hospitalized on two occasions. He came from a materially comfortable background, but with a remote father of whom he saw little and a mother who had expected a man-of-action for a son, who, like her and Oliver's older sister, would love riding, hunting and shooting. Oliver turned out to be a frightened, sensitive, introspective child, who hated horses, had a major cardiac illness for which he was in hospital for nearly a year at the age of 8 (when he was convinced he would die), and who was mercilessly bullied throughout his school years and was himself subject to terrible and uncontrollable rages.

Ancient mariner-like, Oliver clung to his wife and to anyone who would listen to his tale – priest, family doctor, counsellor and then his therapist – in typically ambivalent fashion. Almost all of his relationships were construed in terms of dominance and submission: he saw himself as a dogsbody who had to fit in with other people's demands. At the same time, he harboured enormous resentment towards the people whom he felt were indifferent to his plight, and indulged himself in fantasies of power, success and revenge.

In treatment, he was superficially pleasant and irritatingly apologetic, but gradually became able to admit how furious he felt when the therapist announced breaks irrespective of how they might affect him. Beneath the clinging ambivalent attachment pattern lay a well of unassuaged narcissism and rage.

If the task with avoidant patients is to break open the semi-clichéd narratives they bring to therapy, with ambivalent patients it is necessary to introduce punctuation and shape into their stories – a *making* rather than a *breaking* function. Speech patterns in ambivalent attachment function more to produce a clinging form of attachment than to exchange information or create dialogue. The latter is too dangerous, as it implies intolerable separation and the possibility of losing the secure base.

Oliver tended to arrive slightly late for sessions and to spend the first half hour or so in a rambling monologue recounting what had happened since the previous meeting, usually a catalogue of minor disasters and ways in which he felt let down or ignored. On one occasion, he arrived uncharacteristically on time. I commented on this, perhaps in a slightly sarcastic way. This was certainly how Oliver took the comment, thereby setting up for him a typical bully–bullied pattern mentioned earlier. He then described how his wife had had a row with the mother of one of his son's friends with whom he was due to go on holiday, and had insisted that Oliver ring this woman up, ostensibly to make peace for the sake of the son's friendship. The telephone call had gone horribly wrong and he had ended up attacking the woman, who until then had been quite a close friend, never quite getting to the point, until eventually his wife had had to wrest the phone from him and patch things up as best she could, and so come to some sort of closure.

For Kate the therapeutic task was to prize open her self-justifying narrative and help her to feel the unstructured emotions which lay beneath. Here, close holding and a refusal to be pushed away by an apparently self-sufficient story, combined with an empathic comment, was the therapeutic technique required. In ambivalent attachment, by contrast, the therapeutic task is to help create a story out of the uncontained emotion and unstructured narrative which the patient presents. The patient has to be held at a slight distance, and a more theory-laden intervention can help the patient get a perspective on his emotions.

Unlike Kate, Oliver's reaction to his acrimonious telephone call was not self-justification, but a collapse into misery and self-blame. I suggested that in this episode his son represented the vulnerable part of himself, which he felt had never been recognized by his mother and which he felt I had ignored in my implied criticism of his lateness. His difficulty in coming to the point, I suggested, sprung partly from his tendency to assume that, if he stood his ground as a separate but equal participant in a conversation, he would be ignored or rejected. His moaning style was a way of both hanging onto his attachments and, at the same time, complaining about what he anticipated was the inevitable abandonment which would ensue sooner or later.

In response to my comment, he went on to describe a dream in which *he was walking along a narrow lane near his childhood home. His parents were ahead of him and he couldn't keep up. Suddenly, a landslide of rock fell in front of him and he was unable to see them, and he woke up feeling terrified.* With prompting he decided that the first part of the dream straightforwardly represented the fear of being cut off from the parent-figures on whom he depends, his mother, wife and therapist. Then he suddenly said, 'perhaps *I* am responsible for that landslide'. Momentarily, he glimpsed the terrible paradox of the insecure attachment – how the rage and protest designed to help re-establish contact with others has the effect of creating the very abandonment which he most fears. Oliver also showed disorganized features. Often his account of a situation would be hard to follow, and it was apparent that there was an internal 'psychotic' logic in his mind at variance with the external sequence of events. In disorganized attachment, rage can itself be sort of a last-ditch secure base, both as a way of activating carers to respond and as a 'home' to which, if all else fails, the sufferer can return – often to be followed by physiological states of exhaustion that have charateristics of the secure base.

These two cases can readily be formulated in more conventional psychoanalytic terms. Kate used projective identification to rid herself of her unbearable feelings of loneliness and fury: by hanging up on her friend, she reproduced in her the experience of being cut off which was the leitmotiv of her own relationships. Oliver, in his vicarious telephonic protest about his son's rejection, used his wife's friend as a container for his own unprocessed unhappiness and feelings of rejection. The avoidant person is all container and no feelings; the ambivalent person is overwhelmed with feelings, but with nowhere to contain them. Avoidant people use their objects to do their feelings for them; ambivalent sufferers use others to do the holding, which they cannot sustain themselves. By alerting the therapist to the vocal patterns which express the contrasting attachment styles, attachment theory can help the listener tune into these processes more easily and with greater confidence that they represent reproducible clinical phenomena. In the next chapter, I return to a more theoretical exploration of how attachment ideas can help widen the applicability and relevance of the psychoanalytic perspective in psychotherapy.

Chapter 5

An integrative perspective on change in psychotherapy

Understanding what brings about change in psychotherapy is a key question for researchers and practitioners alike. In this chapter, I try to bring an attachment perspective to bear on one of the crucial differences between cognitive-behavioural and psychodynamic therapies. At the risk of oversimplification, this can be based around the distinction between pre-determined and emergent meanings. Structured therapies like cognitive-behavioural therapy have a set of pre-determined schemata, which, for example, are thought to underlie dysfunctional thinking in depression – a tendency to interpret the world in negative terms and to attribute setbacks to failings in the self. Therapeutic strategies are similarly pre-set; for example, challenging these negative assumptions, building on areas of competence in homework tasks. By contrast, dynamic therapies aim to foster the discovery of emergent meanings (Margison 2001), which come to the fore when an element of instability or turbulence is created within the firm structure of the therapeutic encounter. Thus psychoanalytic psychotherapy may at times appear to lack overt aims or goals. Indeed, Wallerstein (1965: 749) points to the ironic contrast between 'goallessness as a technical tool marking the proper posture of analytic work and the fact that psychoanalysis differentiates itself from all other psychotherapies, analytically oriented or not, by positing the most ambitious and far-reaching goals in terms of the possibilities of fundamental personality reorganisation'. The aim of this chapter is, after looking at the changing theoretical basis of psychoanalytic psychotherapy and relevant findings from psychotherapy research, to use ideas from attachment theory to justify aimlessness as an aim.

Definitions

The word 'aim', which I shall use interchangeably with terms such as 'goal', 'objective' and 'target', can be used to refer to many different aspects of psychotherapeutic activity depending on the time-frame and perspective adopted. Psychotherapy researchers customarily distinguish between *outcome goals* and *process goals*, the former referring to the overall strategic aims of the therapy and the latter to session-by-session objectives (Orlinsky *et al.* 1994). Outcome goals can include symptom reduction, personality maturation, the capacity to form less problematic intimate relationships, enhanced autonomy, reduced dependence on medical services, a strengthened sense of inner freedom and identity. Process goals, on the other hand, refer to the technical means thought necessary to achieve these objectives. In psychoanalytic psychotherapy, these can include forming a working alliance, maintaining boundaries, providing a setting, making transference interpretations, working through and coping with termination.

A third conceptual 'layer', which concerns what might be called *structural goals*, focuses on the connections between process aims and desired outcomes. This also encompasses the links between events in the session and the everyday life of the patient. In what way does a transference interpretation enhance autonomy? How does secure setting lead to symptom reduction, or empathic attunement improve intimate relationships? At this level, we find complex theory-laden aims such as making the unconscious conscious, reducing splitting and the tendency to projective identification (Steiner 1989), 'bringing the trauma into the area of omnipotence' (Casement 1985; Winnicott 1965) or, in Kleinian shorthand, 'from PSP to DP' or 'from –K to +K' (from anti-understanding or anti-knowledge to positive knowledge; Symington and Symington 1996). It is in this intermediate area that attachment theory can make a significant contribution.

These three layers can also be visualized as different time-frames within treatment. Outcome objectives are macro-goals referring to the whole course of a therapy, and even to 'sleeper effects' extending after therapy has finished. Structural objectives are midi-goals: month-to-month changes in the inner world of the patient that the therapy hopes to achieve. Process goals concern the micro-level, homing in on individual sessions or even fractions of them.

Another distinction that needs to be made is between *therapist aims* and *patient aims* for psychotherapy. What the patient wants and thinks she is trying to achieve may be quite different from the objectives of the therapist. Llewellyn (1988) asked patients and therapists what events in a therapy session they thought were most helpful. Patients emphasized reassurance, relief and problem solution; therapists thought the gaining of insight was most useful. This is a particularly complex area in psychoanalytic psychotherapy in comparison with, say, cognitive therapy, since it needs to take into account both conscious and unconscious aims. To be simplistic, the patient may for example *say* he wants to become more autonomous, but unconsciously crave for indefinite dependency, and the same might even be true at a counter-transferential level of the therapist.

From an attachment perspective, the therapist may be acting as a secure base in the traditional physical sense of someone to whom the patient can be physically close at times of emotional disturbance – 'therapy' being a safe space where painful feelings can be explored in the presence of an attuned, reliable and non-threatening other. This is the equivalent of the 'passive immunization' analogy mentioned in Chapter 1. However, the secure base for adults may take the form of emotional rather than physical proximity. Here the therapist is not so much a physical presence as a mental representation of an understanding figure who makes emotional pain bearable – here, therapy is helping to create autonomy and emotional competence. The contribution of the therapist is to a sense of 'being understood' and to the idea that, by gaining some sort of safe vantage point within the self, anxiety and mental pain can be withstood.

The changing context of psychoanalysis

Effective psychotherapy

We do not know for certain what are the effective ingredients of psychotherapy. The debate usually centres around three broad factors – *containment, insight* and *new experience* – with different authors emphasizing one or other as being particularly important (Bateman and Holmes 1995). In attachment terms, containment is readily seen as equivalent to the secure base, and insight equates to reflexive function. But what about 'new experience'? A crucial element here, in addition to reliability, consistency and feeling understood, is the repeated experience in therapy of emotional 'rupture' and 'repair'. In the Strange Situation, the ability of the care-giver to withstand protest and help the child re-establish the secure base following a brief separation is a mark of secure attachment. Similarly, therapy is characterized by a rhythm of separations (at the pre-determined end of sessions and sequence of 'breaks') and reunions, and within sessions by misunderstandings, minor acting out, and so on followed by resolution, with a consequent deepening of empathy (cf. Malan 1976). This alliance rupture and repair is an important therapeutic skill, and provides a very different experience to the entrenched insecure-making responses the patient may have previously encountered (and in adult life helped to create). The capacity for alliance repair is crucial to self-esteem and effective interpersonal functioning.

From repression to splitting

'Healing' – that is, making whole – a divided self remains a fundamental therapeutic aim that has remained consistent throughout the history of psychoanalysis. We hope to help our patients to become more aware of the different aspects of themselves, to become more coherent, more integrated, more 'together'. Early psychoanalytic metapsychology was preoccupied with the 'horizontal' split between the conscious and the unconscious mind, with 'removing the amnesias' (Freud 1896) or making the unconscious

conscious. Thanks to the work of Klein and her followers, the contemporary emphasis is more on 'vertical' splits in which parts of the self are projected into the world, leaving the sufferer feeling depleted, threatened, manically triumphant, and so on. The aim of therapy then becomes not so much to remember what has been forgotten, but to recognize and accept those parts of the self that have been disowned. In working with attachment, those parts of the self sequestered from mirroring responses from the care-giver are similarly viewed as split off – often as an 'alien' presence in the body, or located in a care-giver from whom separation seems impossible – and can gradually be recovered as attachment becomes more secure.

From reconstruction of the past to deepened awareness of the present

Sandler and Sandler's (1984) distinction between the 'present unconscious' and the 'past unconscious' marks another significant shift in the way in which the aims of therapy are viewed. Today's analysis starts not so much with the aim of reconstructing some presumed early childhood constellation from which all present difficulties flow, but from the feelings, phantasies, thoughts, assumptions and impulses that the patient experiences in relation to the here-and-now analytic relationship. Becoming aware of these helps patients see the totality of their responses in a new light, and so widens choice and opens up alternative interpersonal strategies. Hypothetical early childhood relationships provide a powerful metaphor by which these reactions can be encapsulated, but do not necessarily represent either the truth or the cause that will provide a magical key to the patient's difficulties. This change of emphasis from past to present brings psychoanalytic therapy in line with other therapies, such as cognitive therapy, where becoming aware of hitherto ignored 'rules' and assumptions – usually negative or simplistically black and white – similarly leads to greater self-mastery and widened choice. On the other hand, attachment ideas warn against a purely intellectual or 'cognitive' solution to problems, which typically tends to be part of an avoidant strategy in insecure attachment. Attunement implies an emotional responsiveness that goes beyond purely intellectual understanding.

From infantile sexuality to patterns of attachment

Another remarkable change in psychoanalytic thought is the move away from conceptualizing relationships in terms of infantile sexuality to seeing them instead in the light of different patterns of dependency and attachment. The avoidant individual, for example, who shuns intimacy and remains emotionally detached in sessions, might formerly have been seen psychoanalytically in terms of repressed homosexuality. Today's formulation would emphasize difficulties with attachment and fear of the vulnerability to attack that closeness implies. Although this can still be seen 'oedipally' – for example, that the patient fears closeness to the therapist because of paternal prohibition or 'castration anxiety' – these are best seen as useful metaphors rather than descriptions of actual childhood phantasies. Kleinians such as Britton and his colleagues (1989) see 'Oedipus' in conceptual rather than bodily terms – that is, the ability to separate oneself from one's object, to take a 'third position' and so begin to be able to reflect on oneself and one's situation. Even such an uncompromising formulation of the aims of psycho-analysis as Money-Kyrle's (1971) – seeing the breast as supremely beautiful, parental intercourse as supremely creative, and acceptance of the inevit-ability of death – can be seen as a metaphorical expression of more general aims, such as a reduction in neurotic ambivalence, destructiveness and omnipotence. The move from insecure to secure patterns of attachment enables an individual to trust and admire his secure base, to be reassured by the idea of the parental relationship as a guarantor of emotional rather than physical security, and with the help of an internal secure base to face death with equanimity.

From insight to reflective function

We have seen how Fonagy and his colleagues (1995; Fonagy and Target 2000) use the term 'reflexive function' to capture the ability to think clearly and coherently about one's biography. Their research suggests that, in the face of childhood trauma, reflexive function may be a crucial determinant of whether or not this leads to enduring personality disorder. Normally such a capacity is internalized on the basis of the *mother's* capacity for reflexive function, but it can also arise out of relatively brief but good non-parental relationships with, for example, teachers and grandparents or even psycho-therapists. The relevance of reflexive function to the present discussion lies in the use of the word *function*. Achieving 'insight' has always been a central psychoanalytic aim, but there is evidence, both clinical and research, that insight in itself does not necessarily produce change – hence subsidiary notions of 'pseudo-insight', intellectualization, etc. The aim of therapy is not primarily to achieve specific 'insights' into oneself or one's past, however interesting or intellectually satisfying these may be, but rather to develop the capacity or *function* for self-awareness: to identify feelings, thoughts and impulses, to put them into words.

The evidence from research in psychoanalytic psychotherapy

The therapeutic alliance

One of the most robust findings of psychotherapy research is the discovery of the predictive effect of the therapeutic alliance. The Vandbilt group (Strupp 1993) have shown that a positive therapeutic alliance early in treatment is a very good guide to the final outcome of therapy. There has been a great deal of debate about the significance of this finding. Which is most important: the alliance as seen by the patient, the therapist or an external observer? Is the finding tautologous in the sense that a strong alliance is merely evidence of good outcome in the early stages of therapy? It is certainly true that therapists who fail to form a good working alliance with their patients are unlikely to produce much benefit.

It has also been shown that 'patient factors' such as diagnosis and motivation make the greatest contribution to the therapeutic alliance (Horvath and Symonds (1991). The implications of this for our discussion must be that the more disturbed or unmotivated the patient, the greater the care and attention the therapist must devote to fostering a good alliance. What is the therapeutic alliance if not an attachment bond? Techniques such as extended assessment, pre-therapeutic preparation for unsophisticated clients, clear boundaries and therapeutic contracts have an important part to play here if psychoanalytic psychotherapy is to treat effectively the more disturbed patients who form the bulk of referrals in publicly-funded settings. The basic parameters of secure base – consistency, reliability, attunement, rupture repair – are equally relevant to the establishment of a therapeutic alliance. The latter is particularly important in the treatment of disturbed borderline patients where disruption of the therapeutic bond is almost invariable. Like Robert Bruce, the attachment informed therapist must be prepared to try, try and try again to form a bond with difficult patients. It is only once that bond is formed that the controlled turbulence and challenge needed for new meanings to emerge can hope to succeed.

The relationship between diagnosis, technique and outcome

Wallerstein's (1986) study of forty-four long-term analytic patients treated by the Menninger Clinic over a 25-year period remains, for all its methodological shortcomings, a landmark in psychoanalytic psychotherapy research. He found that many so-called analyses were far more supportive than they cared to admit, and that supportive therapy was just as effective, or indeed slightly more so, than so-called classical analysis – although relatively few patients did really well whatever the therapy. These were all highly disturbed patients and the results tend to argue against the commonly held assumption in analytic circles that the more ill the patient, the 'deeper' should be the therapy. There are now several more methodologically rigorous studies looking at the interplay between the maturity of the patient, type of intervention – supportive or interpretive – and outcome, most of which point in the same direction. Horowitz *et al.*(1984), for example, compared outcomes of brief dynamic therapy in patients suffering from abnormal grief reactions. They divided patients into those with 'primitive' defence mechanisms and those using more mature defences. In summary, the less disturbed patients did best with more interpretive therapy, while those using more primitive defences fared best when offered a more supportive slant. The clear implication is that therapists should aim for support, especially in the early stages of treatment, with more disturbed patients. Again, it can be argued that what is called 'support' is no more and no less than the establishment of a secure external base for the patient. More ambitious therapy aims to help the patient to find an internal secure base. Here again (see Chapter 1), the analogy of passive and active immunization seems relevant.

Joyce (1992) found a correlation between maturity as measured by 'quality of object relations' (QOR) and response to transference interpretations. Good outcome was associated with accurate transference interpretations in patients with mature QORs, but where QORs were immature, accuracy of transference interpretations was not linked to outcome. These results can be interpreted in several ways, but in general these results confirm (a) 'different strokes for different folks' (b) indicate that a low frequency of accurate interpretations would be a good process aim, (c) that affective involvement between therapist and patient, within a secure therapeutic framework, is likely to deepen attachment, whether or not it arises in response to a transference interpretation, and (d) disturbed patients may need modification of standard psychoanalytic technique in directions suggested by attachment theory.

Models of change

The assimilation model of therapeutic change

Stiles *et al.* (1990) proposed a Piagetian integrative framework in which they argue that the fundamental task of psychotherapy is what they call the 'assimilation of problematic experience'. They suggest that the patient is troubled by thoughts and feelings which may sit anywhere along a spectrum from 'warded off' through 'vague awareness' to 'problem clarification', 'understanding-insight', 'working through' to 'problem solution' and 'mastery'. This provides a framework both for tracking the progress of a particular difficulty in therapy, and also for conceptualizing how different therapeutic modalities operate, with psychoanalytic psychotherapy working more at the 'left-hand' end of the sequence, while cognitive therapies are focused more on working through and mastery, and less on evocation of 'warded off' (i.e. unconscious) thoughts. It suggests that the aims of therapy need to be understood developmentally and that different aims will apply at different stages of therapy. The initial task is to form a secure base in therapy for the patient; an ongoing need to is to maintain that base and to attend to rupture–repair cycles. Only once that is established can 'warded-off' feelings be faced, explored and tackled with the 'companionable interaction' of the therapist.

Teasdale's 'interacting cognitive subsystems model'

Cognitive Therapy has shown impressive results in treating and possibly preventing relapse from depression. However, cognitive therapists have recently begun to question its applicability to patients with more deeply entrenched depressive symptoms, or those with co-existing personality disorders. Teasdale and colleagues (1995) in particular question the conventional view that cognitive therapy works by helping the patient to question specific *propositional* negative assumptions about the self, such as 'If I attempt this task I am bound to fail'. They argue instead that depression is maintained by what he calls *implicational* affective-cognitive meanings, such as 'I am a worthless person', which lie much 'deeper' within the mind and have a more profound influence than propositional meanings.

In Teasdale's model, change in therapy comes about by tapping into these meanings by a process that involves (a) 'dis-identification', in which the sufferer manages to distance herself from her misery and so see it from the outside, and (b) the arousal of alternative affect that disengages the 'locked in' depressogenic beliefs and leads to new meanings and schemata. Thus, for example, an intervention that suggested that a patient was not so much depressed as sad or angry, linking these to previous loss or trauma, might produce an affective response that in turn might usher in a new less immobilizing meaning-schema, such as 'I am not depressed but in a chronic state of fury'. There are clear links here with attachment theory. The profoundly depressed person is in a state in which all relationships have failed. The illness itself becomes the only secure base to which the patient can cling, and even when things improve will be returned to whenever new threats and stresses arise. Fear of success, which is often seen as patients emerge from a depressive episode, can sometimes be understood in these terms.

'Debriefing' and the treatment of post-traumatic stress disorder

The assimilation and interactive cognitive subsystems models provide a rationale for emphasizing the importance of affective involvement between therapist and patient. We have seen how the formation of attachment is intimately bound up with affective arousal. For therapy to be effective, problematic affect has first to be evoked, brought into awareness and then set in a new context of meaning. In studying the psychodynamics of trauma, Van de Kolk and colleagues (Van de Kolk and Fisler 1996) provide empirical evidence for the view that successful therapy requires a combination of affective arousal and the assimilation of feelings via a new therapeutic narrative. Van de Kolk claims that in severe trauma the normal process of encoding of memory in which events are incorporated into self-schemata is disrupted, and that instead 'raw' sensory experience is stored, probably in the right hippocampal region of the brain. This is so painful that it leads to what Janet (1893, cited in Van de Kolk and Fisler 1996) called a 'phobia of memory'. Therapy for such trauma is based on an integrative 'debriefing' model that includes both psychodynamic and cognitive methods, whereby, via repeated rehearsal, the patient is gradually desensitized to the traumatic memories until they can be faced and brought into a more normal process of assimilation. As we shall see in later chapters, this gradual accessing of narrative forms the nucleus of an internal secure base.

An attachment perspective

Attachment theory offers an explicitly integrative approach to metapsychology and therapeutic practice. I have suggested that the overall goals of therapy can be summarized as the search for *intimacy* and *autonomy* and that the capacity for intimacy arises out of attunement, while a sense of autonomy comes from the successful expression of healthy protest and, where loss is irretrievable, grieving. The aims of therapy are to provide an environment that fosters attunement, is secure enough to cope with relevant protest and, therefore, where new meanings and secure-autonomous narratives can arise.

These ideas are very similar to some conceptualizations of the psychoanalytic process, especially those of Winnicott (1965), Pedder (1982) and Bollas (1992). Attunement is essentially playful and requires the existence of therapeutic space in which patient and therapist can creatively encounter one another. It is here that Bollas's 'unthought known' can be identified and brought into narrative play. Winnicott's emphasis on 'hate', how it is handled and its importance in the development of a sense of self can similarly be related to these attachment findings. Winnicott's idea that an infant needs to be able to say 'Hello object, I just destroyed you!' links with the idea of protest as the basis for autonomy, and with the arrangements of psychotherapy in which the patient is subjected to the mild and controlled stress of regular breaks. Pedder sees depression as arising from an inability to mourn the lost object – to grieve its absence – and in doing so to bring it fully to mind. Thus, to the extent it is absent in the external world, it comes alive once more in the inner world. When this process is blocked, or becomes circular rather than progressive, the lost object cannot be 'reinstated' in the inner world. It is either felt to be irretrievably lost or never really let go of; in both instances, mourning becomes chronic and inhibitory. The capacity for narrative reinstatement – akin perhaps to 'assimilation' in the model of Stiles *et al.* (1990) – depends on an environment in which pain and loss can be integrated into the self through the therapist's capacity to accept protest, tolerate despair and hold the sufferer at moments of hopelessness and with-drawal. In attachment terms, the object is either denied or clung to – but cannot provide a sense of an inner secure base.

The paradox

We are now in a position to return to the dilemma with which this chapter began: How do we reconcile a psychotherapeutic technique that depends on apparent aimlessness with the need to define aims and objectives if psycho-therapy is to be effective and relevant? The resolution of the paradox lies within the nature of the psychoanalytic process itself. To repeat, in the language of attachment theory, the aims of psychotherapy are to help create a secure base within which the patient can begin to face and 'narrativize' past pain and, through the relationship with the therapist, learn the rudi-ments of intimacy and autonomy. A secure base arises out of the responsiveness and attunement provided by the therapist. Attunement is, by its very nature, non-controlling, following rather than leading, affective rather than instrumental. It is 'aimless' in the sense that it cannot legislate in advance for what will emerge from the playful and spontaneous encounter between therapist and patient. This is perhaps a long way round to make a very obvious point and one that all good therapists know in their bones – you cannot prescibe what is going to happen in a session any more than you can prescribe happiness. What *can* be prescribed are the conditions favour-able to secure base; after that, exploration will always be dependent on chance and spontaneity.

The therapist does of course have aims, but these are mainly at a rather general strategic level: to maintain the boundaries of the therapy; to retain the 'binocular vision' that enables her both to engage with the patient and to be aware of the nature of this engagement; to relate the patient's material to a formulation of the intrapsychic issues with which the patient is struggling; and, perhaps most important of all, to be in tune with her own counter-transference. These 'aims' will be a complex mixture based in part on the therapist's training, in part arising from her own unconscious, in part evoked by the patient's transference. The capacity for reflexive function (i.e. to be able to reflect on her aims) is a crucial therapeutic skill. Where this fails and too narrow an 'aim' is imposed, the result is likely to be insecure attachment: avoidant if the patient's psychic pain cannot be accepted by the therapist and so is dismissed, ambivalent if the therapist becomes engulfed by the patient's pain and so is over-involved and, in all likelihood, then unpredictably distances herself from that involvement.

This same point could perhaps be made in more classical terms. Here the aim of therapy might be seen as making the unconscious conscious, or widening 'the endopsychic field' (Rycroft 1985). But it is in the nature of psychic life that a direct assault on the unconscious is likely to provoke extreme anxiety and, therefore, to evoke strong resistance – in both patient and therapist. The aim of therapy is to reduce anxiety via the integrity of the analytic situation and a positive working alliance, so that normal developmental processes can continue unhindered, including those of self-exploration and increasing self-awareness.

Conclusion

Depending on the time-frame, there are immediate, medium-term and long-term aims in psychotherapy. The immediate 'process' aims I have described in attachment terms as the need to become attuned to the patient's affective state, to provide firm enough boundaries to contain healthy protest, and to be aware of counter-transference so that neither aimlessness or control-lingness prevails. These lead to the intermediate aims of fostering of the capacities for intimacy and autonomy and the elaboration of a self-reflexive therapeutic narrative in which pain can be contained and brought within the normal memory system. Long-term aims include the overcoming of symptoms and a shift of psychic equilibrium towards security and exploration in place of inhibition, unboundedness or chaotic dissociation.

I conclude, then, by suggesting that the overall aims of therapy are to set in train the unfolding of a developmental process, either within the therapy itself if it is prolonged, or as a catalyst to 'real life' in brief therapy. At a fundamental level, this formulation does not represent a major change from those of classical psychoanalysis. What is new is the context in which therapy is practised, the introduction of ideas from developmental and psychotherapy outcome research, and the possibility of integrating analytic techniques with those of other therapeutic modalities. Although the personality is subject throughout life to continuous change and renewal, there remains a core identity laid down in the early years which represents a 'destiny' (Bollas 1987) that can be lived out for good or ill. The bringing together of attachment theory and psychoanalysis is simultaneously a rediscovery of core values and an attempt to find bridges and links with other therapeutic approaches. I turn next to some detailed clinical material to illustrate more points of overlap between psychoanalytic and attachment perspectives.

Chapter 6

Disorganized attachment and the 'basic fault'

In the television comedy series 'Fawlty Towers' the 'hero', Basil Fawlty, appears to be a man fundamentally at odds with himself. As proprietor of a small hotel, he is desperate for commercial success and to please his visitors, but his arrogance, incompetence and self-loathing constantly thwart and undermine his purposes. By the end of each episode, he is reduced to a state of abject humiliation, often to be rescued by his exasperated but long-suffering wife. We are mesmerized by this sad, childish, tall 'towering' man – it is Basil himself who is the faulty tower. His self-defeatingness mirrors our own failures. He touches on the ways in which we sabotage our best interests and destroy the objects on which we depend. We squirm and laugh in exquisite discomfort at private humiliations laid bare. We are perhaps in the territory of the 'basic fault', an idea first developed by Michael Balint in the 1950s.

The 1950s perhaps saw the greatest flowering of British psychoanalysis – the birth of 'object relations' as a distinctive position within psychoanalysis (Greenberg and Mitchell 1983). Many of Winnicott's most important papers were written then. Segal, Rosenfeld and Bion laid the foundations of present-day Kleinian psychoanalysis. Fairbairn (1952) published his *Psychoanalytic Studies of the Personality*. Attachment theory was also born out of – and partly in opposition to – the intellectual ferment within the psychoanalysis of that period.

Michael Balint was another central figure, some of whose ideas can be traced back to his analyst Ferenczi, and others, to the emergence of the Independent Group – independent, that is, of the Freudians and the Kleinians – as a 'third force' in British psychoanalysis following the 'gentlemen's agreement' of the late 1940s (Kohon 1986). Balint was interested in profoundly disturbed patients, for whom classical techniques of interpretation along the lines of Oedipal conflict seemed to make little impact. Like Bowlby, he was wary of libido theory and was moving towards a relational theory of the mind, whether three-person at the Oedipal level, two-person at the pre-Oedipal, or at the level of primary love, which he described as a 'harmonious interpenetrative mixup' – a typical Balintian phrase with its own mix-up of the vernacular and technical.

Balint differed from the Kleinians in that, like Ferenczi, he espoused a *deficit* rather than a *conflictual* model of severe psychopathology (Bateman and Holmes 1995), based on failure of 'fit' between the care-giver and the infant. He described, in a devastating catalogue, care that is 'insufficient, deficient, haphazard, over-anxious, over-protective, harsh, rigid, grossly inconsistent, incorrectly timed, over-stimulating or merely un-understanding or indifferent' (Balint 1979: 22). His identification of the 'basic fault' can be seen as a clinical correlate of disorganized attachment.

Retaining the language of libido theory in parallel with this relational approach, Balint defined two paradigmatic ways in which the world and its objects are 'cathected': the 'oncnophilic', in which people cling to their objects (especially intimates such as care-givers) and fear the spaces between them, and the 'philobatic', in which space feels safe, but objects are threatening. Balint's ideas anticipate some of the central concepts of attachment theory. 'Fit' is another word for the notion of maternal 'attunement' that was to emerge from Stern's (1985) infant–mother observational studies and the oncnophil/philobat dichotomy is very similar to Ainsworth's original distinction between ambivalent and avoidant patterns of insecure attachment.

Balint's theories arose out of his experiences in the consulting room rather than from directly observing parents and children. The Kleinians were developing ideas of splitting, projective identification and the interplay between paranoid-schizoid and depressive positions to acount for clinical phenomena arising with highly disturbed and regressed patients. They believed they had found a language with which to reach these primitive levels of the mind, based on the ways in which Klein had talked to her child patients during play therapy: as far as possible, everything brought to a session is related to the transference; a strong emphasis on primitive bodily experience; interpretations of splitting and projective identification taking precedence over repression; and an emphasis on 'death instinct' phenomena such as destructiveness and envy.

Balint differed from the Kleinian approach in several ways. First, he put forward his notion of the 'basic fault' to account for regressive phenomena he encountered with his disturbed patients. He used the geological metaphor of the 'fault' because:

> First . . . this is exactly the word used by many patients to describe it. The patient knows there is a fault within him, a fault that must be put right. And it is felt to be a fault, not a complex, not a conflict, not a situation. Second, there is a feeling that the cause of this fault is that someone has either failed the patient or defaulted on him . . . In geology the word fault is used to describe a sudden irregularity which in normal circumstances might lie hidden but, if strains and stresses occur, may lead to a break, profoundly disrupting the overall structure.
>
> (Balint 1979: 21)

He located this 'fault' at an early stage of development – pre-Oedipal, pre-conflictual, pre-verbal – and argued that it could only be reached in regressed states, which he divided into benign and malignant forms. Benign regression is 'regression in the service of the ego' (Kris 1956): the patient becomes child-like, but in a trusting way, that leads to creativity and a 'new beginning'. In malignant regression, the patient becomes more and more demanding, trying to subvert the analysis into a direct source of gratification rather than an opportunity for growth and discovery. Because 'basic fault' is pre-verbal, Balint advocated quiet holding rather than active interpretation. This was a fairly explicit critique of Kleinian technique, in which he argued that too much interpretation reinforced the omnipotence of the analyst, making the patient feel even more small and inadequate, thereby stimulating oncnophilia (clinging) and malignant regression.

In this chapter, I argue that the notion of the basic fault remains a useful metaphor for contemporary psychoanalytic psychotherapy and one that complements that of the paranoid-schizoid position, but that Balint's ideas about regression need to be revised; that a deficit model and a conflictual model are not necessarily incompatible; and that disturbed patients need *both* holding *and* interpretation if, to use another of Balint's metaphors, basic fault is to be transmuted into benign scar. Furthermore, the notion of 'fault' is central to the conceptualization of incoherent narratives as described by Main in the Adult Attachment Interview (AAI) and is, therefore, suggestive of incoherent attachment patterns in childhood. The AAI rater listens for stories where the logical progression is disrupted and where apparently incompatible or dissociated 'voices' appear to be breaking through. This links with an attachment perspective on narcissism in which, with the failure of an external secure base, the individual takes himself, or part of himself, or his body, as the only source of security and comfort (Holmes 2001).

Clinical material

I shall present material from two cases seen in psychoanalytic psychotherapy, one twice weekly, one once a week. The presentation in each case comes from a particular session, or group of sessions, that appeared to be a turning point or breakthrough. Both patients had been in therapy for several months and had apparently made superficial improvements, but they were still struggling with the fundamental issues that had brought them into therapy and what could be done about them. Both viewed themselves as fundamentally 'wrong' and in some way flawed or faulty.

Oliver: 'I can't cry'
Oliver, the 45-year-old land agent already mentioned, presented for psychotherapy while in the throes of an oncnophilic crisis. After a period of assessment, he started in twice weekly psychoanalytic

psychotherapy, using the couch. In the early weeks, he would arrive rather like the white rabbit in Alice in Wonderland, breathless, puffing, clutching a bundle of papers on which he had made notes in preparation for the session. Despite constant protestations of gratitude (which I found distinctly irritating), it was hard to avoid the suspicion that he viewed me as one among a number of professional helpers – gardeners, accountants, builders, clergymen, estate agents, etc. – most of whom turned out to be useless rip-off merchants who let him down and lined their own pockets.

Despite this, he rapidly became dependent on therapy and it appeared that progress had been made when he was able to admit how angry and abandoned he felt when I announced a break. His extreme sensitivity to rejection and child-like self-centredness (and his 'thin-skinned' narcissism, Bateman 1998) were revealed in this reaction, and in this session he remembered the recurring childhood dream (mentioned in Chapter 4) in which he was walking down a country lane behind his parents in the distance, desperately trying to catch up with them but unable to. This linked with present feelings of being 'left behind', not just by his therapist but by his contemporaries, whom he saw as successful, potent and rich compared with himself.

In time it became apparent that he had from childhood led a Walter Mitty-like existence, comforting himself with daydreams of being powerful, rich and successful, admired and fawned on by everyone. In reality he felt like a worm: constantly at the beck and call of others, especially his long-suffering wife and domineering mother.

As the months went by, things seemed to be going slightly better in Oliver's life. He pulled off a successful business deal. He was getting on better with his son, of whom he was intensely proud. He helped his wife with her business and she told him how much she valued his contribution. He made a number of financial decisions that he knew his mother would not approve of, but nevertheless went ahead. He became more relaxed in therapy, the notes on bits of paper disappeared and, instead of his usual worried disgruntlement, he was able at times to laugh.

Oliver's increasing robustness as these 'non-specific' improvements took hold, enabled me to be more challenging. I tried to get him to define why he really was in therapy. Was it simply to please his wife? He spent his life trying to fit in with others' needs, but what was he really thinking and dreaming about? This was especially relevant to therapy, since he was nonplussed by my lack of directions and, therefore, he found it hard to divine what was expected of him. That was how he habitually related to others: finding out what they wanted, trying half-heartedly to please them, while secretly resenting it, and then feeling let down, and in turn often letting them down. This pattern typified his relationship with his mother as a child.

This culture of challenge reached a point where I asked him to consider seriously whether he really wanted to be in treatment, or was he simply, once again, meeting the needs and expectations of others, especially his wife, while secretly unwilling to change and deeply contemptuous of anyone who purported to be able to help him do so. He came to the next session saying that he was certain that he did want help, but what did *I* want from *him*? I replied that to tell him would, once more, provide him with a script with which to comply, but that 'we' (rather than 'I', thus emphasizing the collaborative nature of the enterprise) could work best if he talked about what he was *really* thinking, rather than what he thought I might want to hear. Then, almost imperceptibly, he began to describe two linked daydreams. One belonged to the past when he had had a brief relationship with a girl who worked in the intelligence service. He described the excitement he had felt when ringing her up at work to ask her out, and that he was privy to the mysteries of the secret service, and the contrast between this excitement and their rather mundane and limited relationship.

Then he talked about a current fantasy in which his son was recruited to the civil service, rose to the top and found out, to his amazement, that his father was in fact the mysterious boss of the whole enterprise. Like the Scarlet Pimpernel, the apparent upper-class buffoon was in fact a courageous and heroic figure. I said little in this session, and he expressed surprise when it was time to stop, saying that he felt unusually relaxed.

In addition to the obvious compensatory aspects of these fantasies they could be seen as expressions of basic fault functioning, as Balint described it. The patient is regressed, immersed in a child-like world of fantasy. He is in a trusting state which Balint called *arglos*. There is a movement towards a fantasy of unity with the primary love object, here in the form of the secret service girl. The patient feels warm and relaxed, and the therapist is not under pressure to interpret. These are secure base conditions, physiologically as well as psychologically. Anxiety has reduced to a level at which a coherent narrative can begin to emerge.

Oliver returned on the following day in a very different state. He was very angry with his next-door neighbour, a farmer to whom he let out several of his fields. His bullocks had broken out, flattening hedges and wandering around in the wrong place with no-one to control them or monitor their movements. The farmer appeared supremely unconcerned. I said that I thought there was a part of himself that, like those bullocks, was out of control, and that he was secretly contemptuous of anyone, including myself, whose job it was to get them back into their rightful place. He replied by describing the rages he used to get into as a child when no-one could control him, and then he went on to talk about a story he had read at primary school about a wood that was threatened by developers and how all the animals clubbed together to save the wood. You were supposed to sympathize with the animals, he said, but he, with characteristic political incorrectness, thought the developer had a perfect right to chop down the wood if he wanted to, even though that idea was totally unacceptable to the teacher.

I said that he longed for the power of the developer, envied the animals, who like his sister, seemed to be preferred by his mother to him. He went on to say how frightened he was by animals as a child, and his terror when he was first placed on a horse at the age of 6. He agreed that it seemed that his mother loved animals far more than people, even her own son. Then he said, desperately, that he just couldn't let people's love 'in'. His wife said she loved him, but he felt himself resisting the feeling: 'It just isn't safe. I would be too vulnerable if I let myself be loved'. I said perhaps the same was true of therapy, he couldn't let it touch him. If he allowed himself to get close and was then rejected he would become a raging bull or go berserk with a chain saw. He nodded and laughed about the tissues in the consulting room: 'You therapists always have boxes of damned tissues. Tissues, tissues everywhere but never a drop of tears. I can't cry – it just isn't safe'. This was perhaps a reference to the earlier session where he had also talked about his inability to feel anything for his wife, and then how he had suddenly seen how awful it was for her to live with him (see Chapters 4 and 10). After this moment of compassion, he had for a short while felt much closer to her. I had compared this with Coleridge's Ancient Mariner, who had suddenly felt pity for the snakes in the becalmed sea, and how that had broken the curse and enabled him to recover.

Although no miraculous breakthrough followed, there was in subsequent sessions a deepening of contact. Oliver's basic fault, his simultaneous terror of and longing for closeness – the approach and avoidance that are the basic polarities of the attachment world view – were now part of our therapeutic vocabulary.

Balint was keen to emphasize the 'non-conflictual' nature of basic fault, perhaps in order to differentiate himself from the Kleinians. This material suggests, however, that basic fault functioning *is* inherently conflictual, in the sense that a fundamental wish or need is associated with an equally powerful anxiety. In incoherent attachment, like Fisher-Mamblona's (2000) goose Feli, there is an approach-avoidance oscillation, but no secure resting point can be found. The sufferer is torn between the longing to have his need met and the fear of the consequences of doing so. Oliver wanted to be able to feel, to cry, to be loved and held, but was terrified of exposing himself in this way to humiliation, rejection, control, ridicule and bullying. He shied away from the possibility of change.

An attachment framework can help make sense of this. Ainsworth (1989) and Bowlby (1988) both suggest that strategies of anxious attachment arise out of the need to maintain contact with an object that is either rejecting (the avoidant or philobatic strategy) or inconsistent (the ambivalent or oncnophilic strategy). This can be contrasted with secure attachment in which a person feels sufficiently integrated and autonomous to allow himself to get close without fear of engulfment and, conversely, feels secure enough to be able to let go and tolerate separation. On one side of Oliver's 'fault line' lay the fear of exposing his vulnerability, on the other his sense of isolation and compensatory daydreams. The apparently self-defeating strategies of his narcissistic personality disorder were an accretion of defences aiming to protect and buttress this fault line. The aim of therapy was, through challenging this defensive carapace, to reveal the fault and so raise the possibility of repair. For those whose fundamental attachment pattern is incoherent and who, like Oliver, have long-established narcissistic defences, this process can be long and arduous. 'Basic fault' essentially refers to the failure of *all* relational strategies; the therapist will be tested again and again before she can be trusted sufficiently for the real story of pain, rage and failure to be faced in a coherent way.

The mutatative response of the therapist was not confined to a Balintian (or Winnicottian) strategy of quiet holding in the first session, important though that may have been. Equally important, in the subsequent session, was the use of the bullock metaphor. The value of this was to bring the basic fault into consciousness by linking the external narrative of the annoying farmer with the internal story of Oliver's fury and rebelliousness. The interpretation acted as a bridge across the fault-line, bringing basic fault, *and* the defences protecting it, into view.

This suggests that effective therapy for basic fault depends on a combination of challenge, holding and linking interpretation – a Kleinian, attachment-influenced and interpersonal triad perhaps. It further suggests that neither a pure deficit nor a simple conflict model is adequate to account for the clinical phenomena. Oliver's interpersonal difficulties may well have originated in the 'deficit' of poor parenting, with a disengaged father and a self-preoccupied and controlling mother who never got onto her son's wavelength. But his response to these deficits – clinging to his mother/wife, while at the same time maintaining an absolute emotional distance – set up an unbearable conflict within him, a sense of failure and the impossiblity of resolving a dilemma that led him to see himself as fundamentally faulty. These ideas can now be tested in the second case, a woman who also saw herself as suffering from an irremediable basic fault.

Jane: unable to say 'I love you'

Jane, an unmarried successful businesswoman, was referred by her GP because of episodes of depression and feelings of emptiness which had failed to respond to simple counselling and anti-depressants.

Despite an effervescent personality and friendly open manner, and well above-average good looks, Jane saw herself as ugly, a failure and a coward (a 'wimp' as she put it), who had achieved extraordinary success in her field as a clothes designer due to luck and chuztpah rather than any inherent ability or flair. She expected at any moment to be revealed for the fraud she felt she was. She described herself as a workaholic, useless in her private life: 'I don't cook, my house is a mess, I don't keep fit, I have a boyfriend who likes me but who I don't deserve . . . *I* am a mess, that's the way it's always been, that's the way it's going to stay'.

She was the youngest of four children – and saw herself as a 'mistake' whom her parents regretted throughout her childhood. She felt she could never please parents who valued only beauty and action. 'Unlike my adored older sister, I was ugly and shy: I could never dare to go to dance classes, ride horses, do well at school or have boyfriends like her'. Her lack of physical prowess in childhood fed into her sense of defective narcissism. At 19 she left home for the first time and travelled to the USA. A turning point seemed to be a bungee-jump which she had steeled herself to do after an hour of vacillation. Having pushed herself to overcome the fears which had so restricted her as a child, she didn't look back. She returned home, started her business and went from strength to strength – but always keeping her feelings of despair at bay by constant work.

The main theme in the early weeks was control. Jane found the open-ended structureless sessions difficult, and she constantly tried to prod me into offering advice, questioning if I would like to hear her dreams or could suggest topics for 'discussion'. She made me feel redundant. She was her own therapist, presenting a packaged analysis of what was wrong with her, but without any spontaneous expression of feeling or live 'material' with which to do useful work. Nevertheless, she seemed to prosper. Her depression, which had brought her into therapy, remained at bay, her business went from strength to strength and, to her amazement, her boyfriend (whom she secretly despised) told her he loved her (this immediately after a session in which she had talked about the fact that no-one had ever said that they loved her). She had, of course, been unable to reciprocate.

As time went by, her fear of spontaneity and of not being in control in sessions began to have an increasingly deadening effect. There was no feeling of development or carry through from session to session. We seemed to be going round and round in circles. I began to challenge her inability or unwillingness to tell me about her feelings and the day-to-day happenings in her life. It was as though she was talking about someone else, someone she knew quite well, who just happened to be her. She was always an object, never a living subject in the room. I tried to link this with what she had told me about her parents – a father who was grossly insensitive and who always seemed to her to put her down ('if you tell him not to sit on that table, the first thing he will do is sit on it'), and a self-preoccupied narcissistic mother for whom Jane had always been a disappointment, even now that she was so successful and could buy them a house and look after them.

She would complain about her boyfriend – she just stayed with him out of convenience and fear. She didn't find him exciting sexually, but they got on well as companions. She thought of leaving him, but 'I could meet the most brilliant lover . . . and not be able to stand him except in bed'. When I suggested that *our* intercourse might be rather disappointing to her, or that she was playing out the theme of disappointment from her childhood with her boyfriend, only this time *she*, rather than her parents, was in control, she dismissed these as idle speculations or challenges that had little impact – she insisted that she was *here* wasn't she, what more did I want, was that not proof enough that she took therapy seriously?

One week she rang up and said her car had broken down and asked me to pick her up from town! I refused. She arrived by taxi a quarter of an hour late and was amazed at the end of the session when I stopped at the usual time, rather than adding on the quarter of an hour she expected. She started her next week's session by saying she would probably not be here next week, she had to go on a business trip the next day and wouldn't be able to fit in her therapy. I felt marginalized and irrelevant – again a form of projective identification perhaps, in which she was letting me know what it felt like to be seen as unimportant. I suggested that this might be her way of getting back at me for the missing quarter of an hour the previous week. She laughed and said '*no-one* does that to *me*', an acknowledgement that it had been a relief in some way that I had stood up to her.

Then, as usual, she started on her litany of self-criticism, covering familiar ground. I said I would like her to talk about her feelings. She seemed genuinely puzzled by this and was clearly unable to differentiate feelings from thoughts: 'What exactly *are* feelings?' I said that her difficulty with feelings could be linked with the bungee-jump or what it symbolized. By taking that plunge she had freed herself from fear and low self-esteem, but to do the jump she also had to banish her feelings. Her fear now was that if she allowed therapy to become important in her life, she would revert to her pre-bungee-jump state.

She then started to talk about how she had lain in bed that morning in her boyfriend's cottage, and looking around her had been horrified by the squalor which she subjected herself to: 'I could have a big house, a lovely garden, surround myself with beautiful things . . . only yesterday my accountant told me I am a rich woman'. I suggested that she hoped that I, like her accountant, would open her eyes to her inner riches, but that that also meant looking at her 'squalid' feelings, and that was very frightening.

She didn't respond, but went on to talk about a salesman who worked for her who had rung her up with all sorts of excuses about why he wasn't meeting his deadlines, but that basically he was lazy and a con-man. I said that a part of her was lazy and didn't want to do the work necessary if psychotherapy was to be helpful and how she wanted to con me by not talking about her feelings. She blushed and said 'That's IT – you're spot on'. She then said that her boyfriend had rung her up recently and had said 'I love you', and how, much as she wanted to, she just could not say the same thing back to him. I said that perhaps to say you love someone is to run the risk of being controlled by them, and that if she let me know or her boyfriend know about her feelings she might be in our control, just as she was controlled by her mother as a child. She ended the session by talking much more tenderly about her mother and how she is getting old and won't be around for ever.

She parted by saying that perhaps she would come next week after all – but in the event, she didn't. Nevertheless, this session did mark something of a turning point and she became more open with her feelings in subsequent work. In the end, and not without many misgivings, she did marry her boyfriend and soon after the wedding ended therapy, perhaps somewhat prematurely.

At first sight, this sequence might seem far removed from Balint's formulation of basic fault: no obvious regression, no 'arglos' (quiet trusting togetherness between patient and analyst), all too obvious conflict between therapist and patient, and a patient whose difficulties appear to lie in the three-person sphere of rivalry with her pretty sister. Yet Jane undoubtedly did feel that she was faulty, and in the moment of 'that's it' her fault line seemed to have been touched, a place she so vigorously defended up to then, and once again after it. Also, that point seemed to centre on a pre-Oedipal two-person dilemma: her terror of being alone with another person, her inability to love. As with Oliver, she expressed an inescapable conflict – she wants more than anything to love, but to do so is to lose control, and that is what she fears more than anything. Also, like Oliver she was brought to that point by a sequence of challenge, linking interpretation, and holding. The challenge was a double one. By insisting on her talking about her feelings I was showing that I took her seriously, and by refusing the extra quarter of an hour I was refusing to pander to her, which would have been, in Balint's terms, a fragment of malignant regression. The transference interpretation brought the displaced affect into the therapeutic relationship. When I accused her of being the lazy one, the con-person, she was initially shocked and furious, then relieved and moved. All this in the context of holding, not just in the sense of non-judgemental listening and taking her seriously, but also holding her to her commitment to regular therapy. This fierce holding can be seen in the context of a movement from insecure to secure attachment. People who are insecurely attached both need and fear their secure base, endlessly oscillating between approach and avoidance. To help overcome their fear of the secure base, they may have to be held tight even as they struggle and resist, and only thus gradually come to discover that their fears are groundless, that trust is possible and that a coherent relational strategy can work both as a source of security and a jumping off point for exploration.

I have tried to describe moments in therapy when a bedrock interpersonal difficulty is finally reached, often after a sense of not getting anywhere. Basic fault implies a contrast between superficial and structural work, or, in the vernacular of systemic therapy, between the 'second order' and 'first order' change. Balint formulated the concept in the context of psychoanalysis rather than psychoanalytic psychotherapy, and specifically to address the problems of more disturbed borderline patients as opposed to the 'three-person' Oedipal problems with which psychoanalysis started. Basic fault may take a different shape when seen in the setting of weekly psychoanalytic psychotherapy. The opportunities for regression are less, so what is seen is not so much Balint's 'beyond conflict' state of calm regression (although that can occur, as it did in the first of the two sessions with Oliver), but rather some manifestation of basic fault *and* of the patient's protective defences against it.

The key is Balint's 'two-person situation'. When the therapy begins to tackle the fundamental relationship with the therapist and the extent to which the patient can view therapy as providing a secure base, that is when basic fault begins to manifest itself. Transference interpretations are key tools touching basic fault, since they force patients to face their attitude towards intimate relationships as it confronts them here and now with the therapist. Challenge is an integral part of this – the geologist's hammer that penetrates through the defensive accretion to the fault line beneath. But, as Balint implies, patients will only feel safe enough to reveal basic fault if they feel sufficiently held in an atmosphere of acceptance.

This updating of Balint can be linked to some current integrative developments in psychoanalytic psychotherapy. The idea of a basic fault can be related to Luborsky's (1984) 'core conflictual relationship theme' or Ryle's (1995) 'reciprocal role procedures', both of which try to capture the essence of an interpersonal difficulty. The proposed sequence of challenge, linking and holding is implicit in Blatt and Behrens' (1987) formulation of the nature of therapeutic action – a combination of 'gratifying involvement, experienced incompatibility, and internalisation'. They argue for an integrative approach similar to that advocated here:

> We take exception to those analysts who view the major task of analysis as interpretation and confrontation and who stress the importance of

guarding against gratifying the needs of the patient. We take equal exception to those who consider the major task of analysis as establishing an empathic bond and who stress the need to guard against disrupting the patient's narcissistic illusions of omnipotence in the therapeutic alliance.

(Blatt and Behrens 1987: 293)

Attachment theory suggests that timing and sequencing are crucial here. *First* the secure base must be established, *then* comes challenge and confrontation. This applies both to the overall strategy of therapy and within sessions. Challenge in the first 5 minutes of a session, before the therapist has been re-established as a secure base after the preceding day, weekend or week's break, will lead to decreased empathy and retreat by the patient into their characteristic pathological secure base posture. Challenge in the mid-point of the session will foster emergent meaning. Implicit too in Blatt and Behrens' statement is that therapists must guard against ambivalence-reinforcing collusion or avoidance-fostering bullying (cf. Dozier *et al* 1994). Secure base arises out of a middle path between the two.

In both the sessions reported, a crucial element appeared to be a transference-type interpretation in which the patient's narrative of external events was linked with their internal world and the interpersonal situation between patient and therapist. This can be viewed in the light of the possible meanings of the term 'transference' (literally to carry across). First, the carrying over of psychic material from one sphere to another – here from the patient's investment in an external dispute to their own conflict with the therapist. Second, as a translation in the sense of conversion of meaning from one language to another – in this case, from the language of secondary process to that primary process. To this a third can be added, translation in the sense of a *movement*, in which a static, rigid structure becomes more fluid and mobile. Therapists must always feel free to move around in their mind and within the 'space' of the session, rather than being boxed into a corner either by the patient's demands or their own theoretical rigidity (cf. p. 18).

This image of mobility contrasts with the geological picture of the basic fault metaphor and reminds us that basic fault *is* no more than a metaphor – as are many useful psychoanalytic ideas. There is in reality no 'fault', but rather an enduring disposition to enter into a particular pattern of interpersonal relationships, a pattern established in childhood and permeating all significant interactions, including that with the therapist. In so far as basic fault is a metaphor, it is open to several interpretations and modifications. I have also suggested that the basic fault concept can be linked, via the empirical findings of attachment theory, with a robust interactive model which suggests that in neurosis there is a trade-off between the need for security on the one hand and to maintain contact with the object on the other. Main

(1995) describes the 'fluid attentional gaze' of the securely attached child who can move from loving attachment to care-givers to excited exploration of the world in one swoop. This can be contrasted with the fixed clinging-ness to people (ambivalence/oncnophilia) or avoidant adherence to things (philobatism) of insecure attachment. Basic fault captures at an experiential level the inherently conflictual aspect of this: the patients' simultaneous longing for and fear of closeness and the rigidity that this imposes on their relationships.

Psychoanalytic psychotherapy tries to 'translate' this rigidity into move-ment. It does this in a number of ways: by strengthening other aspects of the personality so that the basic fault zone becomes less crucial to survival; by helping the patient to see that people are inherently flawed and thus reduce narcissistic investment in perfection; by showing that men and women are not in reality made of stone and that shaking and moving the basic fault does not necessarily result in disintegration. In each of these tasks, humour is often a crucial ingredient. We are all at some level 'faulty towers'. By learning to laugh at ourselves, a fault can become a rich seam of pleasure and self-knowledge – although laughter can of course at times be a manic defence against sadness. In the next chapter, I turn to a more sombre theme, the transmission of insecurity across the generations.

Chapter 7

Attachment and the 'storied self'

Evolutionary theorists have long recognized that human evolution takes place mainly by cultural rather than genetic transformation. Intergenerational transmission is psychosocial psychiatry's genome project – an ambitious collaborative attempt to map the ways in which one generation shapes the psychological architecture of the next. Like the genome project, it has the potential to highlight pathological developmental pathways and to suggest ways in which they may be ameliorated.

Dawkins only half-jokingly coined the term *meme* as the unit of cultural evolution. A meme is an item of behaviour or an idea that is transmitted 'by leaping from brain to brain via a process which . . . can be called imitation' (Dawkins 1976). Humans, especially babies and young children, are mimetic experts. The most striking example of this is, of course, language acquisition. Infants are confronted by James's (1890) 'buzzing booming' world of sounds and sensations, yet manage to construct from this the syntax and grammar of their own language. How do they manage – to adult students of language – this seemingly impossible task?

The answer seems to be two-fold. First, the infant is never alone. Learning a language is an interactive process. Without a care-giver who acts both as an imitative model and a shaper and pedagogue, the child will never fully enter the linguistic universe. Second, the child is biologically predisposed to learn language, possessing a cerebral mechanism which Chomsky (1972) called a language acquisition device (LAD). Taken together, these two forces ensure that every neurologically normal child will learn to speak.

What is the relevance of this to psychotherapy? Psychotherapy is concerned with the language of emotions. Like language, emotional life, while being fundamentally biologically based, is learned, experienced and lived in a relational context – a central axiom of the attachment perspective. We learn both to speak and to feel on and from our mother's lap. There is the same predisposition to become attached – and perhaps, to acquire 'mental mechanisms' such as splitting, projection and repression – as there is a linguistic imperative.

We are held together both as individuals and as a society by relationships and by language. Lacan (1977) was the first to articulate clearly the profound connections between the psychoanalytic notion of an inner world and the linguistic universe: 'the unconscious is structured like a language'. I take this to mean that there is a grammar and syntax – structure and rules – to emotional relationships, of which we are largely unaware, yet which have a determining effect on how we feel about ourselves and those whom we love and hate, and which we have learned – like a language – within the microculture of the family.

This chapter explores how the way we talk about ourselves and our feelings – and so, ultimately, the way we experience ourselves and our relationships – is *transmitted* from generation to generation, and also can be *transmuted* by the process of psychotherapy. Bowlby (1988) developed attachment theory both as an extension of and in opposition to psychoanalysis, so I start by considering psychoanalytic models of parent–child influence. The empirical evidence outlined in earlier chapters shows how *handling* in infancy connects with *narrative style* in adulthood. I try to link this with Fraiberg and co-workers' (1975) notion of 'ghosts in the nursery' and to show how, if psychotherapy is a species of 'ghostbusting', psychological health requires a realignment of a person's relationship to their 'ghosts', so they neither dominate nor need to be denied.

For Freud, the basic mechanism of inter-generational transmission was *identification*. Central to the Freudian vision is an *active* baby, creating a world – both inner and outer – out of the influences that are presented to her. Identification starts from the incorporation or introjection of the breast-mother through the act of feeding. 'We are what we eat' is perhaps physiologically naive, but captures this primitive notion of cannibalistic identification. Piaget (1954) used a similar digestive metaphor for his fundamental schema of learning: *accommodation*, bringing food in proximity to the self in the stomach, followed by *assimilation*, in which it is broken down and turned into 'me'. Accommodation corresponds to the imitative aspects of identification, assimilation to the process by which what is learned is brought within the provenance of the self. As we shall see, a bad object may fail to be incorporated in this way and remain as an accommodated but unassimilated malign influence within the personality, liable to undermine or hijack constructive impulses.

For Freud (1923), identification was central to psychic life, forming the nucleus of the self–other axis, determining both narcissistic and relational pathways: who we would like to *be* (for little boys the father) and whom we want to *have* (the mother). Identification is also the basis of the ego-ideal/superego system (Freud 1923). Another aspect of identification centres on the ways in which the ego deals with the pain of loss by 'identification with the lost object' (Freud 1917). If the developmental process is seen as a series of losses, the ego becomes a 'precipitate of abandoned cathexes'. The self is composed of an amalgam of relationships, past and present. A sense of self arises out of the capacity to shape these influences into a coherent whole, one that is both unique and yet clearly a link in an inter-generational chain.

Klein, Fairbairn and their successors took this latter model, derived from Freud's and Abraham's speculations about melancholia, and made it the basis of object relations theory. The inner, or representational, world comprises the introjected objects – both good and bad – of the child's early life. These form a self–other template that acts as a model for subsequent relationships. The individual may identify with either 'end' of these valencies – passive or active, victim or abuser, sufferer or carer, and so on.

In these models, however, the relationship between external factors – parental handling, culture, ideology – and the inner world of fantasy and feeling is not clearly articulated. Attachment theory, by contrast, is an explicitly relational model in which there is no *a priori* inner world onto which some degree of external influence is inscribed. Relationship is present from the start, and the constraints of different attachment patterns are what makes for more or less adaptive identifications. There is a never-ending process of interactional pattern that plays itself out through the generations. Notions such as 'the self' or an 'identificate' are abstractions from this process. The following example suggests that the capacity to acknowledge this identificatory process is an important component of psychological health.

Peter

Peter, a businessman in his thirties, presented in a state of depression and panic. Whenever he became close to a woman and the possibility of commitment raised itself, he would become depressed and angry and sabotage the relationship – this had happened again and again. Peter worked for his father, whom he idealized as everything he would never quite be: intelligent, successful, powerful. At the same time, he hated him and painfully remembered the daily humiliation of being forced by him to make conversation at the dinner table as a child and becoming tongue-tied. Being able to articulate his feelings in therapy was a great relief, although there was always the suspicion that the therapist, like his father, would somehow use Peter's confidence to do him down.

In the course of psychotherapy, Peter began to see how, unconsciously, he was constantly seeking his father's approval, an approval that was never overtly forthcoming, even when he knew that his father was secretly pleased with him. He glimpsed at how this fruitless search bound him to his father and had prevented him from leaving the family firm and setting up on his own. Lacking a secure paternal introject, whenever he was called upon to 'be a man' and commit himself to a partner, he was beset with doubts and anxieties. He feared either that he would *become* the hated father (and so was intensely anxious about the possibility of having children of his own) or that he would fail to live up to the ideal father he felt he should be.

His relationship with his mother was equally ambivalent: as the oldest child he never really forgave her for having two more children. He resented her intrusiveness but relied on her always being 'there' for him, whatever went wrong in his life.

His autonomy and self-esteem were compromised by these ambivalent identifications. The process of transmission from one generation to the next was blocked – literally in his inability to conceive of himself as a parent. Peter's *father's* 'ghosts' (*his* parents had both died in a car crash when he was 10 years old) so influenced his handling of Peter (over-protecting and yet depriving him of approval on the grounds that everyone should learn to stand up for themselves as he had had to) that vitality could not be passed down to the next generation.

Through these partial and ambivalent identifications, a loss was transmitted in an unassimilated way from father to son. Peter's avoidant attachment style arose out of a childhood need to remain close to a father who could not himself tolerate closeness. This 'identification with the aggressor', or avoidant attachment style, led him to perpetuate a rigid pattern of unsatisfying relationships. For the curse to be redeemed – for the ghosts to be put to rest – two things were necessary. First, Peter had to have the opportunity to develop a non-avoidant relationship with the therapist, who became a more or less secure base in which he felt free to express feelings without fear of rejection. Second, he needed to become aware of the ways in which his own self-experience was shaped by his father's fantasies, and that his father's behaviour was in turn the product of what had happened to him as a child.

From this attachment-based perspective, the two ingredients of new experience plus insight remain central (cf. Chapter 5), but this is seen in terms of establishing a secure base and the emergence of narrative competence. The new attachment pattern is forged out of both the patient's and the therapist's attachment history (Dozier *et al.* 1994), and the focus of insight is as much on the previous generation as it is on the patient himself.

Object relations theory focuses primarily on the psychic activity of the baby and how through identification one generation is 'pulled down' into the next. Bion, Bowlby and Winnicott were all, although in quite different ways, concerned with an interactive or interpersonal model to which parent and child are equal contributors. Leiman (1995) brings together a Winnicottian perspective in his model of interpersonal learning which takes place at the 'zone of proximal development' (Vygotsky 1978). In the transitional or play space, the parents' task is to give meaning to the child's experience: a movement is recognized as a gesture, babbling is identified as the beginnings of speech. Thus the parent's capacity for empathy, to set limits, to put her own feelings to one side to focus on the baby, and what the baby 'means' to her (the one on whom she will lavish the love she feels she never had, the sibling who displaced her, the brother who was preferred to her, and so on), all these factors will determine the quality of parent–child interaction and so influence how the baby comes to understand herself and her world, and how fantasy transmits itself from one generation to the next.

As introduced in Chapter 3, Winnicott's notion of maternal *mirroring* is a key concept in theorizing this process. According to Winnicott (1967), when the mother looks at the baby, 'what she looks like [i.e. to the baby] is related to what she [i.e. the mother] sees there'. As discussed above, this clinical insight has been expanded by Gergely and Watson (1996), who suggest that an attuned mother helps her infant identify feelings by mirroring behaviour that has two characteristics. First, the mother's facial expressions of emotion are 'marked' by exaggeration, so that the child can see that they are 'pretend', not real. Second, they are contingent on the child's feelings, so that they arise only when he or she appears to be experiencing a particular emotion (a response that in itself has a soothing function). Here we see the beginnings of a possible representation of, or story about, the self and its feelings. 'Marking' separates out self-representation from ordinary perception. It is as though the mother is saying 'this is a little play about you and your feelings'; contingency ensures that the play hangs together. 'Marking' can be related to the highlighting, figure/groundedness of the narrative self (who I tell myself I am); contingency is linked to the sense of a coherent and unitary self. Both, too, may form a basis for the beginnings of the sense of an inner world – a 'place' in which experience can be projected, represented, thought about and creatively assimilated.

Attachment research suggest links between these observations of early life and the narrative self in adults. The way a parent talks – and, presumably, therefore thinks – about him or herself links forward with attachment patterns into the next generation, and backwards to their own attachment experiences in childhood. Reflexive function, it is believed (Fonagy 1997), is a key determinant of whether mothers whose own childhoods were traumatic will have infants who turn out to be insecure in the Strange Situation. The capacity for reflective function appears to be protective against psychological vulnerability in the face of environmental difficulty, an important finding for psychotherapists, since a large part of their work could be seen as enhancing reflective function in their patients. Clearly, too, reflective function is related to autobiographical competence: to tell a story about oneself in relation to others, one has to be able to reflect on oneself – to see oneself, partially at least, from the outside, and this in turn depends on the experience of maternal mirroring. The maternal mirror is the basis of the 'inner mirror' or representational world whose establishment is part of the task of psychotherapy.

While attachment emerges from parental handling, narrative style has to do with the individual's relationship to herself. Between the Strange Situation and the Adult Attachment Interview (AAI), a process of internalization has taken place, which comprises an individual's awareness of herself, her significant others, the relationships between them, and her awareness of, and ability to report on, these phenomena.

What, then, can we say about the origins of these kinds of awareness and their relationship to security and insecurity? Meares (1993) has developed an hypothesis based on what he calls 'self-narrative'. He starts from Winnicott's (1971) notion of the child's need to be able to play 'alone in the presence of the mother' if a stable 'true' (in attachment terms 'secure') sense of self is to emerge. By providing a quiet background presence, the mother, in a typical Winnicottian paradox, enables the child to forget her and to concentrate on the self-exploration that is the essence of solitary play. If, on the other hand, the mother is unavailable, inconsistent or unattuned the child will be forced to think about her parent and so be liable to develop a distorted representation of herself.

Meares (1993) studied tape recordings of the type of speech used by 3 to 4-year-olds during this solitary play. Following Vygotsky (1978), he calls this 'inner speech', although at this particular stage in linguistic development it is audible and therefore available for scientific study. Inner speech has specific features that differentiate it from social speech. Rather like Freud's (1911) contrast between primary and secondary processes, inner speech is disconnected and incomplete, words flowing into one another by association rather than following a logical progression. Audible 'inner speech' stops rather abruptly around 5–6 years of age. It is reasonable to speculate that self-awareness, which is so bound up with a sense of self, privacy, awareness of emotional truth and falsehood, the ability to plan and to reflect on emotions, is a continuation of this play talk described by Meares.

What started as an interaction, shaped by the attachment dynamic, has become internalized, so that the child now has within herself an inner mirror, or inner eye, within which emotional thought can be represented and creatively modified. Acquiring inner speech means becoming intimate (the word 'intimate' provides an etymological link between emotional proximity and communication) with oneself: knowledge of oneself goes hand in hand with knowledge of others. If required, the playing child can report on the goings on of her inner world; for example, 'I was pretending the mummy had gone away and the baby was sad'. As an adult, perhaps during an AAI, she might be able to say, 'When my parents separated, I used to pretend that my doll's mother had gone away and then returned'. Analytic psychotherapy recreates the childhood situation of being 'alone in the presence of another': 'free association' is, perhaps, none other than inner speech externalized once more.

The acquisition of inner speech is a developmental function. We can imagine how it could be disrupted in ways that might correspond with insecure patterns on the AAI. If the mother is unavailable, the child may be so concerned with maintaining proximity to her that he or she will be unable to play and so find an inner voice. This, in turn, leads to dismissive narratives and difficulty with intimacy. Preoccupied narratives reflect unmetabolized pain that has not been transmuted into the metaphor of play: the sufferer is searching for a safe container and using whoever happens to be at hand for that purpose – here feelings may be evacuated via 'projective identification'. If the parent has been intrusive, the child's self-narrative may be contaminated with the parental narrative, always thinking and feeling what is expected rather than what might have emerged had more child-centred parenting been available.

Finally, if the environment is traumatizing, the whole 'containment/self-narrative' envelope may be obliterated, leaving lacunae and discontinuities in the texture of inner reality and its representation in inner speech. This links with the notion of a child's 'theory of mind', as developed in the psychoanalytic literature by Fonagy (1991), Leiman (1995) and Hobson (1993). Fonagy argues that traumatized children lack a 'theory of mind' in the sense that they have difficulty in seeing others as having feelings, intentions and desires, any more than they can accurately define their own inner world. If there is no inner mirror, there is no capacity for mind in Fonagy's sense.

Faced with aggressive or sexually intrusive parents, the normal process of 'secondary inter-subjectivity' in which a child shares her experiences of the world with her care-givers via visual cueing, imitation and so on, is inhibited. To perpetrate his cruelty, the abuser has to remove from his consciousness the knowledge that the child can experience fear, pain, disgust, and so on (the ultimate example of this is the abuser who then murders his victim in an attempt to obliterate mirroring altogether). The child grows up in a world in which her feelings – and meanings – are discounted or obliterated. At the same time, the child is dependent on the abuser and may indeed be strongly attached to him. There is often a vicious circle, based on the attachment dynamic, in which the more the child is traumatized, the more she clings to her attachment figure, who thereby is encouraged to perpetrate further abuse, and so on. The abused child is likely also to deny the existence of her abuser's mind, since not to do so would be to face the unacceptable fact that those one loves and on whom one depends have malevolent intentions towards one.

The autobiographical self can be seen in terms of an inner object with which an individual has a relationship, comparable to 'external' relationships that can be understood in terms of different attachment styles. At a clinical level, the psychological fluidity of the secure-autonomous individual can be contrasted with the relatively static and defended positions of avoidant or ambivalent attachment.

Gergely and Watson's (1996) ideas suggest that there is a close relationship between the development of the self and secure attachment. 'Marking' enables one to distinguish one's own feelings from those of others and is thus a bulwark against the excessive use of projective identification. Where 'marking' breaks down, which may be particularly the case in ambivalent attachment, the child may be unable to distinguish her feelings from those of the mother: 'Is it my feelings I am seeing myself in the mirror, or hers?' Contingency is related to the 'truth' of one's feelings, helping one to ensure that there is a correspondence between an emotion and its representation. Here avoidantly attached children may be especially vulnerable, since they have not had the wrappedness of attention that is needed for them to 'find' their feelings in the mother-mirror.

Bowlby's (1988) formulation of what I am calling the 'inner mirror' was the idea of internal working models – maps of the self and its relationship to others, constantly checked and updated in the light of new experience. As will be discussed in more detail in the next chapter, those who are securely attached can (a) distinguish between their own experience and that of others, (b) represent and so tell the story of their feelings, and (c) have the capacity to break up their stories and reform them so they are more in keeping with the flux of experience. Ambivalent individuals are so close to their feelings that they cannot achieve the objectification – in White and Epston's (1990) terms, 'externalization', akin to Gergely and Watson's (1996) 'marking' – needed for a working story. Avoidant people, by contrast, cling to a stereotyped version of themselves and their past and feel threatened by the idea of the constantly updated narrative – again, in Gergely and Watson's terms, one that is checked for contingency – that is characteristic of creative living.

Ghosts

This attachment-based account suggests the beginnings of a theory of inter-generational transmission. Whatever is transmitted from generation to generation – a story, a fantasy, a script – acts as a ghostly presence or organizing principle around which psychological development can take place. It provides a necessary coherence, structure and shape for the emergence of psychological structure. The story may be 'good' (secure) or 'bad' (insecure avoidant or preoccupied), but at least it is some sort of map that helps its bearer to know who she is, where she comes from and where she is likely to go. Incoherent organization (disorganized attachment), by contrast, which seems to arise out of the most damaging kinds of childhood experience, provides chaotic, confusing or contradictory messages for the next generation, in many cases leading to psychopathology. Perhaps in a few exceptional individuals who are able to transcend this confusion, this may be strengthening: they seem able almost to create an identity *de novo*, and in doing so may become the innovators (in evolutionary terms, the benign mutations or 'hopeful monsters') of the next generation.

Fonagy and Target (1996) see the function of psychotherapy as helping the patient to move from 'psychic equivalence mode' to 'pretend' mode. In the former, 'ghosts' are terrifyingly real, whereas in the latter, without devaluing the importance of pretence and imagination, they are ultimately seen as insubstantial remnants of the past – figures in a mirror, shadows rather than current perceptions.

The idea of ghosts goes back to the famous paper of Fraiberg *et al.* (1975: 387–8) and perhaps behind that to Ibsen's famous play:

> In every nursery there are ghosts. They are the visitors from the unremembered past of the parents, the uninvited guests at the christening. Under all favourable circumstances the unfriendly and unbidden spirits are banished from the nursery and return to their subterranean dwelling place . . . but how shall we explain another group of families who appear to be possessed by their ghosts? While no one has issued an invitation, the ghosts take up residence and conduct the rehearsal of the family tragedy from a tattered script.

Fraiberg's model links the archetypes of Pereault's 'Sleeping Beauty' fairy story with the developmental research we have been considering. In 'Sleeping Beauty', the curse of the uninvited guest lies dormant until Sleeping Beauty reaches puberty. Everything pointed and aggressive is removed from the palace, but in vain. Evil cannot be eliminated this way; the repressed will surely return. The princess pricks her finger and the blood (menstrual blood surely) starts to flow. The only solution now is total repression – the princess, and everyone else in the palace (her inner world), falls into a deep sleep. Only love will redeem 'the curse' (a menstrual reference); that is, the phallic insistence of the prince who cuts his way through the forest that has sprung up around the princess's sexuality. Like pubic hair, the mysterious forest is both an invitation (a mark of sexual maturity and availablity) and a covert of concealment, a warning to the unwary. The prince's kiss is an 'ah-ha' moment, like a good interpretation which brings those who are only partly living to life again. Now the story can be told and the ghosts (and the princess!) layed.

Leaving aside the sexist implications of female passivity in this story, Fraiberg's key point is that it is the *parental* ghosts who come to haunt the psyche of the next generation. A Kleinian reading of 'Sleeping Beauty' is entirely possible – the bad godmother contains the split off and projected hatred and disappointment of the 'Kleinian' infant, the reconciliation with aggression represented by the prince and the spindle exemplifies the depressive position – here 'haunting' is intrinsic to psychological functioning: none of us fully transcends the paranoid-schizoid position. But from an attachment perspective, early developmental history is the point at which the parental psyche hands on its legacy to the next generation. What cannot be represented in the parental mind will, through the constraints of insecure attachment, find its way into the unconscious psychic life of the child. As

Fonagy *et al.* (1995: 248) put it: 'The *child's* behaviour in the Strange Situation may then be a direct function of the child's cumulative experience of *maternal* behaviour in response to stress' (italics added). In other words, the child 'picks up' maternal responses to his own distress, which then shape his self-experience, just as his mother picked up her response to the child's grandparent's behaviour, and so on. Inter-generational transmission is by definition a three-generation theory.

Implications for psychotherapy

What are the implications of this for the practice of psychotherapy? As stated earlier, the AAI is innovative in that it concentrates as much on the style and form of a narrative as it does on its content. If psychotherapy works, at least in part, by providing a 'corrective emotional experience' (a point once hotly contested within psychoanalytic circles), it is likely to be because the therapist offers similar conditions to those underlying secure attachment: attunement, handling of protest, responsiveness, mirroring, and so on.

But these 'non-specific factors' (already discussed in Chapter 5), common to all psychotherapies, form only the background to the preoccupations of practitioners and their patients. Most therapists are concerned primarily with *content* and *cognition* – handling is taken for granted, once a therapeutic alliance has been formed. Inter-generational transmission appears as a *story* handed down and lived out by the protagonist in the family drama. Reflexive function (which is essentially a revival of the psychoanalytic notion of insight) brings together story *and* style, in that reflexions necessarily take a narrative form, but it is the *capacity* to reflect (i.e. reflexivity as a psychological function) which seems vital to psychological health, and acquiring that ability is a mark of progress in therapy.

There are three distinct stages involved in coming to terms with inter-generational transmission in psychotherapy. The first consists of becoming aware of the ways in which present feelings and behaviour are dictated by past experience – getting in touch with one's ghosts. This can be painful, especially as these influences from the past are so deeply ingrained, affecting every aspect of self-experience at a physiological level. It is as though ghosts are inscribed on (and in) the body.

The second phase usually consists of an attempt to expel these ghosts by violently differentiating oneself from what appear to be alien influences. This is the phase of anger towards parents and existential protest about the loss, trauma and inadequacy to which the sufferer was exposed. The patient hopes that, through the benign influence of psychotherapy, a new self will emerge, unscathed by the past. There is an emphasis on the creative self and the ability to find new solutions and patterns rather than be trapped by the dead hand of the past.

But this project can only be partially successful. Like it or not, we are made up of our past and cannot escape its shaping influence. There is no such thing as a self-made man or woman. The third phase, therefore, consists of coming to terms with our ghosts, of seeing how the parents whom we blamed so bitterly were themselves products of their own history. The patient (and the 'patient' at this point is also a facet of ourselves) comes to see that if things had been different, as he so fervently hoped they might have been, 'he' would not have existed and so the attempt to rewrite history is an impossible project, a product of the residual omnipotence and narcissism which is so essential to survival and yet so beguilingly misleading. Now he can begin to forgive his parents, to empathize with their pain and, in the end, to be grateful to them for bringing him into the world – the only world there could have been – with its mixture of joy and suffering.

These phases are, of course, never so neat in clinical reality as I have depicted. In psychoanalytic psychotherapy, each is played out within the transference, in which, initially, the patient will attempt to replay her attachment history with the therapist. These transferential feelings, as she becomes aware of them perhaps for the first time, are a reminder of the infantile self which silently shapes our destiny. Then, at some point, the therapy will be angrily repudiated, overtly in some cases ('I've found a faith healer, a new lover, a new anti-depressant, *that's* what's made me feel better'), more subtly in others, through missed sessions, slavish devotion that conceals bitter disappointment, gradual disengagement from therapy, and so on. Finally, with luck, there is acknowledgement and gratitude for the help that has been given, acceptance of what has not been achieved, appreciation of the obstacles which lie ahead.

Alison

Alison had been in once-weekly psychoanalytic therapy for several years. Her presenting problem was her depression and failure to sustain relationships with men. Much of the work focused around her father, a violent and abusive man who had terrorized her throughout her child-hood, and who had continued to make sexual advances to her as an adult. She experienced her mother as a depressed, downtrodden yet controlling woman to whom she longed to get close but seemed for ever out of reach. These themes were incessantly played out in the transference in one guise or another. She saw her therapist, like her father, as impossible to please, however much she ingratiated herself or pleaded with him ('tell me you like me – that is all I need to feel better', etc.). She was determined to be a 'good' patient, to free associate, talk about the past, cry or do whatever she thought was required, but always failed since the issue was spontaneity, and it was that which she feared more than anything. Worse still, she became at times *like* her father, intruding on the therapist's privacy, bombarding him with her requests to be liked, dictating his responses ('don't you dare say a word in exoneration of that man, I can't bear it').

At other times, the mother theme dominated and she became a passive suffering victim, rejected by men, hopelessly depressed, crippled (her mother had been a polio victim) by the traumatic horrors of her childhood. Now the therapist became the neglectful mother, silently standing by while she suffered, wrapped up in his own concerns (her mother would say, 'Have you hurt yourself, dear, go and ask somebody to get you a plaster', as she desperately tried to capture her attention) and apparently indifferent to her unhappiness.

For many years, therapy was the main focus of her life. Much improved in her external circumstances, she gained a measure of autonomy and self-respect. Her depression faded, but still the possibility of ending treatment was unthinkable and her relationships with men, while far more meaningful and satisfying, continued to be problematic.

In the seventh year of therapy, she came to a session following a 2-week holiday break with a 'confession'. She had three men in her life she said: her therapist, her current lover, and a former lover who still wished to be with her. 'I have decided that you are interchangable. When one of you is unavailable, I simply turn to the other'.

At this point, an image came into the therapist's mind of a children's film he had seen recently, 'Babe', in which a talking piglet was separated from its mother, and was offered instead three mechanical teats. 'So we are rather like teats offered up to a baby separated from its mother', he suggested. She said how scared it made her to hear him say that: 'Now you know that all my flattery and insistence that you are special and indispensable is merely a ruse to keep you interested in me'.

She then recalled an image from around the age of 4 in which she was lying in a large empty dormitory in the boarding school where she grew up (her parents ran a 'progressive' school for middle-class children during the 1950s, making sure that their own children were given no special favours compared with the other pupils), trying to get to sleep, feeling frightened and abandoned. The therapist remarked; 'It is not surprising that during the break you needed a substitute 'teat' while I was away, just as you would have needed to conjure up the image of a comforter while you were all alone at the age of 4'.

Then, suddenly, she made a positive link with her father almost for the first time in therapy. He was a foreign national and had been interned during the war. Her mother was pregnant with her when he was taken away, and she was 3 when he was finally released. '*He* must have felt abandoned when he was in that internment camp. No wonder he resented me when he came out, I had had my mother all to myself during that time'.

Next, quite unexpectedly, she recalled that her aunt had once told her that early on in their marriage her mother and father had been very much in love. She saw that without that love, or at least without their desire, she would not exist. They had given her the gift of life, however much that love and mutual desire had later turned to hatred, and however terrifying and painful at times that life had been. Paradoxically, this realization of her ultimate helplessness made her feel stronger and more free. Momentarily she no longer saw her father as a huge and terrifying monster, but as a flawed and vulnerable human being like herself. He inhabited her, not just to crush or eliminate her, but as an inescapable part of her history. The evil teat became a sad ghost whom she needed to set free. As she got more in touch with the aggression that lay behind the idealization of her therapist, so she was able to relinquish her intense dependency and ambivalent attachment. The fluidity of a more secure attachment enabled her to develop an inner mirror in which she could begin to see her father for what he was.

Coda

This chapter began with a rather grandiose comparison between inter-generational transmission and the genome project. The latter, if successful, will raise enormous ethical problems for future generations. If our fate is, to some extent, inscribed in our genes, how much of this do we want to 'know' – as parents about our children, or as individuals about ourselves. Certainly the argument for 'knowing' is a powerful one, both practically – by analogy with those who suffer from phenylketonuria but can be entirely healthy if they eat a special diet – and at a philosophical level, in that knowing more about the past and one's genetically determined future may deepen one's capacity to live fruitfully.

Understanding inter-generational transmission in psychotherapy can make an important contribution to this debate. Santayana's much quoted (and misquoted) dictum that 'those who cannot remember the past are condemned to repeat it' is supported by the findings of contemporary AAI research. If it is confirmed that reflexive function is truly protective against the pathological consequences of adversity in childhood, then we can say that it really is 'good to know' or, rather, to be able to know. Fonagy (1991) has, I believe, deliberately described reflexive function as a *function* – that is, a psychological attribute – rather than sticking with the more conventional notion of 'insight'. What is protective is not specific insights into particular historical events – indeed, there are circumstances in which traumatized people may need to be able to forget – but the *capacity* to introspect, to see oneself from another point of view and to put one's feelings into a context.

Psychotherapy enchances reflexive function in different ways depending on the model used. Cognitive therapy explicitly gives the client the task of attending to her 'automatic thoughts' and later of trying to modify them. Systemic therapies, especially in their current narrative guise, aim to help families identify the 'scripts' by which they live, and by honouring their past become less in thrall to it. In analytic therapy, by attending to her counter-transference reactions as a guide to the 'pull' exerted by the attachment needs of the patient, the therapist attempts to develop a shared picture of the unconscious interplay between them. The story of the therapy – an arena of shared reflexion – becomes a replay of the patient's history, but now one that she can represent in her inner mirror and from which she can begin to detach herself.

Inter-generational transmission challenges us to make something of what we are made of. We are – willy-nilly, narcissism or not – part of a continuing story. Stories exist in time, and however much we long to return to a pre-storied pre-symbolic existence, we cannot escape from time. Art captures time and, in doing so, tries to make it timeless: flux becomes fixed. As readers, observers or listeners, we enter the imaginary world that the artist has created, freed momentarily from the dictates of the past. But what we encounter there is the beauty of coherence and unity. As we open ourselves to this process, our capacity to reflect on ourselves – our reflexive function – is strengthened.

Art and psychotherapy thus both inhabit Santayana's paradox, which I see as an expression of the tension of living in a world of modernity, one to which attachment theory can add a scientific angle. I end with two literary examples of this tension – of the pull between the historical imperative of traditionalism and post-modernism's insistence on the primacy of an ever-renewing linguistic universe.

Scott Fitzgerald's *The Great Gatsby* (1926) has been described as the Great American novel. Its theme is the American Dream – the dream of the poor boy who can become a millionaire, and all for the love of a woman whose class position made her inaccessible, and who married her 'own', not for love, but for propriety. But the dream shatters, and at the end Gatsby, and his rival Wilson, are both dead, murdered by each other. Gatsby's success is based on a wholesale avoidance of his past; he rewrites history, is a liar and a cheat.

The unattractive anti-semitism of the book links this cheating and Gatsby's money-making with Jewish dirty-dealing. We can contrast this paradigm of tragedy in which ghosts, if denied, become avenging furies (there is an echo of Oedipus here), with the work of, say, Isaac Bashevis Singer, which celebrates the continuity of Jewish family and cultural life as it extends in time from the pogroms of the seventeenth century to the holocaust, and in space from the Warsaw ghetto to the Bronx.

The ultimate pathology of modernity is, like Gatsby, to deny the past and its transmission across the generations; of traditional society to remain in the grip of the past and to be unable to celebrate a creativity and renewal.

Singer's work teems with ghosts, which at first intrude and dominate the protagonists' lives, seeming to trap and enmesh them in traditionalism, but in the end come to be accepted as part of the unexplained mystery of life. The task of psychotherapy is, through offering an experience of secure attachment, to help find a middle course: through recognition of, but not enthralment to, the ghosts of the past, helping its patients to live more fully in the present. This link with literature will be taken up again in Chapter 10 and leads to the third main theme of this book – narrative – which forms the subject of the next chapter.

Chapter 8

Attachment and narrative in psychotherapy

Joseph Conrad's *Heart of Darkness* (1912) begins and ends on a packet ship moored on the River Thames, with the narrator Marlow sucking at his guttering pipe, forming a frame with which the reader has been taken on a compelling and horrific journey into the interior. The book is a story within a story, framed by the river itself, whose reaches, unlike stories, are unpunctuated – stretching in a spatial continuum from London across the oceans to the heart of the Congo, and in time from the present day back to the Roman invasion of Britain.

This contrast between the structure and boundedness of story, and the fluidity and formlessness of reality, forms the background to this chapter. This is also an opposition between artifice and nature, which can been expressed psychoanalytically as a contrast between the innocence, however bizarre, of the dream narrative and the patchwork of fragmented associations and the 'day's residues' which a dream evokes. Bollas (1995) takes this as a general paradigm for the activity of the unconscious, which he sees as continuously fashioning lived life into stories that appear to cohere, and then dismantling and dispersing those stories in the light of further experience. I shall follow this theme throughout this chapter, which is both an exposition and a critique of the 'narrative turn' (Howard 1991) in psychotherapy. I consider first some general aspects of narrative and then its application to psychotherapy practice. My aim, consistent with the overall thrust of the book, is to weave together contemporary psychoanalysis, attachment research and narrative theory into a common story.

My main contention is that narrative forms one half of a duality that lies at the heart of psychotherapy. This dichotomy can be expressed in a number of different ways: narrative and its deconstruction; prose and poetry; secondary and primary processes; story and image; 'when . . . then' and 'present moment'; then-and-there and here-and-now. Things go wrong, I shall argue, when the balance of this duality is disrupted – too much prose and not enough poetry, or vice versa. Psychopathology, which I approach largely through attachment theory's distinction between the various types of insecure attachment, can be seen in terms of an excess of one or other element. Let us begin with two contrasting clinical stories.

The constrictions of 'story'

Tom, an unemployed youth living with his parents and 15-year-old sister, was referred by his family doctor for help with his 'compulsive gambling', which was causing enormous concern within the family. When Tom was interviewed on his own, the story that emerged was as follows. He had been unemployed for most of the time since leaving college 2 years previously. Both his parents were working. During the day, while they were at work and his sister was at school, he would take items from the house such as video machines or his father's tools, sell them to his friends and then proceed to spend the money on fruit machines. Things had come to a head when he had smashed the family car, which he had taken without asking and was driving without insurance, while on his way to a local gambling arcade.

Tom, a shy and young-looking 20-year-old, described how difficult things had been since leaving college, how he had been unable to settle in a job and how his father had had a period of unemployment, which meant that they had lost their home and had to move into a smaller house. He had missed his dad dreadfully when a lack of local jobs meant that he had had to work away from home. When asked about his 'winning fantasies' in gambling, he spoke of how he dreamed of restoring both the family fortunes and his own reputation within the family.

When Tom was interviewed with his parents, a rather different picture emerged. Tom's father, clearly a good man at the end of his tether, was constantly criticizing his son; Tom's mother was obviously depressed, sitting mostly silently with tears running down her face. They explained how they were convinced that Tom was 'on drugs': he was pale and tired all the time, irritable and monosyllabic, just like the descriptions in the leaflet a friend had given them. They were then asked to confront Tom with this possibility in the session. Tom denied using drugs (as he had in the individual session, apart from admitting to occasional cannabis), while the parents looked non-plussed. The therapist suggested that his exhaustion and irritability might reflect depression rather than drug dependence. As Tom's father continued to express his exasperation – saying how they had several times been on the point of throwing Tom out but could not bring themselves to do so – the boy became visibly upset. The therapist reminded him of what he had said about his feelings while his father had been away. 'I missed you dad . . .' he said tentatively. Father was stopped in his tracks and looked tearful. With prompting he began to say, 'You're not a bad lad, son, it's just that you do bad things'. Tom went on to say how he felt an outsider in the family, while his parents and sister formed a cosy little threesome. Again mother and father looked upset, and mother began to say how she felt caught between her husband and son, and how, against her better judgement, she gave in to Tom's demands for money.

The session ended with the parents determined to be firmer with Tom, if necessary locking valuables away during the day, and with Tom and his father giving each other what seemed like a genuine hug of reconciliation.

At the start of the session, this family seemed trapped within a very restricted 'story' of their situation. Seeing Tom as a 'compulsive gambler' or a 'drug addict' made some sense of their distress, if only to medicalize it and so shape it in such a way that they could elicit help. The purpose of the psychotherapy was to introduce some perturbation into this rather rigid narrative, to disperse it for long enough for a new story to coalesce, one with more complexity, allowing for a greater range of emotional expression. The new story was one of a lost youth trying to rescue his family fortunes, of parents torn between lenience and violence, of the looming impact of unemployment. The crucial moment in the session came when Tom told his father he missed him, and father responded by becoming tearful. At that moment, he seemed to listen to his son again and see him as a person, not as a clichéd 'story'. Momentarily, both escaped from their stereotyped version of events into a new envelope of shared feeling.

In this example, there is a movement from a secure but narrow 'illness narrative' through the dangers but creative possibility of uncertainty and unstoried immediacy to the possibility of a new and less constricted narrative. Here, then, there was an excess of 'story'. In the second example, by contrast, we see *un*storied disturbance and emotional danger in search of a therapeutic narrative that might provide a satisfactory fit with experience.

Searching for a story that fits

James, a successful teacher plagued by depression, arrived at his fifth session 7 minutes late. Despite an apparently positive therapeutic alliance, the therapy was not going well – both therapist and patient were struggling to find a real focus with which to work. James tended to tell lots of stories about his situation and his life, but no real pattern emerged, certainly nothing that could be useful to him. In this session, both James and his therapist knew he was angry with him – James had asked the therapist to run a seminar for a group of teachers at his school, but the therapist had declined, on the grounds that it would interfere with the therapeutic process.

James started the session by explaining that he was late because he had been helping a friend pull his car out of a ditch. The therapist mused to himself on the different possible stories of which this incident could form a part. He offered a fairly conventional transference comment: 'Perhaps you are hoping I will pull you out of the ditch of your depression – you are showing me the way'. No, this did not seem to fit. James spoke of his need always to be looking after others – family, fellow-teachers, pupils and now the friend who was stuck in the ditch. This linked with James' childhood story: a feeling that his mother never really liked him, and was always fussing over his sister and brother. This led onto James' feeling of rejection over the therapist's refusal to speak at the seminar. Together, the therapist and James pieced together a new story: by being late he was saying 'I am angry with you. You don't care about me. You are more interested in everyone else. Right, *I'll* show you how people should be helped. I'll get them out of their ditches even if you leave me in mine'. Immediately James began telling the therapist how helpful something he had said in a previous session had been. The therapist commented: 'Do you notice how much your own aggression seems to threaten you? No sooner do you criticize me, than you have to tell me how wonderful I am, perhaps for fear I will retaliate or abandon you'. James laughed – a confirmatory response that the new story was on target.

Here the affective response confirms that a story has been found that fitted. The previous example seemed to illustrate the opposite: tears marked liberation from the constrictions of the old story. The work of psychotherapy is to find 'stories' that correspond with experience. This may mean disrupting clichéd stories in avoidant attachment, or reaching for a narrative that can better comprehend the confusions of everyday feelings in ambivalent attachment. Affective responsiveness seems to be one way of gauging how successful this process has been. But how does one establish the truth or otherwise of a narrative? Can a story be emotionally true, while being factually incorrect, or vice versa?

Can there be a science of narrative?

Jerome Bruner (1986: 16) argues that there are two kinds of approaches to truth:

> A good story and a well-formed argument are different natural kinds. Both can be used as a means for convincing another. Yet what they convince of is fundamentally different: arguments convince of their truth, stories of their lifelikeness. The one verifies by eventual appeal to procedures for establishing formal and empirical truth. The other establishes its truth by verisimilitude.

As an advocate of narrative, Bruner's use of the word 'verisimilitude' is risky, given its OED definition of 'having the *appearance* of being real or true'. Critics of psychotherapy might argue that this is a concession that the stories elaborated in psychotherapy can lay no more claim to the truth than can myths or fairy stories. How can this charge be answered?

Bruner's response, I believe, would be that there *is* truth in myths and fairy stories – emotional truth rather than factual truth, which can be judged not by scientific standards, but by such tests as whether the story rings true, feels 'right', is satisfying, coherent or touches the listener emotionally. Ironically, a play has verisimilitude if it compels the audience to remain in a state of 'suspension of disbelief' for the duration of the performance. Similarly, psychotherapeutic case histories could be Brunerian 'good stories' that have a paradigmatic value in their own right, even though by the standards of a 'well-formed argument' by themselves they prove nothing.

The criteria of a 'good story' certainly apply to psychotherapy. A psychotherapist is constantly using her intuition to evaluate the patient's narrative, asking herself if it makes sense or hangs together, questioning aspects that don't quite fit, probing clichéd phrases and well-worn narratives for what might lie beneath. The quest is always for a more elaborated, all-embracing, spontaneous, individualized, flexible story that encompasses a greater range of experience.

This evaluative activity, akin to aesthetics, is part of the 'art' of psychotherapy. But can there also be a science of narrative, including one that encompasses the narrative aspects of psychotherapy? One response is to concede that the quest *is* fruitless and that there can be no science of psychotherapy. The hermeneutic school of psychoanalysis, of whom Spence (1982) and Schafer (1992) are leading exponents, argues that what matters in psychotherapy is not objective or 'historical' truth – which is, in their view, in any case inherently unknowable – but 'narrative truth', something akin to Bruner's verisimilitude.

The main drawback of this position is the implication that a psychotherapeutic narrative is no more or less likely to be true than any other account of the patient's distress, whether religious, narrowly 'organic' in the psychiatric sense or delusional. My objection to this position is not based on a fear of losing the respectability which the mantle of science confers. Nor would I want to deny that psychotherapy is, among other things, a moral rather than a narrowly scientific discourse, in which questions about what it is to lead a good life and to flourish as a human being are central (Holmes and Lindley 1998). My main worry about the hermeneutic turn in psychotherapy is that it threatens to cut psychotherapy off from aspects of science – especially from evolutionary biology and developmental psychology – where dialogue is both necessary and possible.

The contribution of attachment research

While the immediate goal of psychotherapy may be to remove symptoms, behind that lies a set of more general and more ambitious objectives – to help an individual to flourish, to foster well-being, and so on. These can be seen in terms of the development of a strengthened and more versatile set of selves; for example, a more secure self, a more creative self, a more coping self, a more resilient self, a more autonomous self, a self with a greater capacity for intimacy. In contrast with the Cartesian *cogito*, narrative theory sees the 'I' not as a fixed and pre-existing entity, but as an autobiographical self, formed out of the interplay between agency and contingency, needing to be 'told' to another – or storied – before it can come into being (Brockmeier 1997). The telling of a self implies a built-in dialogical structure. There is always an Other to whom the Self is telling his or her story, even if in adults this takes the form of an internal dialogue.

We have seen how types of dialogue link with patterns of attachment. This suggests that there may be objective criteria – coherence, succinctness, relevance, etc – by which to evaluate the 'verisimilitude' of a clinical narrative. It also points to powerful links between the 'narrative truth' of the clinical situation and the 'historical truth' of the patient's actual biography.

Patients seek help in a state of uncertainty and confusion. Something is 'wrong', but they do not know what this is, or what to do about it. Footsteps may have to be retraced: a story is needed that will both explain how they arrived where they are and point the way forward. Psychotherapy, like art, 'holds a mirror up to nature'. The patient learns to put his or her feelings into words; these are then 'reflected back' by the therapist ('marking'); the patient then rechecks this reflection for its congruence/contingency/ verisimilitude – whether it 'feels right'; finally, a representation or story is formed. In the remainder of this chapter, I shall explore the formula: *raw experience plus meaning equals narrative*. The patient learns to build up a 'story-telling function', which takes experience from 'below' and, in the light of overall meanings 'from above' (which can be seen as themselves stored or condensed stories) supplied by the therapist, fashions a new narrative about her self and her world.

A story is linked to what I am calling 'raw experience' via a world of meanings. It is likely that the capacity to make this link is a developmental function, mediated by early attachment experience. The attuned mother responds to her infant's affective state via identification, based on her *own* 'lexicon' of feelings (Fonagy's 'reflexive function'). A 'story' is *offered* to the infant ('Oh you're feeling cold, bored, cross, wet, tired, hungry . . .'etc.), which in turn forms the germ of that *child's* reflexive function. If the caregiver is avoidant, the range and complexity of the stories will be limited; if she is intrusive, they will fail to match the child's experience. The care-giver does not just sooth her infant, she also *symbolizes* the soothing process. In later life, the child in whom this has failed may lack both the capacity for self-soothing (so characteristic of borderline patients) and the ability to talk about or symbolize her distress.

Narrative in clinical practice

How does the psychotherapist function as an 'assistant autobiographer'? I shall now consider some ways in which the narrative principles so far elaborated impinge on the psychotherapeutic process.

Narrative as a therapeutic technique

The first task of the therapist is to assist the patient to tell her story. The starting point will be some form of distress: desires have been thwarted or hopes dashed. The attachment research outlined above suggests that secure attachment is marked by coherent stories that convince and hang together, where detail and overall plot are congruent, and where the teller is not so detached that affect is absent, is not dissociated from the content of her story, nor is so overwhelmed that her feelings flow formlessly into every crevice of the dialogue. Insecure attachment, by contrast, is characterized either by stories that are over-elaborated and enmeshed (un-'marked'), or by dismissive, poorly fleshed-out accounts that lack contingency-testing. In one it is barely possible to discern a coherent story at all; in the other the story is so schematic or vague that it lacks the detail upon which verisimilitude depends.

Starting with the assessment interview, the therapist will use her narrative competence to help the patient shape the story into a more coherent pattern. With an enmeshed patient, the therapist will introduce frequent 'shaping' remarks or punctuations such as 'We'll come back to what happened to you as a child in a minute; first let's hear more about what is troubling you right now'. The 'We'll . . .', 'Let's . . .' construction brings therapist and patient together as joint authors of a new story. This is the beginning of objectification, but also a model for an internal observing ego (or self-reflexive self) that can listen to and modulate feelings. Shaping a story is the narrative version of the modulation and responsiveness of the security-transmitting care-giver.

With a dismissive patient, the therapist will elicit narrative in a different way, always searching for detailed images, memories and examples that bring perfunctory stories to life. 'What was your mother like?'; 'Can you remember an incident that illustrates that?'; 'When did you first start to feel so miserable?'; 'When you say you feel depressed, what does that feel like?'; 'Whereabouts in your body do you experience your unhappiness?'

In both cases, the therapist offers intermittent summarizing or 'marking' remarks that serve to demarcate 'The story so far', and to confront the patient with a narrative construction against which to measure the raw material of their experience. Some of these comments may be purely, yet pointedly, descriptive: 'When you were talking about your relationship with your husband, you appeared to be apathetic and defeated, yet when you started to tell me about your children you became quite animated!'. Others will be more general and overarching: 'You seem to be confident about your relationships with women, including your mother and girlfriends, but to feel much more uncertain when you come to speak about men'. These kinds of intervention would perhaps be classified as 'pre-interpretations', yet by translating a shared experience into verbal form *are* interpretative in the sense of carrying over experience in one medium ('raw experience', affect) into another (words, narrative conventions).

As therapy proceeds, the shaping process becomes less obvious and is probably most evident in the therapist's rhythms of activity and silence, the balance between verbal interventions and 'mmm . . .'s, grunts and indrawn breaths. Like an attuned parent, the effective therapist will intuitively sense when the patient needs stimulus and direction to keep the thread of narrative alive, and when she needs to be left alone to explore her feelings without intrusion or control. Sometimes, especially when the therapy feels stuck, the therapist may simply describe or tell the story of what has happened, either in a particular session or sequence of sessions: 'You started off today seeming rather sad and finding it hard to focus, then you began to talk about how difficult you always find Christmas, then you mentioned your friend's aunt who died suddenly . . .'. This story may well then provoke a realization or moment of insight, such as 'Oh . . . it was Christmas when my grandmother died, I always feel a bit down at this time of year . . . maybe that is why'. This will mark the end of this narrative sequence; the narrative is dispersed (or 'cracked up'; Bollas 1995), mingled with new experience, until a new narrative sequence emerges.

In psychoanalytic psychotherapy, the transference becomes a 'meta-story' that shapes the overall therapeutic interaction. Each session consists of a number of narrative episodes: what happened on the way to the session, an argument at work, something that happened with a partner, a memory from childhood, and so on. Luborsky (1984) has shown that most therapy sessions contain roughly three such episodes. Let us say the patient starts the session before a holiday break by talking about an incident at work in which his boss asked him to do a job, but without showing him clearly how it was to be carried out. The therapist might comment, 'There seems to be a story here about being left to fend for yourself without proper support'. This might then prompt the patient to talk about how his parents left him in charge of his younger brother without explanation, and how frightened and angry he felt about this. This, in turn, may lead to a sudden realization about how upset he is about the coming break. A core story is emerging about abandonment and the response it evokes.

Implicit in my argument so far is the view that psychological health (closely linked to secure attachment) depends on a dialectic between story-making and story-breaking, between the capacity to form narrative and to disperse it in the light of new experience. Like Main's (1995) securely attached child shows with her 'fluidity of attentional gaze', so in adult life narrative capacity similarly moves between fluidity and form, between structure and 'de-structuring', construction and deconstruction. This capacity ultimately depends on being able to trust both non-possessive intimacy and healthy aggression, which form the basis of much psychotherapeutic work. Intimacy provides the closeness needed if meaning and experience are to be woven into narrative; trusting one's aggression enables these stories to be broken up and allowed to reform into new patterns. The attachment perspective I have adopted suggests three prototypical pathologies of narrative capacity: clinging to rigid stories, being overwhelmed by unstoried experience, or being unable to find a narrative strong enough to contain traumatic pain.

Nodal memories: deconstructing dismissive narratives

Just as language is infinite but based on a finite number of simple grammatical rules, so, despite the potentially limitless capacity of memory, most people have a small number of prototypical memories that epitomize their fundamental relationship to others and to the world. These often concern important transition points in the life history – the birth of a sibling, a first day at school, and so on. They might be called 'nodal memories' in the sense that they represent a concentration of the assumptions, fantasies or working models about the self in relation to others. They may be actual or imagined. The individual usually 'reads' a particular meaning into them which acts as an organizing principle around which they organise their present-day experience.

One patient learned that she had been left in her cot for 5 hours after her birth. In her mind, this represented (and explained) all her subsequent feelings of cutoffness and rage about being abandoned by lovers, friends, and so on. Another dreamed of the Post Office tower in London, 'A phallic symbol if ever there was one', he said glibly. A third focused all his feelings of being intruded upon by his mother, and lack of recognition for his achievements by his father, on his circumcision as a baby.

In the process of psychotherapy, these nodal memories become reworked. First, they have to be unpacked – 'cracked up' in Bollas' (1995) terms – and then reassembled, taking on a new perspective. The woman in the cot came to see that her mother was simply following the child-rearing fashions of the day, and that her furious attempts to be self-sufficient – to mother herself – had cut her off from the good things her mother did have to offer. In the second case, what really seemed to fit was not the psychoanalytic cliché of the phallic symbol, but the tower as an image of communication, a way of linking with others, which this lonely man so desperately craved.

The man who so resented his circumcision, now a successful test-pilot, came to see how his phallic prowess and fear of having his wings clipped flowed from his longing for a father to whom he could get access (the father had abandoned the family when the patient was 15) and who would see him as an equal. In each case, the patient comes to see that there are many versions of the same story. Therapy provides an opportunity for the patient to begin to see himself from the outside; to forgive parents as well as to blame them; to see and own his contribution to circumstances, rather than viewing himself as a helpless victim; and to recognize that there are occasions in which fate deals us cards over which we have no control.

Changing the narrative context of memory

Dave was in his mid-fifties when he suffered from a prolonged depression triggered by being made redundant from the firm in which he had worked his way up from the shop floor to be factory manager. His father had died in the war when he was 2, and his widowed mother struggled to make ends meet for herself and her two children. He had always tried to be a 'good' boy, to help his mother, had worked hard, and was an indefatigable servant of his employers as well as father-figure to those who worked under him. In his depression, he alternated between attacking himself for his failure to prevent the firm from going into receivership and violently attacking his bosses for their financial mismanagement. In one typical moment of recall, he vividly and guiltily remembered an incident from childhood in which he had been at the cinema with some other boys. One of them proudly produced a half-crown which he stated that his dad, whom he claimed was 'very rich', had given him – and then accidentally dropped it. Dave immediately offered to help him retrieve it, which he did, whereupon he walked out of the cinema with the money in his pocket. Fifty years later this scrupulously honest man was still berating himself for this callous act of theft. When the therapist gently suggested that perhaps he had felt that he, as a fatherless child, was entitled to purloin the money that this boastful son's father had given him, there was a sudden shift in the session as tears came to Dave's eyes. A new *context* for his obsessive, guilt-laden story had been created, one which encompassed his pain as well as his crime.

'Negative capability' and ambivalent narratives

This chapter began by contrasting the security of narrative prose with the poetic impulse to make contact with the 'thing itself', suggesting that psychological health might depend on a balance between these opposing psychic tendencies. The prosaic structure of narrative contains, reassures and soothes, but may also constrain, control and distort. Lyric poetry can be a liberation from story, enabling us to see the world with fresh eyes, but its capacity to fragment meaning takes us dangerously close to the limits of understanding. In the previous section, we saw how, starting from nodal memories, psychotherapy can helps break up stories and so broaden the range of admissible experience. Equally, there is often a need to find ways of capturing the confusion and vagaries of overwhelming feelings.

Here Keats' 'negative capability' – the 'ability to remain in doubts, uncertainties and mysteries' – is vital. The therapist has both to be able to tolerate confusion, while trusting that a meaningful pattern will eventually emerge.

Finding a narrative thread

Naomi's sessions were confused and rambling, moving rapidly from topic to topic and from past to present and back again. She was tearful for much of the time, and seemed to 'flop' into her chair, gazing imploringly at her therapist, without ever clearly stating what was wrong or what she wanted. She 'didn't know why she had come . . . she had had a bad week . . . lots of worries about her 15-year-old son who was getting nowhere at his school . . . it all started when she discovered that a friend had also been raped by the same man who had raped her when she was 17 . . . her mother was dying then so she couldn't tell her or her father, they had too much to worry about . . . with two small kids and a new husband it's difficult to find time to talk . . . She met her first husband almost immediately after her mother's death . . . it was a relief to get away, the atmosphere was so sad . . . it was odd when her father remarried after her mother died, she couldn't get used to him holding hands with a new woman . . .'.

Gradually piecing together the story of the rape and her mother's illness seemed to help. She had left home at 16 after many rows with her mother and was working as a nanny. When her mother became ill she was expected to return home to look after the house. The rape happened on the way back from a party with a man she hardly knew. She described it in graphic detail. She arrived home. Her father called out 'All right?', as he always did. She could not bring herself to tell him, he was so worried about her mother. All this was 20 years ago, but it seemed like yesterday, she was not much older than her son is now. He, like her dad, is so difficult to talk to. Now things began to fall into place. The therapist commented: 'You did not talk to your mother, just rowed, and then she died; you could not burden your father; now you worry about your son, but can't talk to him; in coming for help you are looking for someone who will listen to the story you kept to yourself all those years ago'. 'I did tell my doctor – but he told me to forget about it, he wasn't much good, he committed suicide in the end'. Now at last a pattern was emerging – of painful feelings of loss and worry, of wanting help but never quite trusting it, of clinging on with words – the long rambling stories at least mean someone is there, even if they can't really hear what is said. The therapist mused, 'Perhaps you are wondering if I will be able to take it, or whether I will get angry, and let you down like the others, whether I am *really* prepared to listen to how distressed you are.'

Here there was a movement, from fragmentary and often poetic feelings, images and themes, through a period of confusion to a resolution in which a more solid interpretative story or pattern emerged. This is a familiar pattern with enmeshed narratives. The session starts with laying out the jigsaw pieces; an edge or container is formed; then images begin to come together – here a cloud formation, there a face; finally, there is a rapid period in which the pieces fall into place and the full picture appears at last.

Stories in search of a voice: working with trauma

The attachment framework followed throughout this book suggests four patterns of narrative styles in psychotherapy practice: secure, coherent; avoidant/dismissive; ambivalent/preoccupied/enmeshed; finally, trauma-organized narratives, often revealed by disorganized/incoherent with fractures in what at first sight may appear to be a smooth narrative envelope.

In the case above, Naomi had been traumatized by the rape, but she was able to talk about it to some extent, and with a little prompting could give a detailed and convincing account of what happened. For others, memories of traumatic events are associated with such unpleasant emotions that they are avoided in a phobic way. At the extreme of this is traumatic amnesia or repression. We shall see in the next chapter that there is evidence that in these situations memory for trauma is organized differently from 'normal' memory. The person will recall images or physical sensations but not a coherent sequence of events. As already mentioned, if asked to recall the trauma during neuroimaging, there is activity in parietal regions of the non-dominant hemisphere (Van de Kolk and Fisler 1996), while normal memories evoke dominant hemisphere activity. This suggests that traumatic memories have not been processed into a verbal, narrative form, but remain in a 'raw' primary process state.

Trauma breaks through (or 'pierces', the etymological origin of the word) the self–other dialogue that underpins thought and language. The self – the narrative self – is obliterated, and all that remains are dissociated images and sensations. When it is a care-giver who is responsible for the trauma, then this likelihood is increased, since, as suggested earlier, the perpetrator is the very individual whose responsibility is to help with the process of symbolization and soothing.

Feelings of shame, typical of trauma survival, are an elaborated version of this: one is an outcast, unworthy of attachment, rejected of men. Basic trust has broken down. Therapy can help, but often with extreme difficulty. The sufferer has to feel sufficiently held to risk the extreme emotional pain that may be associated with recall of the trauma. Some means of symbolizing or mirroring raw experience is required – often poetry, drawings or guided fantasy are first steps towards the elaboration of a coherent narrative of the trauma. The therapist becomes witness, but how can she possibly grasp the unthinkable? She stands for the part of the victim's self that could not bear to look at what was being done to her. By revealing the story to herself, the victim fears she will again become enmeshed in her story, unable to escape. Previous narrative defences, such as psychic numbing, dissociation of feelings from story, selective forgetting, or even fragmentation of personality, will be challenged as a more coherent and often unbearably painful account emerges, but one that seems to correspond more closely with experience.

Thus the trauma victim is often initially avoidant, and later becomes potentially trapped by her story. Turning trauma into narrative in therapy requires a sequential process, starting with the overcoming of avoidance by imagery, and later moving to a more objective, distanced position where the victim can identify with the therapist's benign concern. I shall try to show in the example below that the minor aspects of trauma that can be played out symbolically in the transference helps with this process, since it becomes shared and therefore potentially narratable.

The role of the therapist

Working with traumatized patients tests not just the skills of the therapist but also her personal strengths. Her moral maturity will be exposed, especially her ability to use her own feelings in the service of the therapy, without allowing them to direct, dominate or intrude upon the patient. Wadell traces the evolution of George Eliot's sensibility from her early novels, which, Wadell argues, 'suffer from an intrusive imposition of self, a persistence of personal elements that block her creative vitality', to her mature novels, which

> seem to produce a force and refinement of writing which is wholly distinct from that which seeks to express aspects of character which are superficially much nearer to her own experience in the sense of personal longings and aspirations. The danger *then* . . . is the imposition of feeling from the outside, resulting in sentimentality and pseudo-emotion. The emotional space necessary to, and produced by, that distinctness invites an identification on the part of the reader with . . . the inner qualities and characteristics of the object rather than the external and more available ones.
>
> (Williams and Wadell 1991: 56)

A similar maturity would be a goal for a therapist who will inevitably draw on her own experience and preoccupations in her identification with her patients (see Chapter 1), but at the same time has to find a distance – Wadell's 'distinctness' – which enables her to allow the patient's imagination to flourish, unimpeded by contol or manipulation. Thus the therapist's attachment style, and *pari passu* her narrative style, will be an all important element in determining the outcome of therapy. Enmeshed therapists tend to impose their own narrative on patients or get bogged down in interminable stories that have no end, while those with avoidant styles may fail to pick up on vital emotional cues and jump to unwarranted conclusions. The therapist's task is to be attuned while retaining her balance, a position I have called 'non-attachment' (Holmes 1996), as the following concluding anecdote tries to illustrate.

Non-attachment as trauma narrative emerges

After more than a year in weekly psychotherapy, Dave, already mentioned above, revealed with intense shame that he had been at approved school in his late teens. He then said that he had been admitted to psychiatric hospital around that time, a fact he had only vaguely alluded to before. Then he spoke of the circumstances leading up to the admission. It seemed that he had doused some rags in petrol, wound them round his legs and set fire to them. As he spoke of this, the therapist sat silently, wrapped with attention, picturing vividly this now ponderous silver-haired man in late middle age as a 17-year-old. There was still a mystery to unfold. How did it all hang together? What 'made' him do it? Dave spoke of his naval school, to which, as a bright naval rating's orphan, he had a scholarship, and the contrast between his schoolmates' parents who appeared on speech day in their officers' regalia, while his mother and stepfather never came (they could not afford the train fares), and if they had would have shamed him with their shabbiness; of his envy and contempt for these well-heeled lads who had no inkling what it was to suffer.

All this seemed relevant to his feelings about his 'posh-accented' therapist, to whom he was strongly attached and yet could not fully trust. This too was sensed 'impersonally' by the therapist – he could *feel* the hostility, the longing, the envy, the dependency, but in an objective way that seemed to have little to do with him as a person. At this intense moment *he* did not exist; he was a projection of his patient's inner world and yet, at that moment, felt intensely alive and very much himself. Then Dave made the missing connection: one of the staff at the approved school was sexually abusing the boys in return for cigarettes and had made advances to Dave. He was deeply ashamed about this coercive propositioning which touched his longing for closeness (still speaking of his never-known dead father as if he were a close companion), his anger at the abuse of that craving, his embarrassment and confusion. This was what had led up to the episode of self-harm. As he listened, the therapist felt the story almost as if it were happening to him, yet impersonally – both fully involved and at the same time watching, observing, still able to protect the boundary of the session, both for himself and the patient.

This is an inadequate attempt to capture an intense moment in therapy – moments which occur regularly but infrequently. Perhaps, in the end, this is what therapy is *about*: the emergence of a story that is both intensely felt (captures 'raw experience') and has an objective validity (congruence, contingency, verisimilitude). The therapist's specific contribution to this process is as witness, holder of the narrative boundary, 'subjective-object' (in Winnicott's terms), facilitator, and one who is able both to lose himself and remain true to himself in the process. Winnicott (1965) wrote of the importance of 'bringing the trauma into the area of omnipotence'. In the transference, the therapist becomes both the longed for and the abusive object – but because transferentially rather than actually so, one that is potentially transformational. Dave's therapist was responsible for creating a dependency and with that the hope that, at last, Dave would have the enduring inner object – the missing father – he so longed for. At the same time, that hope was constantly ('sadistically') dashed by the realization that his father *could* never come back to life again.

Such moments of insight, however significant, can never be points of arrival. Each story is there to be revised in the light of new experience, new facets of memory, new meanings. In this chapter, I have tried to bring to life the cycle of narrative construction and deconstruction which I believe is central to the therapeutic process. I have argued that narrative has its psychobiological origins in the 'marking' and contingency of maternal mirroring. I have traced the links between infant attachment patterns and adult narrative styles. I have tried to show how in psychotherapy the therapist shapes patients' story-telling and mirrors their affective experience in a way that leads to a more secure sense of self. In the next chapter, I turn to a more detailed examination of the relationship between attachment and trauma, especially when it is abusive.

Chapter 9

Abuse, trauma and memory

An attachment perspective

Attachment theory starts from the power of adults to protect and provide security for their children. In abuse, this fundamental biosocial contract between adults and children is ruptured: adults use their power for their own ends rather than those of the child. In the first half of this chapter, I look at abuse and trauma from an attachment perspective; in the second half, I consider how these phenomena may influence the workings of memory and the constructions of personal narrative.

The dictionary definition of abuse includes the following synonyms: perversion, improper use, violation, adulteration and defilement. Implicit in these meanings is the notion of a normal or proper use against which ab-use can be measured: violence and the physical or moral rupture of integrity; transgression of sexual propriety; and from defilement the notion of fouling – the introduction of the unclean and excremental into a world of cleanliness and innocence. Any of these meanings, and more, may be triggered off in the listener when abuse is mentioned. To these we can add the Kantian notion of the wrongness of using fellow human beings as a means to an end rather than as an end in themselves.

Classifications of abuse usually list four main types: sexual abuse, physical abuse, emotional abuse and neglect. Implicit in the notion of abuse is the idea that each of these is a perversion of what a child might rightfully expect from his or her parents or care-givers. Equally, it seems likely that abuse will have a powerful impact on a child's attachment style, both as a trauma in itself and in view of the context in which abuse is likely to occur.

I will start with some preliminary remarks on similarities and differences between an attachment and the psychoanalytic perspective on abuse. As mentioned in the Preface, psychoanalysis puts desire at the centre of its thinking. Parents are their children's first libidinal objects. What is traumatic and confusing about sexual abuse is that the adult world, rather than containing and holding the child's desire, reciprocates. The fruit of the tree of knowledge is eaten before the child can digest it – with resultant shame and loss of innocence, and premature expulsion from the world of play and plenitude. This use of biblical imagery shows how the notion of abuse taps into primal fantasies, and how abuse can become a metaphor for all that is evil and demonic – often one that is uncritically accepted as the cause of all psychic ills.

From Kleinian psychoanalysis came the idea that parents are not just the object of the child's first love, but also of their hatred. Intrinsic aggression and inevitable frustration of desire leads to murderous hatred in the baby, which, as with libido, is ideally contained and detoxified by the care-giver, so that, gradually, the child learns to cope with feelings of disappointment and deferment of gratification. In physical abuse, this process is perverted: rather than absorbing and buffering the hatred, the adult retaliates, using the child as a container for *his* deprivation and pain. In systematic emotional neglect, the adult refuses the inevitable intimacy of the parent–child relationship and the projective processes that implies. In a further perverse twist, the adult may see the child as deliberately inflicting misery upon him. Following the talion law of the primitive psyche, in the perpetrator's eyes abuse then becomes an act of justified revenge. Perversity can also afflict victims of abuse, which, when unravelled, is a form of protest and retaliation. This flows from identification with a bad or useless self, good only for exploitation and abuse. It is as though the abused person says to the world, 'you have treated me as a worthless object, so that is what I shall *be*'.

As we have seen, attachment theory starts not with libido, but from the overwhelming need for adults to provide security for their young if development is to proceed safely. Bowlby (1988) observed the extreme vulnerability of young mammals to predation (as many a fox, which has managed to drag off a newborn lamb for his young only to find his cubs fallen prey to terriers, would testify) and hypothesized that behavioural and psychological mechanisms which ensure proximity between adults and their offspring at times of danger are built into our nervous system through natural selection. The perverse paradox of abuse from an attachment perspective arises from the vicious circle in which an adult, usually a care-giver, is *both* the attachment figure to whom the child turns for protection and the source of threat which gives rise to the need for that protection. The more frightened or in pain the child becomes, the more the child clings to the perpetrator.

Abuse and attachment

It is tempting to speculate that different forms of abuse may connect with different parental patterns underlying anxious attachment. Avoidance arises in the context of parental aggression – child battering is the extreme example of this, and the frozen watchfulness of the battered child is perhaps a caricature of avoidant wariness. Childhood sexual abuse by parents or stepparents may tap into ambivalent attachments in which, as described at the start of this chapter, the child clings to a care-giver who alternates between being sexually intrusive and threatening or rejecting. Parental neglect, which, taken to the extreme, is a form of abuse, might link with disorganized attachment, in which the child despairs of finding any workable strategy for activating protective behaviour in his care-giver.

This is, of course, over-schematic. In clinical practice, the distinction between the different types of insecure attachment is not so sharp, with mixed patterns being common, for example, in eating disorders. This makes psychological sense, since avoidance and ambivalence are mirror images of one another: the avoidant person longs more than anything for intimacy, while ambivalent individuals crave autonomy, but both are too fearful to risk reaching out for what they really want. Thus anxiety lies at the core of insecure attachments (if that statement is not a tautology), and it is the failure of the secure base providing care-giver to alleviate anxiety that inhibits the capacity to develop both intimacy and autonomy.

Two ways of looking at abuse from an attachment perspective are to be found in the literature. Heard and Lake (1997) emphasize the shift from secure/companionable interactions to those organized around dominance/submission. The latter strategy enables the weaker party to afford a measure of protection from a stronger individual, but at a price in terms of intellectual and emotional development. Fonagy (1997) links Bowlby's (1988) notion of 'incompatible working models' with disorganized attachment and dissociative disorders, which are common in those who have been sexually abused. Where the abuser is a member of her family, the victim is likely to dissociate, both as a way of dealing with the pain and fear of the act of abuse itself, and also because the abuser who inveigles her into his room is the same person who behaves 'normally' in the public family context. The child thus has two incompatible internal working models of, say, stepfather-with-family and stepfather-as-abuser, and of herself in those two contexts as well. This will lead to a disrupted or incoherent attachment strategy and, ultimately, to the victim resorting to an aspect of the self or her body as a pathological secure base (cf. Chapter 2).

Aggression and protest

The Strange Situation Test centres around the way in which the infant responds to separation. The 'normal' response involves healthy protest – the parent is 'punished' by the child's cries and sometimes aggressive clinging for the act of abandonment. The capacity to protest, show appropriate aggression and to 'ask for help' (at the age of one by vocalization rather than verbalization) are marks of secure attachment, while insecure children are more likely either to be unable to protest or to be locked into unassuaged aggression. This picture can be linked with the Winnicott–Bion model of a 'breast' (i.e. attachment figure) able to 'metabolize' the rage and hatred of the frustrated infant, and return the feelings to the child in a detoxified form.

Security arises in part out of the ability of the care-giver to accept and contain protest without retaliation or rejection.

This is relevant to abuse in a number of obvious ways. First, a precondition of security is the ability to defend oneself when necessary, either by standing one's ground or by recruiting the support of a secure base adult. Secure people are not afraid of their aggression and can express it openly, or, when necessary, contain and soothe themselves appropriately when their anger is aroused by pain or fear. Inhibition of protest and appropriate rage is an almost universal accompaniment of abuse: how can one expect an adult who has harmed one to accept and 'metabolize' one's protests? A second, related point is that potentially abusive parents are in any case unlikely to be able to contain their children's aggression, doubtless because it triggers off their own feelings of uncontainment *vis-à-vis their* parents – the intergenerational pattern of abuse playing itself out here – and so will retaliate against or neglect the protesting child.

A third point concerns a key feature of sexual abuse, the inability of the child to let her parents know what has happened, or, if tentative moves towards disclosure *are* made, to be met with disbelief, rejection or punishment ('how dare you accuse your stepfather of such a thing, go to your bed at once you filthy-minded child'). Here the child's experience is invalidated or disconfirmed, with consequent distortions in self-understanding. In secure attachment the responsiveness, 'marking' and contingent responses of the parent help the child clearly to distinguish between self-experience and that of the care-giver. In insecure attachment, by contrast, especially in ambivalent and disorganized patterns, this differentiation is shaky, such invalidating responses serving to confirm pre-existing confusion and self-doubt.

Developmental pathways

Single episodes of abuse are far less likely to have far-reaching effects on the personality than is repeated abuse, suggesting that context is all-important, both in determining whether abuse occurs in the first place and, if it does occur, what its consequences are likely to be. Insecure or secure attachment patterns describe developmental pathways representing patterns of repeated parent–child interaction in a particular family constellation. These pathways, if suboptimal, do not 'cause' abuse, but represent one of the many factors, which acting in concert, can either promote or prevent abuse. Although what we call 'abuse' can be identified as definably inappropriate use of aggression or sexual transgression between adults and children, single or repeated events take place against a background of ingrained patterns of already established behavioural interaction between parents and children. Where isolated episodes of abuse do not have long-term consequences, these are likely to be secure attachment patterns. Much more commonly, insecure behavioural patterns are internalized as 'internal working models' – which, in the case of children who are abused, will tend to be (but are not necessarily) maladaptive and hence, in the psychiatric sense, precursors to pathology. An abused child will carry with her into adulthood a set of assumptions – such as 'if anything goes wrong it is my fault', 'intimate contact with men is frightening and disgusting', 'I must submit to others' demands if I am to gain any safety at all', and 'the way to escape from intolerable situations is to split my mind from my body' – that will provide a breeding ground for disturbed relationships and anxiety or depression in later life.

Thus the overall context within which the abuse occurs is equal in importance to the abuse itself: a depressed and unresponsive mother; a stepfather, himself perhaps abused, at the end of his tether; unemployment, chronic ill-health, low self-esteem, and a myriad of other psychological and social factors which provide a backdrop to the abusive act (Belsky 1993).

From a clinical or preventative perspective, this contextual and 'cumulative trauma' must be accorded due weight. Given the dramatic and overwhelming nature of post-traumatic stress disorder (PTSD) symptoms such as flashbacks and phobic avoidance of the psychophysiological correlates of the abuse (the smell, sounds, level of lighting, terror, disgust, unwanted excitement, feelings of being trapped alone, or preparedness for self-sacrifice to protect siblings), it is tempting to focus exclusively on the trauma itself. In practice, both trauma and context need to be addressed. Indeed, in therapy with adult survivors of abuse, many months may be needed to build up a picture of the developmental context before the details of the trauma itself can be talked about.

Post-traumatic stress disorder as a syndrome was originally understood in the context of the Vietnam War and superseded the notions of shellshock and battle fatigue developed by psychiatrists and psychologists in the First and Second World Wars. The long-term effects of sexual abuse have many features in common with PTSD, and some have even tried to conceptualize borderline personality disorder (60–70 per cent of sufferers have experienced sexual abuse) as a form of PTSD (Gunderson and Sabo 1993). Herman *et al.* (1989) wrote of 'complex PTSD' to capture the long-term effects of cumulative trauma and its impact on internal working models. One of the key questions for both PTSD and abuse is to ask what determines whether such trauma will or will not be 'traumatic', in the sense of producing major psychiatric symptomatology or the distortions of personality development found in borderline personality disorder. An attachment perspective can help unravel some aspects of this.

Earlier it was suggested that a number of apparently perverse features of borderline personality disorder can be understood in attachment terms. In self-cutting, for example, the body is used as an 'object' that is simultaneously attacked and acts as a source of comfort – self-cutters regularly report a temporary period of peace and calm following self-injury. Abuse interferes with the child's acquisition of the capacity to self-soothe: the parent whose soothing actions are normally a template which gradually becomes internalized, instead cause pain and fear. The child then turns to the body as a surrogate secure base for self-soothing. The 'secondary gain' of showing the wound to professional carers further mobilizes attachment behaviours. The inappropriate use of alcohol and drugs similarly blots out pain physiologically, and provides a feeling of being held and divested of responsibility similar to that which is sought when attachment needs are activated and assuaged.

Narrative and attachment

Only a minority of abused children will go on to develop borderline personality disorder. In children faced with adversity, a number of protective factors have been identified (Belsky 1993), including the existence of at least one good relationship – perhaps with a grandparent or teacher – attractiveness, sporting ability and the impact of psychotherapy (Styron and Janoff-Bulman 1997). Another aspect concerns the capacity to 'narrativize' painful experience. As discussed in the previous chapter, neuroimaging techniques suggest that traumatic memories are processed in the brain in different ways from non-traumatic ones (Van de Kolk and Fisler 1996). Most memories are stored in the brain in the form of 'stories', sequences of events that can be verbally recalled and in which the sensory and emotional aspects of the memory remain in the background. Traumatic memories seem to exist in a 'raw' sensory form, in which a coherent verbal account is hard to elicit. They are also often 'near the surface' and easily activated by cues that share features with the traumatic situation, triggering associated emotions such as panic and fear. Abuse can inscribe itself in the very way in which we think and speak about ourselves. The incoherent narrative style associated with abuse presumably reflects traumatic memories threatening to break through into consciousness, kept at bay by only partially successful attempts at verbal papering over cracks.

In the absence of a secure base, the child's capacity to develop self-narrative, and ultimately a self-reliant and positive sense of self may be compromised. If the child cannot rely on the parent to be there consistently, without interference or neglect, then his play and thoughts will be tinged with anxiety; if care has been abusive, the very coherence of thought patterns and the integration of affect with cognition may be disrupted.

Some attachment-inspired authors (Fonagy 1991; Hobson 1993) have linked the above empirical findings with the philosophical question how do we know that other people have minds? They argue that secure attachment experiences can only be provided by care-givers who see their charges as sentient beings, centres of their own personal universe. Conversely, in abuse the victim is seen as an object without feelings or memory, and indeed may be coerced into denying her own experience. The title of one of Bowlby's (1988) late papers 'on knowing what you are not supposed to know, and feeling what you are not supposed to feel' captures this confusion beautifully. We know that other people have minds, the argument goes, because we ourselves have been treated as people with minds. The care-giver's view of us becomes internalized not just as our view of ourselves, but also of others. From this follows concern for the object and awareness of others' needs that is so often distorted in survivors of abuse.

Memory and abuse

A fierce debate has raged on the question of memory and abuse. From an attachment perspective, abused children are likely to have disorganized attachments and incoherent narrative styles. This means that their capacity to hold onto a personal narrative is profoundly compromised: reality and fantasy may be confused, fact and fiction conflated, and the normal capacity (which is installed early in development, around the age of 3 years) to distinguish between what is the case and imagination (which will inevitably be stimulated by real events) impaired.

For Freud, the clarity of memories, as opposed to the hazy quality of dreams and phantasy, was the method by which we decide on their veracity; thus an 'ultra-clear' phantasy (which may arise in those who have been subject to trauma generally) can easily, by perceptual 'mis-attribution', be labelled as a memory (a point originally made in the eighteenth century by Berkeley).

Recent findings from cognitive science help us to unravel some aspects of memory in relation to abuse. For example, 'infantile amnesia' (Lindsay and Read 1994) is virtually universal for the first 2 years of life. It seems likely that there is a neurological/maturational basis for such a lack of memory, and that the advent of language around 2 years is linked in some way with the beginnings of what Tulving (1985) calls 'episodic memory' – that is, the ability to recall specific events and situations. That is not to say that the experiences of the first 2 years of life have no effects, or are not in some way 'laid down' in the nervous system. Quite the contrary: Tulving differentiates the episodic memory system from what he calls 'semantic' and 'procedural' memory. Semantic memory refers to the 'grammar' of our lives: the rules of relationships that are just as ingrained as are actual happenings, which Byng-Hall (1995, after Schank 1982), calls 'event-scripts'. Procedural memory would be akin to Segal's (1991) 'memory in the body', the somatic sensations of intimacy, rejection, satiation, frustration, and so on that form a psychophysiological substrate to the sense of self (what we and the world 'feel' like), and is presumably related to parental handling in the early months of life including attachment experience.

Again, the radical distinction between memory and forgetting assumed by some authors is questionable. We now conceive of a much more fluid relationship between consciousness and the rest of the mind. We may be completely unaware, dimly aware or consciously suppress painful feelings and memories or, at times of stress and depression, feel overwhelmed by them.

> *The return of the repressed*
> Jonathan, a depressed teacher in his forties, 'knew' that his father had been an alcoholic and had died when he was 11, that his brother had died in a road accident a year later, and that his mother had had a depressive breakdown soon afterwards, but he never talked about these events to anyone, even, as he put it, 'to myself'. It was only when he began to be overwhelmed with feelings of sadness and futility around the time that his son reached the age of 11, and he was himself slightly injured in a minor road accident, that he sought help. In the setting of therapy, vivid images from the past came flooding back – the mixture of sympathy and disgust he experienced when he helped his father to walk to the off-licence.

In working therapeutically with abuse survivors, memories may take one of three forms. First, the patient may be helped to get in touch with current thoughts and phantasies of which she is dimly aware, but has failed to attend to, or to realize how much they may be influencing day-to-day moods and behaviour. Second, there may be the emergence of genuinely repressed traumatic memories, as in classical psychoanalysis. Third, and most contentiously, there are putative memories that may be inherently unrecoverable in 'semantic' form – if they date to a time before the age of 2 – but which may be inferred from the patient's history, collateral evidence and behaviour in relation to the therapist.

Changing clinical experience

Dissociation and classical hysteria are comparatively rare in contemporary clinical practice. We are just as likely to encounter patients who are overwhelmed with memories from the past which they cannot quell or cope with as we are people suffering from classical repression. As Alvarez (1992) put it, some people need to learn to forget, given the high incidence of traumatic abuse to be found in the histories of the borderline patients who seem to be the modern equivalent of Freud's hysterics (Bell 1992). They really do suffer from their reminiscences. From the perspective of attachment theory, enmeshment in past pain is just as much a manifestation of insecure attachment as are avoidance and dismissal.

What we call 'memory' is an active system (Loftus 1993), (a) which depends on the state of the organism and its relationships at the time of the experience, (b) which is actively worked on ('processed' or assimilated) sub-sequently and given meaning, and therefore (c) which, in so far as it is congruent with the assumptive world or 'internal working models' by which the individual lives, will become part of a store of memories which can be used to guide action and to reinforce a sense of self, but, if not, acts as a potential source of conflict and self-division. Finally, (d) conscious memories and their meanings are continuously updated in the light of later experience (which, surely, is what makes psychotherapy possible). Unassimilated or unconscious memories are not available for such reworking.

The attachment literature suggests that 'processing' of feelings is only possible when an individual feels secure, since exploration is necessarily inhibited if the individual is in a state of tension. Each of the main types of insecure attachment produces a specific impairment of memory. The avoid-ant individual simply suppresses her memories and would perhaps be closest to Freud's original formulation of hysteria: memories are not available for assimilation since they have to be experienced in the present before they can become part of the past. The enmeshed individual, by contrast, is overwhelmed by painful memories from the past: her problem is not remembering but forgetting. In disorganized attachment, which is seen most frequently in relation to deprivation and abuse, there appears to be no coherent overall integrative strategy: the individual has a tendency to dis-sociate from painful experience, and presumably therefore memories from one another, leading to a lack of overall structure of personal meaning. The childhood origins of such patterns emphasize the interpersonal aspect of memory. Secure holding is needed if a child (or troubled adult) is to be helped to distinguish between fantasy and reality, to separate the real from the unreal. The style of an adult narrative is more likely to give clues as to the history of such holding, or its absence, than is the specific content of the story that is being told.

Janet saw hysteria in terms of dissociation, but dissociation is not in itself a pathological process. We all have multiple selves, both contemporaneously (husband, lover, friend, etc.) and across time ('Can the person who stole that half-crown be "me", the upright citizen, and which is the "real" me?'); we can act a part, dissemble, deceive others and sometimes ourselves. What seems to be different in hysteria is not dissociation itself, but the lack of awareness that one is dissociating. The crucial capacity here is self-awareness, or reflexive function, a key requirement if secure attachment (and therefore the ability to process memories) is to be achieved in the face of adversity.

To return to Tulving's (1985) classification of memory systems, it appears that episodic memory rests on a substrate of semantic and procedural mem-ories which reflect the interpersonal context at the time of the experience. As suggested in the previous chapter, most individuals have a store of relatively few *prototypical* or *nodal memories*, which seem to encapsulate their view of themselves and their past and are integral to personal identity and meaning. These are 'episodic' – in the sense that they appear to record actual events – but they also typify semantic and procedural elements. The work of psychotherapy often centres around these nodal memories as they are unpacked and recontextualized in the new setting of the therapeutic relationship.

A nodal memory recontextualized

Jamie, a highly avoidant and schizoid bisexual man, who had grown up in a rough working-class area in Glasgow and had left home at the earliest opportunity to go 'cruising' in the local bars, had a recurrent dream in which he was standing by the door of his mother's flat, unable to leave because she was holding his testicles. When he came into therapy he interpreted this as: 'She's got me by the balls'. Towards the end of therapy, he began to see the same image as an expression of her acknowledgement of his vulnerability, an attempt to cradle him and protect him from violence – his own and that with which he was surrounded.

Recovered memories and false memory syndrome

In the light of this discussion, I will now briefly comment on the controversy surrounding recovered memories and the so-called false memory syndrome. We now know how erroneous and simplistic was Freud's pre-1897 model of hysteria: symptoms equal repression equals abuse, therefore therapy equals remembering equals recovery. But there is still truth in these original ideas, especially in relation to childhood abuse. Memories are often kept out of awareness. When they do surface, they threaten to overwhelm the sufferer, who often develops symptoms which in the nineteenth century might have been labelled as 'hysteria': feelings of panic, nausea, dizziness, sexual difficulties, and so on. The 'recovery' of memories often arises out of a contemporaneous trigger, such as a relationship difficulty or a child reaching the age at which the sufferer was abused. Such people appear to have been deprived of the soothing and comfort associated with secure attachment and, as suggested in Chapter 2, may turn to drugs, self-harm, eating disorders, and so on as a vain attempt at self-soothing. Self-harm soothes because it distracts from mental pain, a dissociative technique that many traumatized people discover as a way of enduring the pain and humiliation of abuse. Chaotic relationships, alcohol and substance abuse, and eating disorders serve the three-fold function of distraction, possible endogenous opiate release and evoking protective behaviour in others (De Zulueta 1993).

The epidemiological evidence suggests that total amnesia for trauma and abuse is rare, although, as mentioned, amnesia for events before the age of 2 is almost universal. In one study of women known to have been abused in childhood, only 20 per cent had no recollection of it (Lindsay and Read 1994). Much more common are patterns of unassimilated memory coloured by insecure attachment patterns: facts are recalled but not feelings, or the sufferer develops trance-like states in which past and present are confused.

At worst, 'false memory' can arise out of simple errors of logic. *Post hoc, propter hoc* bedevils discussions of causality in psychotherapy generally. Even if the simple recovery of memories did lead to a cure – and there is very little evidence that it does – that in itself would not prove that the forgetting of memories was necessarily pathogenic. Childhood trauma and abuse undoubtedly comprise significant vulnerability factors for adult psychiatric disorder, but are not in themselves causative (Mullen *et al.* 1993). A simple error of logic is that of the 'undistributed middle'. Thus the argument 'bulemic women have often been sexually abused in childhood, you are bulemic, therefore you must have been sexually abused – even if you have no recall of it', is logically unsound, although apparently widely believed by therapists (Poole *et al.* 1995).

Conclusion

In conclusion, *memory is a construction* and is therefore inherently fallible. Attachment theory can help understand the different ways in which memory can fail. An important finding from the Strange Situation Test is that attachment status with one parent is uncorrelated with that for the other, at least at the age of one. It is possible for a child to develop a number of attachment patterns, each of which appears to be stored independently in the brain. This presumably has survival value, just as the symmetry of organs means that if one is damaged the individual can continue to function. Thus, despite abuse, if a person has had at least one relationship that allowed for the development of reflexive function, she may well survive without major relationship or emotional difficulties. Autobiographical competence – the ability to describe one's past, however painful, clearly and coherently without denial or being overwhelmed – is a manifestation of secure attachment and reflexive function. Freud thought that putting trauma into words was curative, but it is more likely that *secure attachment and concomitant reflexive function* underlie *both* resilience and narrative competence.

It follows that the recovery of memories will not in itself necessarily be curative. Indeed, an enmeshed and intrusive therapist–patient relationship in which trauma is endlessly rehearsed may merely reinforce ambivalent forms of insecure attchment (cf. Dozier *et al.* 1994). The therapist must create a secure base for the patient from which she can begin to recover and re-evaluate her past. As we have seen, secure attachment follows from responsiveness, attunement and the capacity for healthy protest. Intrusiveness and inconsistency are associated with ambivalent attachment; in so far as 'suggestion' is intrusive and compromising of autonomy, Freud was correct in his eschewing of suggestion. A major aim of therapy is to enhance reflexive function, through providing the patient with an opportunity to experience, consider and master her feelings in relation to the therapist. It is this that makes Sandler and Sandler's (1994) 'present transference' as important as any recovery of memory.

The importance of present transference

Alison, mentioned in Chapter 7, a woman in her forties, felt that her whole life had been ruined by a tyrannical and abusive father. In therapy (as in the rest of her life) she was placatory and compliant, endlessly trying to guess what the therapist wanted from her, so that she could earn the approval from him which she felt had never been forthcoming from her father. On one occasion her therapist had to change the time of her session slightly and rang her at home to arrange this. In the subsequent session she described her initial reaction, which was to think 'Good, now he owes me a favour, he really *will* have to care for me this time'. When the therapist failed to offer her the praise or encouragement she craved, she became first self-pitying and then angry, and finally revealed how intruded upon and abused she had felt by the therapist's telephone call. 'Reconstructing' her father's abuse was important, but it was also familiar territory, which in itself had not alleviated her pain. 'Finding' her authentic anger in the present was a necessary step towards turning her abuse from continuous torment into a painful memory.

As our lives progress through time, we are constantly creating a past. To experience the present – joyful, neutral or painful – we have both to let go of the past and to preserve it. From her dark perspective, Melanie Klein (1986) saw life as a series of losses, and equated maturity with the depressive position in which loss and the hatred it evokes are reconciled with attachment and love. As we have described, later Kleinian writers have seen depressive position function in Oedipal terms: the ability to separate oneself from one's mother and 'allow' her to be with one's father (and siblings). This creates a 'third term', a distance, a space within which thought and words can arise (Britton *et al.* 1989). For Klein (1986), loss is bearable because, in healthy development, the lost object is 'reinstated' in the inner world. This 'reinstatement' is inseparable from memory. In Sonnet 29, Shakespeare starts in narcissistic despair: 'When in disgrace with fortune and men's eyes/I all alone beweep my outcast state' and then, suddenly, he remembers his beloved:

Yet in these thoughts myself almost despising
Haply I think on thee, – and then my state
Like to the lark at break of day arising
From sullen earth, sings hymns at heaven's gate;
For thy sweet love remembered such wealth brings
That then I scorn to change my state with kings.

This poem spontaneously came to mind while working with an utterly miserable, borderline patient who seemed to see no hope and no future. It prompted me to remind her that she had lost touch with the one good relationship in her life, which was with her father (who sadly had died when she was in her teens). This produced at least a temporary shift towards a more positive mood in the session. For Shakespeare the 'good object' was not just his beloved, but the poem itself within which she (and in the early sonnets, he) is reinstated. Similarly, it is the psychotherapist's task to help the traumatized patient to find not just good memories, but to provide the setting that can prompt the words to describe them, in such a way that they no longer distort the present as in false memory syndrome, nor are lost in an irretrievable past as in classical repression. In the next chapter, I look in more detail at the role of art in helping overcome trauma, once again using examples from Alison and Oliver's therapy.

Chapter 10

Art, attachment and psychotherapy

For the psychotherapist, exploration and creativity are one of the most important of the attachment domains. This chapter starts with some remarks about the origins of creativity, then looks in detail at Wordsworth's famous 'Ode on Intimations of Immortality'. There is then a discussion, with some clinical examples, of the use of art in the therapeutic context.

One way of looking at art in therapy is to see it in much the same way as Freud viewed dreams: a covert expression of hidden impulses, the task of the therapist being to 'read' the unconscious meaning which the artefact both reveals and conceals. Thus, for example, Freud (1928) discussed a story by Stephan Zweig in which a middle-aged widow, whose sons no longer need her, is attracted to a young man whom she sees at a casino. Her first glimpse of him are his hands as they place his bets. She decides to 'rescue' him from his addiction to gambling and, in the process, ends up in bed with him. He promises to renounce gambling, she gives him money for his journey home and they part. But later the next day she discovers, to her despair, his hands once more playing the tables at Monte Carlo.

For Freud the emotional power of the story lies in its covert account of the struggles which beset young men concerning masturbation. Gambling equals masturbation: compulsive, guilt-laden, promising immediate gratification but ultimately dissatisfying. The affair with the older woman reflects the deepest repressed longings of a young man, to regress to an infantile state of physical union with his mother, while her part in it can be seen in terms of a failure to mourn the loss of her sons, and a wish to recreate an idealized caring relationship. Gender themes are also played out in this story – the masculine wish to merge once more with the mother, and terror at doing so, the female longing for closeness with a man as compensation for her loss of the mother.

In this discussion, we see both the limitations and potential of a psychoanalytic approach. To our contemporary ears, the equation of masturbation with gambling appears simplistic, not least because, unlike Freud, we are no longer living in an era in which 'masturbatory insanity' is taken seriously by the medical profession. Nevertheless, the suggestion that compulsive gambling, like drug addiction, promiscuity or repetitive self-harming, might represent or symbolize compensatory self-soothing activity when a person's external relationships have failed, and that this in turn may arise out of early deprivation or trauma, are ideas which fit readily into the idea of a continuing need for a secure base in adult life.

The key concept here is that of symbolization. Ernest Jones (1916) elaborated on Freud's ideas on symbolization, arguing that a symbol, like an image in a dream, is a disguised representation of an unconscious thought that has been banished from consciousness. Furthermore, he claimed that symbols are intimately bound up with the body, or the self and its immediate relationships. He distinguished between symbolization and sublimation, the latter being the 'healthy' expression of unconscious meaning in which the force of unconscious drives had been sufficiently attenuated.

The early analysts were keen to make links between sophisticated sublimatory activities and early bodily functions. Thus Freud suggested that the craft of weaving arose out of female shame about penislessness and the concealment of the fact by pubic hair, while Fenichel (1946) argued that the origins of musical ability are to be found in the infant's pleasure in belching and breaking wind. Today, this can look like reductionism at its most absurd, yet there is no doubt that the body and its functions do provide a basic reference point for metaphor: to take the most obvious example, roundness tends to be a fundamental female symbol, straightness a male one. Artistic production is necessarily physical: the hand that draws the line or string, the voice that speaks or sings, the body that mimes. Freud's contention that the unconscious is preoccupied with the fundamental corporeal facts of existence – birth, feeding, sex, parenthood, illness, death – which tend to be symbolized in dreams, daydreams, fantasies and art, remains as true today as when it was first proposed. Furthermore, contemporary evolutionary theorists now argue that artisitic creation may be a form of sexual selection – ultimately a way of showing off to secure a desirable (i.e. biologically fit) mate.

By contrast, Jones' (1916) distinction between symbolization and sublimation has not stood the test of time. It seems more parsimonious to see symbolization as a universal human activity, which may be inhibited in insecure attachment. Metaphorical thinking is a basic psychological function (Ogden 1997). Rycroft (1985) argued that a balance between primary and secondary processes – between the capacity for symbolization and for logical thought – is a precondition for psychic health. He is critical of the Freudian view of the unconscious as a 'seething cauldron', riven by conflict and clamped down by repression. For him, primary process is the source of creativity, playfulness and pleasure to which a securely attached individual has ready access.

Segal (1991) distinguishes between what she calls symbolic equation and symbolic representation, like Freud illustrating her ideas with a discussion of masturbation. One patient, a violinist, had been unable to play since the onset of his psychotic illness. When asked why, he replied: 'Do you expect me to masturbate in public?' Another, also a musician, had dreams about the violin that connected with masturbation, but which did not interfere with his capacity to play. In the first case, there had been a *failure* of symbolization, a symbolic 'equation', but no metaphorical link. In the second, the patient had sufficient reflexive function to be able to think about his feelings and his body and work on them in therapy.

In Freud's (1920) 'tripartite model', he saw the mind as being divided into three parts – id, ego and superego. Here the ego has a synthetic function, bringing the individual in relationship to the reality principle while at the same time attempting to satisfy the pleasurable desires of the id and the prohibitions of the superego. From the perspective of the arts, the structural model suggests that the ego's function is to create forms of expression in which perceptions and feelings arising in the id can be symbolized, while at the same time arranging a moratorium on the strictures of the superego. From an attachment perspective, the 'superego' is the critical parent of the avoidant child. In secure attachment, the art or music room or stage are places – Winicottian spaces – where normal social rules are relaxed, where 'anything goes', where 'messes' can be made, loud noises are permitted, unrestrained gestures, leaps and bounds are encouraged or, in the case of drama, where predictable personae can be relinquished as the individual tries out the feelings associated with different characters.

The capacity of the ego to contain, to hold things together, to create a mental space within which feelings can be expressed is crucial to artistic practice. From an attachment perspective, the inner world is furnished via the individual's primary relationships, and the ego is imperceptibly transformed into the idea of the self. Sense of self arises out of relationships with objects, which may be benign or persecuting, secure or insecure, depending on childhood experience.

Daniel Stern (1985) argues that the sense of self emerges out of activities which can be seen as fundamental to artistic activity. He sees maternal 'attunement' as a key theme in which the parent taps into the infant's rhythms of activity, vocalization or physical expression. Thus, for example, a mother may be playing with her child on the floor. The child might be 'singing' in a rhythmic fashion and the mother will pat him or bang the floor in time – this is what Stern calls 'cross-modal attunement', the vocalizing senses being linked with kinaesthetic sense. This, Stern argues, will strengthen the child's sense of himself as an abstract centre of being, not tied to any one sensory modality, mirrored by the mother's responsiveness. The mother acts here as an 'auxiliary ego', helping to create a temporary artistic 'form' as she joins in with the infant's vocalizations, and reflecting back to him a pattern that is not identical to his own creation, but is sufficiently related ('in tune') for the child to begin to sense who 'he' is.

This sequence of (a) form, (b) activity, (c) reflection and (d) re-internalization of the reflection is fundamental to the creative arts and so to art in therapy. If Stern's model is correct, it can be traced back to the primary I–Thou relationship of infancy. We discover who we are through our actions and artefacts. Initially, a parental presence is needed to shape the ability of the child to use first his body as an instrument and then to offer the tools of self-expression – the spoon to bang, the pencil to scribble, the music and the 'bouncer' with which to dance. Later an internal dialectic is created in which part of the self interacts with the medium of artistic expression, which, in turn, is scrutinized and shaped by a more reflective part of the self, which will, for example, question whether something feels artistically 'right' or not. Art in therapy can help the discovery and strengthening of the sense of self. Art is always communicative, even for the lonely artist in his garret. It is always an attempt to get in touch with the self, through an external medium, which in its origins requires the presence of another. The artist is 'attached' to his artefact as though it were a person, but can play and experiment with a relationship that both has a life of its own and is completely under his control.

This discussion has moved from consideration of psychoanalytic meanings in art – the hidden Oedipal longings revealed in the Zweig short story, for example – to the fundamentals of artistic production itself. Both have central therapeutic value. Through looking at himself, with the help of a therapist, in his pictures or poems a patient may understand preoccupations previously hidden from his conscious understanding. He may find he has depths of which he was unaware, and feel a strengthened sense of worth and self-esteem as his creativity becomes more accessible. At the same time, the very act of artistic production creates the container for feelings that may have been lacking in childhood and puts the patient into a state of relatedness to himself and the world that may have been stunted in the traumatic environment in which he grew up. Art enables the object to be created in imagination, to be grieved, attacked, separated from or transformed in a way that was impossible in the course of abusive or constrained development.

I now turn to a specific example of the interplay of childhood experience and creativity and draw out some conclusions relevant to psychotherapy.

Wordsworth's Ode

Let us start with some brief biographical facts. Wordsworth was 32 years old when he wrote the Ode, about to marry Mary Hutchinson and planning a secret visit to France to say goodbye to Annette Vallon, who he had met 10 years earlier at the time of the revolution and by whom he had had a daughter, Caroline, whom he had never met. His mother had died when he was 8, after which, with the help of his sister Dorothy, he had become a passionate nature-lover.

The famous starting epigram calmly sets out the underpinning theory and the state of mind which, after much struggle and difficulty, the poem finally achieves:

> The child is father to the man
> And I could wish my days to be
> Bound each to each by natural piety.

The unspoken theme of the poem concerns how it is possible to maintain continuity in the face of loss and trauma – not just immortality in the religious sense, but also in the sense of 'going on being', symbolized by the notion of the eternal spirit.

Wordsworth's initial image for loss centres on vision, in both its literal and ecstatic – as in 'visionary' – sense. He mourns the loss of the 'celestial light' which 'I can see no more'. Then comes the ambiguous line, the sort that linguists delight in:

> To me alone there came a thought of grief

Was it Wordsworth only who was troubled by grief, or was it because he was 'alone' and orphaned that grief hits him? In either case, the answer comes immediately – perhaps too immediately, like a consolatory thought – almost a cognitive behavioural intervention – that pushes away the unhappy feeling rather than fully experiencing and thinking about and metabolizing it:

> A timely utterance gave that thought relief
> And I again am strong
> The cataracts blow their trumpets from the steep
> No more shall grief of mine the season wrong.

True, he 'gives sorrow words', turns the feeling into an 'utterance', but somehow it all seems too easy at this stage. Off he goes in an almost manic peon: 'all the earth is gay', everyone is happy and joyful, man and beast: 'The fulness of your bliss I feel'. Then suddenly, once more the shadow returns:

> Oh evil day! If I were sullen
> While Earth itself is adorning
> This sweet May morning . . .

This is a super-egoish thought – 'how *could* you *dare* to spoil other's joy with your misery?', which, turned around, could read as the rage of the bereaved, railing against the mother who left him, and fate for 'forcing' him to abandon his youthful love.

Then, for the first time in the poem, he moves into what Britton (1998) calls his 'thoughtful' as opposed to manic mode:

> . . . there's a Tree, of many, one
> A single field which I have looked upon
> Both of them speak of something that is gone
> The pansy at my feet doth the same tale repeat
> Whither is fled the visionary gleam?
> Where is it now, the glory and the dream?

There is still a problem to be solved, simple ecstasy won't do. Nor, in the long run, will simply clinging to a secure base, although that will be a necessary first step. There is something that needs to be thought through. He turns to what at first is a purely intellectual solution, which is not to say that it is not deeply helpful. It is the simple but profound idea that heaven is not where we are going to, and therefore about which we can know little, but *where we have come from*, and therefore about which we know everything, *if only we could remember it*. To help with that remembering is part of poetry's task.

'Our birth is but a . . . forgetting', sure, *but*

> Not in *entire* forgetfulness
> And not in *utter* nakedness . . .
> Do we come/from God who is our *home* (my emphases)

If we can build on the remnants of past love we will be able to find a home, a secure base, which can help us to withstand mortality and loss and change and breaks in continuity.

But why do we spend so much time trying to forget our celestial past? Why, returning to the visual imagery, does growing up involve a fading of the vision into the light of common day? Wordsworth's answer is once more to be understood in terms of the contrast between a manic and 'thoughtful' solution. Earth is a stepmother, anxious to distract her foster children from their loss, offering them the 'pleasures of her own', much, perhaps, as Dorothy might have done to try to console her grief-stricken younger brother, and vicariously, herself, at the time of their mother's death.

Now we come to stanza 8, the apex of the poem, where the contradictory feelings with which the poet has been struggling are juxtaposed most starkly. It starts with an echo of Wordsworth's great epigrammatical paradox: the child as parent, sage, best philosopher, mighty prophet, 'eye amongst the blind', tall in his might and freedom, in contrast to his actual physical size. Here, perhaps still a little manic. But then comes the rub: why, oh why,

> . . . with such earnest pains dost thou provoke
> The years to bring the inevitable yoke
> Thus blindly with thy blessedness at strife?

This is a *cri de coeur* with which psychotherapists are all too familiar: the patient who has 'everything going for him', but who is unable to value what is good within him, and who self-defeatingly manages to make himself and everyone around him miserable.

The remainder of the poem is a resolution of this paradox; a resolution which is itself a paradox, since it takes a paradox to undo a paradox. There *is* joy:

> The thought of our past years in me doth breed
> Perpetual benediction . . .

But it is not a simple harking back to good times that helps – to the 'delight and liberty' and 'new-fledged hope still fluttering in his breast' (Wordsworth reminding himself here of his revolutionary, and perhaps sexual, fervour at the time of the French revolution), to the 'mad endeavour' – but rather, and here's the paradox,

> . . . for those obstinate questionings
> Of sense and outward things
> Fallings from us, vanishings;
> Blank misgivings of a creature
> Moving about in worlds not realized,
> High instincts before which our mortal nature
> Did tremble like a guilty thing surprised.

It is only *because* we know that joy is transient, because, unlike the lambs and other animals, we suffer and tremble and experience loss, that we are able to value the dim recollections of 'the eternal silence'. If we take suffering seriously, rather than running away from it, pain points us to its resolution. Without pain there could be no healing, just as, in the Buddhist schema, the first step towards overcoming suffering is to accept that suffering is inevitable. The bereaved boy can look back beyond his misery to 'those first affections', 'that immortal sea/Which brought us hither', and know that he *was* loved, and that the memory of that love cannot be taken away from him.

And now, in the final two stanzas, at last the tone of the poem becomes relaxed and eligiac. With his new-found security, the poet does not have to rush manically to imitate the lambs, but can join them 'in thought'. He can accept that although nothing will bring back the 'hour/of splendour in the grass, of glory in the flower', there is no need any longer to grieve. Suffering transformed in this way becomes soothing. The 'philosophic mind' is able to see 'through death'.

This new perspective, encompassing and accepting loss, goes beyond it to something deeper. The object can be reassured in its turn that all will be well: 'forebode not any severing of our loves'. The 'habitual sway' of everyday Nature can be enjoyed unambiguously, no longer passionately adored perhaps, but also not hated for reminding the poet of how things were and can no longer be. The poet has 'come through' (as Lawrence put it), he has won his palms in a race in which the only way to win is to lose, and to know that one has lost – echoed 150 years later by Bob Dylan when he sings 'there ain't no success like failure/And failure ain't no success at all'. The blown flower reminds us that change is unchanging. Humility, fear, empathy for nature, acceptance of transience, takes us to a place 'too deep for tears'. Whatever chaos and loss rage around us, there is a 'heaven-haven' with the power to calm and comfort us, and move us towards a state of acceptance and non-attachment that is beyond suffering. Ultimately, by embracing change we can help overcome our vulnerability to it.

Poetry and psychotherapy

I want now to draw out some links between poetry and psychotherapy from these reflections on the Ode. First, it is important to approach poetry, as much as patients, 'beyond memory and desire'. Our initial task is to open ourselves to the poem as it stands, to attune and align ourselves to it, and try to enter the mind of the poet, without imposing our own models or pre-conceptions, seeing avoidant attachment here, manic defence there, and so on. Such theorizing is permissible, but only after we have fully grasped the poem (or the patient) in its own terms.

Second, poetry is based on words, but words used in a very special way. For Lacan (1997), the word is the paternal Oedipal sword, categorizing and separating, and disrupting the primary narcissistic fusion of subject and object, of mother and child. So here's another paradox: poetry uses words to re-establish that lost pre-verbal unity. Poetry's means to make those connections are rhyme, rhythm, metre, repetition and, above all, simile and metaphor, which, in different ways, reach out across the divide between the words, re-establishing connectedness – or attachment. This happens at the level of meaning, but also physiologically. Rhyme and rhythm link bodies across the spaces that separate them, evoke the soothing sounds of parents with their infants, and the 'mmms . . .' and 'Let's sees . . .' of psychotherapists with their patients.

Third, in both poetry and psychotherapy, there is a dialectic between form and content – the one firm, the other open-ended. Like psychotherapy, poetry creates a structure, a container, a set of rules and parameters which allow feelings to arise spontaneously. Poetry, like dynamic therapy, is a device for generating 'emergent meanings'. 'Difficulty' seems to be inherent in this process. Unlike prose, where meaning is usually manifest and transparent, we have to struggle to understand a poem with its concentrated latent implications and reverberations. I must have read the Ode many times, but there are still parts that are obscure and resist explication. Deciphering a dream can be similarly difficult; and how often do we finish a session with a patient and say to ourselves 'I really didn't understand what was going on there'? This aspect of responding to both poetry and what goes on in psychotherapy can be seen from an attachment perspective as the shifting balance between disorganization and coherence. We have to be able to tolerate the poem's obscurity, and the consequent feeling in the reader of splitting and falling apart of meanings, secure in our 'negative capability', and in the knowledge that a resolution will emerge, given time, attentiveness and faith. Similarly with patients we have to attune ourselves both to their and our own feelings, without knowing in advance what they 'mean', or how they fit into a pre-determined schema.

A poem, arising apparently from 'nowhere' and out of 'nothing', becomes an object in its own right with which the poet, and later the reader, has a relationship. The poet/reader speaks to the poem, and the poem speaks back to the poet/reader: 'my words echo in your mind'. A poem is an artefact, but once the first words are down on the paper, it has a life of its own with which the writer/reader can relate. A dialogue emerges where previously there was silence, emptiness, loneliness. Writing poetry can, like undergoing psychotherapy, be seen as 'narcissistic', self-indulgent even, but both use narcissism to overcome narcissism – as Jung said, we have to first find our self before we can lose it. With the help of the therapist, the psychotherapy patient begins to learn how to talk to and listen to himself. Where previously there was just a 'blob' – as many patients describe themselves and their misery – a subject and object emerge.

But where is this object to be found? It is certainly not 'on the page', any more than the music which we hear exists on the score. The poem exists in inner space, projected, as it were, onto an internal screen within the mind. Poetry is seen and heard in the inner eye and ear; to understand a poem, we have to be able to 'see' its meaning, hear its music, bring its visual and auditory imagery to life within ourselves. Similarly in psychotherapy, the patient is brought into touch with his representational world where his true feelings, and ideas about himself and those to whom he is close, are projected.

What kind of a thing or 'object' is a poem? It is neither entirely 'out there' on the page, nor wholly 'in here' in the mind of the poet/reader (a poem, ultimately, has at some level to be comprehensible, i.e. available for external scrutiny and evaluation). It can be described as an 'external–internal object', a 'self-object' (Kohut), a 'transitional object' (Winnicott), a 'poetic third' (Ogden) arising out of the inter-subjectivity of poet and reader. In the language of this book, its rhythms and music give it the characteristics of a secure base in that it has the power to soothe, but also to contain and hold firm in the face of powerful and often unbearable feelings. This 'poetic third' is an extension of Ogden's notion of the 'analytic third', the transferential relationship that is both real and an illusion created by the patient's mind.

In both therapy and poetry, there is an idea of 'movement' as the poet struggles with the emergent meaning of his poem, and in the course of psychotherapy, both in the individual session and over time. In Kleinian thought, this movement is always along the continuum paranoid-schizoid position to depressive position. Britton (1998) sees Wordsworth moving from a manic identification with nature as an escape from mental pain, to a depressive position characterized by thoughtful and more distanced acceptance of pain and joy.

It seems to me, however, that Kleinian thought makes coming to terms with loss as the key to psychological maturation a much more straightforward process than in fact it is. There is a paradox, or at least a difficulty, at the heart of depressive position that can easily be glossed over. How *do* we come to see that the object we hate and the object we love are one and the same, that sadness and joy are often intermingled, that without pain there can be no happiness? First, this is not merely an intellectual move, any more than Wordsworth has got himself out of his dilemma by his idea that we come from rather than are going to heaven. He still has to *feel* his way free, as do our patients. Second, there is an inherent mystery in the reconciliation of opposites. To move from Wordsworth to T.S. Eliot (1952), on the one hand:

Time past and time future
What might have been and what has been
Point to one end, which is always present

– whatever our hopes and imaginings, our actions and achievements, in the end all we have is the present moment. On the other:

If all time is eternally present
All time is unredeemable

– without a notion of history, of how things might have been and might be, different redemption (or psychotherapeutic cure) is impossible. Finally,

Human kind
Cannot bear very much reality.

As Freud was fond of saying, 'neurosis is in essence a turning away from reality'. Poetry and a preoccupation with the inner world may be a distraction from reality, but it can also provide us with the strength and security we need to face it. We must be careful not to over-emphasize the 'reality' of loss, at the expense of the inner reality of our attachments which relationships and creativity provide. Poetry and psychotherapy create transitional objects, self-objects or an internal secure base with which the 'fort' and 'da' of loss and refinding can endlessly be played.

From an attachment perspective, as for Wordsworth, loss is always equipoised with connectedness. Without the containing presence and later the internalized representation of the therapist, or the poem, or the idea that we still trail some residual clouds of glory, the movement from paranoid-schizoid position to depressive position is impossible. Without the analytic or poetic third, the sufferer is stuck with his nihilism and his narcissism. With the help of a poetic secure base we can relax enough to listen to footfalls in the memory, follow them down the passage into the rose garden. Psychotherapy is not just about a grim coming to terms with loss. Like poetry, it also, and necessarily, puts us in touch – physiologically, emotionally, cognitively – with our 'first world', so that, with luck, we can live more fully in our 'second'.

The uses of art in therapy

How does all this relate to actual practice of therapy? The analytic therapist might argue that she does not *need* art materials, journals, stories or poems, because everything that the patient says or does is an unconscious kind of poetry, the unravelling of whose meaning is her primary job. Focusing on pictures or music might prove a distraction from this task, an *enactment* by the therapist that could be counter-therapeutic if it enables the patient to hide behind her pictures, rather than face up to real interpersonal anxieties. Even dream-interpretation, so close to the heart of psychoanalysis, has to be undertaken cautiously, endless discussion of dreams being on occasion not work on self-evident messages from the unconscious, but an avoidance of painful aspects of the therapeutic relationship – anger, envy, disappointment or undeclared love.

Of course, many patients in long-term analytic therapy do bring poems, pictures or other artefacts into their sessions. It would be churlish as well as foolish for the therapist to ignore these enactments. Being in therapy puts patients in touch with previously unmetabolized feelings. The experience of being contained within therapy provides a model which the patient often spontaneously tries out for himself, and art or writing, as already suggested, is in itself a containing space for holding and thinking about feelings.

The analytic therapist, therefore, might argue that while access to creativity is often a mark of progress in therapy, it is peripheral to the analytic process itself. The analytic interchange is in itself a creative activity – a 'verbal squiggle game' which calls on the spontaneity of both therapist and patient. There are, of course, occasions when the arts of artefacts enter into this process. Two examples follow by way of illustration.

Russian dolls

Alison, mentioned in Chapter 7, had been in analytic therapy for 8 years. Outwardly successful, she suffered from depression and found it difficult either to live contentedly alone or to sustain close relationships. She had vivid memories of the scorn her father had poured on a picture she had made at school of which she had been rather proud. She habitually tried to please her therapist, while at the same time secretly trying to manoeuvre him towards giving her the love and praise which she so desperately wanted. She gradually progressed and began to think about ending therapy. At the Christmas break preceding the appointed ending at Easter, she presented him with a wrapped gift. He thanked her, said that he would open it later and, using standard analytic techniques, invited her to talk about the meaning of the present. Alison was insistent – he must open the present now. He did. It comprised a nest of Russian dolls. 'Open them up' she insisted. She then described how she had found the dolls in a junk shop and found that the 'baby' doll was broken. Using modelling clay, she had then painstakingly repaired it, so that it was almost indistinguishable from new.

This was a decisive moment in therapy. Alison had at last been able to show some assertiveness; the doll clearly symbolized and summarized the work that had been done over the years. The outer dolls stood for her many false selves, effective, but ultimately unable to hold her close to others or maintain self-esteem. The work of therapy had centred round the need to repair her 'inner child', facing the impossibility of altering the damage that had been done, but which, though still wounded, now felt much more whole.

Here the use of an artefact had spontaneously broken into the analytic frame with beneficial results. The therapist had protected his technique but was flexible (and human) enough to adapt to the needs of the moment. In this example, it was the patient who brought art into the treatment. In the next example, it was the therapist who did so.

The ancient mariner

Oliver, first mentioned in Chapter 4, went away on holiday for a week with his wife. On his return he reported that the first few days had been pretty bad and that he had felt very cut off from his wife. They had then had a row, in the course of which he had suddenly seen how awful it must be for her to have to live with him. He was filled with compassion for her and, in his words, 'the barriers suddenly came down' and they were able to remain close for the rest of the holiday. As he was listening to this story, the therapist had a vivid image of the famous passage in Coleridge's *Ancient Mariner* in which the parched, sleepless and guilt-ridden mariner, whose companions are all dead, watches the water-snakes in the sea and, in a moment of compassion for his fellow creatures, 'blesses' them. At that moment, the albatross falls from his neck, he is able to sleep at last, wind returns, rain falls and his companions wake from the dead. The snakes, symbols of evil, are suddenly seen as innocent living creatures, symbolizing perhaps the mariner's own projected evil with which he has suddenly come to terms. As he forgives himself, so his depression lifts.

All this seemed to fit Oliver's plight so well that the therapist risked telling the patient of this parallel. Fortunately, Oliver was able to respond, and compared his early presentation to the ancient mariner who clutched at anyone who would listen to his story. As the therapy continued, the phrase 'an ancient mariner situation' became a shorthand for various emotional states of guilt and desperation, but also a byword for compassion and the possibility of escape from depression.

The purpose of these examples is to show how, like it or not, aspects of art will infiltrate themselves into psychoanalytic work. Patients will use often art as a container for feelings, especially in once-weekly therapy where sesssions may not be available when needed. A theme running through this book has been the difference between the actual presence of a secure base with the need for physical proximity at times of distress, and the idea of an 'internal' or representational secure base which can itself reassure, or lead to emotional proximity to loved ones, who may include therapists. Art lies in an intermediate zone between the two: an artefact is a physical object, but its value lies in its emotional power to soothe and provide meaning to inchoate experience. Art, in this way, can be an internal/external secure base. We shall see, in the next chapter, how attachment to money can play a similarly ambivalent role in the psyche.

Chapter 11

Money and psychotherapy

According to Freud (1913), 'Money matters are treated by civilised people in the same ways as sexual matters, with the same inconsistency, prudishness and hypocrisy'. From an evolutionary perspective, there is nothing surprising about this: people will exaggerate or conceal their resources from others either to gain an advantage or to prevent envious attack.

Money thus equals security, and the way in which people relate to money is powerfully indicative of attachment styles: avoidant individuals for whom money 'means nothing', the ambivalent types who cling to their hoard, or those disorganized people for whom money difficulties seem inextricably bound up with their psychological problems. In this chapter, I speculate about the meaning of money both generally and specifically in therapy, with such a classification in mind.

Money is one of the great inventions of civilization, comparable with the discovery of written language, fire or the wheel – although to state that quite so baldly sends a slight *frisson* of danger down the puritan spine. Money is primarily a means of exchange, and human relatedness is based on exchange. Mother and infant exchange smiles, parents exchange the labour of loving and upbringing for the chance of genetic survival. Exchange enables the diversity of the human race to be put to good use. You exchange the fruits of your labour for those of mine; I benefit from your special skills and opportunities and vice versa. But if I am to scratch your back and you to scratch mine, we have to be in physical proximity, which feels good, but also imposes severe limits on those with whom exchange is possible. Money widens the scope of reciprocal altruism and allows for exchange to take place at a distance and between strangers. But money also objectifies the arbitrary differences between people, breeding envy and greed as a consolation for emptiness and loss. It both brings us together and alienates us from others and ourselves.

Simple exchange, or barter, precedes the existence of money and occurs in money-free societies or even among non-human primates – societies to which, as the corrupt grip of money tightens, late capitalism yearns to return. But the introduction of money into the system enables exchange to be extended both in time and space. I give you something, you pay me money rather than goods; I can 'cash in' my gift whenever and with whomever I want. Money turns arithmetic into algebra; money is the universal 'X' in the equation of exchange, a Babel fish (Adams 1978) that allows one good to be translated effortlessly into another.

Before the twentieth century, money could be defined as a portable object of value that is convertible into other objects of value (Wemmick's 'portable property'; Dickens 1861/1994). Thus money is both a desirable in itself – an object – *and* a symbol. To compare it with language, it has properties of both onomatopoeia and abstract meaning. The outcry when Britain went 'off the gold standard' marked a movement away from money as an object in itself towards its role as pure symbol. Today money is not so much gold in the bank or in a sock under the bed, but paper, plastic and the flickering of electronic quicksilver. Like physical versus emotional attachment, it has moved from being a thing to an idea.

Although in the unconscious meanings are freely exchangeable, for Freud the body and its drives was the signified to which all the protean transformations of meaning could ultimately be traced. Similarly, money does have a universal 'real' characteristic in that it always implies *quantity*, and this is its ultimate reference point. With money we are almost always interested in 'how much?' Money is therefore a *measure* of something: how big we are, how good, how much we are worth, how powerful, how lovable. Money appears to be a measure of value. But even value cannot always be equated with an amount – we can have too much of a good thing. Money can be equally a 'good' or a 'bad' thing, and this applies psychotherapeutically as much as it does in any other sphere. Let us look, then, at the positive and negative sides of the coin as they apply to psychotherapy.

In praise of money

Graham Greene (1955: 162), in *The Quiet American*, argues provocatively:

> They had been corrupted by money and he had been corrupted by sentiment. Sentiment was the more dangerous because you could not name its price. A man open to bribes was to be relied upon below a certain figure, but sentiment might uncoil in the heart at a name, a photograph, even in a smell remembered.

For Greene, as a Catholic, corruption (i.e. sin) is inescapable – the only question is, what form will it take? In this passage, Greene suggests that money provides a safer framework for morality than ideology or 'sentiment'. The same is surely true of psychotherapy. A therapist who sees her patients for love will be far less predictable and professional than one for whom there is a sound financial contract. Therapists who sexually abuse their patients often claim that they were only meeting the patient's need for closeness or helping them to overcome sexual inhibitions – following their 'sentiment' or instinct that their patients need sexual help. But such therapists are highly selective in their favours, and never provide them to all patients, irrespective of gender or attractiveness – they are driven by 'sentiment', not money.

An attachment perspective on exchange argues that, despite the discrepancy of power between care-giver and care-seeker, there is always an exchange of some sort. Ultimately, the parent provides a secure base for the child in return for genetic survival (see Chapter 3). Similarly, financial exchange forms part of the framework of safe therapy, akin to the need for regularity of time and place, and consistency of approach. In private practice, this is an explicit part of the therapeutic contract. In publically funded therapy, patients who show excessive gratitude, worrying perhaps that they are getting 'something for nothing', may sometimes have to be reminded that, in the National Health Service, they have a right to treatment, that they have paid our salaries via taxation, and that if they were not ill and 'bothering' us, we would be out of a job.

In private practice, patients need to know that therapists are not simply holding them in therapy as a meal ticket and that, faced with a choice between the patient's best interests and her own, the therapist would always opt for the former. Reick (1922) tells the story of a millionaire who offered him indefinite financial security in return for one therapy session a day. At first he was tempted by this prospect, which would have enabled him to devote the rest of his time to writing and research, but realizing how this arrangement would compromise his therapeutic freedom, quite rightly refused.

Publically funded therapy might seem to offer better prospects for disinterested practice. The therapist can be as tough as she likes with her patient, knowing that her salary does not depend directly on any particular case. But removal of direct financial links between therapist and patient may breed therapeutic arrogance (hence the need to audit and evaluate the effectiveness of therapy); and cosy collusive relationships have attractions beyond the narrowly financial.

What are psychotherapy patients paying for?

What is the 'good' which we offer our patients in return for money? A patient comes to therapy searching for an escape from alienation or alleviation of mental pain. A therapist is quintessentially a stranger, someone who is 'outside the system' within which the patient feels trapped, not infrequently experienced as a system bounded by instrumentality and the power of money. Patients hope that therapy will restore them to themselves. They are more or less aware of the need for the impartial undivided attention, benign concern and the capacity to set limits that is our biological birthright, and which has so often been lacking or perverted in their lives. It may seem curious that the message of therapy is often a painful one – learning to cope with loss and separation is intrinsic to most successful therapy outcomes. But people will pay for almost anything that offers them greater autonomy and an ability to feel more deeply: rock climbing, the painful acquisition of musical skills, or psychotherapy.

The parable of the talents emphasizes the transformative power of money: put to work, money can multiply itself a thousand-fold; buried for security, it lies idle and tarnishes. If therapy is to be successful, patients have to take risks and invest something of themselves in it – time and commitment at least, and in private practice money as well. Therapy is 'work' in the sense that it implies that effort needs to be applied for some change to come about. Resistance is central, and resistance implies labour. In the course of therapy, the patient may discover something 'that money cannot buy', but in our society the overwhelming metaphor for value is money (Haynes and Wiener 1996). I often ask patients at assessment what they would choose if they could have their heart's desire, or had a fairy godmother who could grant their every wish. Some understand immediately, others look blank. Since the inception of the National Lottery, however, everyone now understands if asked, what would they do if their numbers came up.

Therapy usually comes to an end when the patient feels that the 'return' on their investment no longer justifies the outlay and they can make better use of their money. Often when patients come into therapy, they are out of touch with their resources – their talents; by the end there is often a feeling of excitement at the prospect of the surplus that will now be released which therapy has up to now consumed. An internal secure base has replaced the need for an external one in the form of therapy.

The discussion thus far illustrates the universality of the money metaphor. Money represents both reality – the reality which safeguards the boundary of therapy – and the dreams which arise within the safe space enclosed by that boundary. Payment for therapy counteracts patient and therapist omnipotence: the therapist is not so wonderfully 'good' that she does not need recompense for a treatment that depends on her skills as well as her personal qualities, and the patient is not so magisterial that the therapist is privileged to treat her for nothing. Within that framework anything is possible; fantasy is bounded by reality, of which a fee is a key component.

Therapy is sometimes compared with prostitution. Perhaps the therapist's attention or 'love' is no more the 'real thing' than the prostitute's temporary exchange of her or his body in return for sex. What difference is there, so the argument goes, between the prostitute who ends her 'session' by saying 'time's up love', and the therapist who callously interrupts the patient's distress to announce that it is time to stop, with the implication that there is another patient waiting, not to mention a fee to pay? There are obvious parallels, but also vital differences. The prostitute, like all professionals, has to split her private from her professional self. She may be feeling fear, pain, disgust, hatred, boredom or exhaustion, but these must be concealed from the client so that she can continue to act her part. The therapist, by contrast, is required to attend to her counter-transferential emotions and to make use of them in the service of therapy. To be effective, the prostitute must abandon authenticity; the therapist must be true to herself.

A brothel is a place in which fantasy is translated into enactment. In the consulting room, this process is reversed: the patient learns to distinguish fantasy from reality and to substitute thought for action. Some patients, especially if they have been sexually abused, approach treatment as though it *were* a kind of prostitution. Some offer themselves to the therapist, hoping that by divining his every need they will gain the attention and admiration they so desperately crave, even at the expense of prostituting themselves. Others view the whole process as a form of whoring; they can only see themselves as one in a line of clients, accusing the therapist of betrayal and callousness as he switches his attention promiscuously from one person's distress to another as the hour chimes.

The therapist has to be sensitive to these ways in which money may permeate the matrix of therapy, without denying the fact that doing therapy is a job for which she expects to be paid. The therapist who insists that she 'does it for love' is in danger of colluding with the fantasy of a child's exclusive possession of the mother, based perhaps on her own ambivalent attachment needs. Money, like language in the Lacanian framework, is the guarantor of Oedipal reality. Here money comes to stand for the power of the father to withstand these regressive forces. But it is not just the therapist and her other patients who have the power to separate the individual from her heart's desire; the fact that, indirectly or directly, the patient pays, provides a developmental push towards differentiation that is the positive side of the Oedipal situation.

Filthy lucre

If denial of money stands for denial of three-person psychology, over-valuation of money is equally fraught with psychological danger. Midas discovered that money can't buy you love – you can't eat or drink gold, be warmed by it, or lie comfortably on it at night. For St Paul it was not money but *love* of money that was the root of all evil. Money and love are separate realms: the danger lies in confusing them. When Christ said 'render unto Caesar' he underlined his remark by pointing to a coin with Caesar's head on it. God and Caesar should not be confused. But what if Caesar becomes a God? This was what Marx (Bottomore and Reubel 1963) saw as the essence of capitalism. In his discussion of *Timon of Athens* he shows how Shakespeare depicts the 'yellow slave', the 'glittering precious gold':

> . . . that will make black white, foul fair;
> Wrong right; base, noble; old, young; coward valiant . . .
> Will knit and break religions; bless th'accurst;
> Make the hoar leprosy ador'd; place thieves . . .
> . . . damned earth,
> Thou common whore of mankind . . .
>
> (Bottomore and Reubel 1963: 180–1)

But money is not just earth; it is earth transformed by labour. Marx saw both the transformational quality of money and its capacity for perversity:

> . . . the transformation of all human and natural qualities into their opposite, the universal confusion and inversion of things; it brings incompatibles into fraternity . . . It is the universal whore, the universal pander [Pander was the go-between who spoke Troilus's love to Cressida] . . . the divine power of money resides in its essence as the alienated and exteriorised species-life of men . . . What I as a man am unable to do . . . is made possible for me by means of money. Money therefore turns each of these faculties into something which in itself it is not, into its opposite.
>
> (Bottomore and Reubel 1963: 181)

For young Marx money disrupts a natural order, just as for Lacan language separates the infant eternally from the realm of true desire. Both retain a prelapsarian vision which is 'pre-Oedipal', and, in Fenichel's (1946) phrase, 'pre-pecuniary'. The deification of money is a perverse response to pre-Oedipal emptiness. If I cannot have love, then at least I will have money; my unsatisfied greed turns to money-lust as I amass my fortune; by seeking riches at least I deprive others of the goods which I imagine them to enjoy. In Orson Well's *Citizen Kane*, all Kane's money cannot bring Rosebud back from the fire, but at least it can comfort him in his loss and, through inciting envy, punish the world for having inflicted it upon him. Here money has become the pathological secure base that compensates for a lack of real security and attunement.

In therapy, love without money is an illusion, a denial of Oedipal reality; money without love is a perverse attempt to compensate for pre-Oedipal failure. Therapists who are simply in it for the money will be unable to reach their patients' deepest longings; therapists who pretend that money does not matter risk creating a collusive denial of reality. Money belongs to the Oedipal phase and the advent of the father in the child's mind. The pre-pecuniary world is maternal, pre-Oedipal. We need to experience boundless love – and its limits.

The paradox of money is that it can *be* the reality, but symbolize the fantasy. For something new to emerge, there has to be intercourse between these two principles. Sex is 'spending' – and, at the height of passion, leaves us 'spent' – but what it produces is something that is not just sex. Money is needed for new birth, but money that only begets money is sterile.

In a typical piece of early analytic brilliance, Ferenczi (1952) traced the origins of the love of money from the infant's excitement and interest in faeces (his first 'gift'), through playing with mud and sand, to collecting stones until the coprophilic patient becomes a miser admiring his heap of gold. He even suggests that the love of music may have its origins in farting! These classical psychoanalytic theorizings are a manifestation of the monadic universe of early Freud. Music can only arise from the child's own body, rather than from the interactive pattern of singing and rocking of the mother–infant dyad – not to mention genetic ability and social conditioning! An attachment perspective sees the world of the infant as interactive from the start. Neither love nor money can be understood outside of relationships. What matters is the symbolism of the use to which the object is put, its relational coordinates, than with the object itself. *How* a person handles their money – or their sexuality, or their attitude towards death – becomes the main issue.

Thus, denial of the significance of money may represent a regressive wish to return to the pre-pecuniary state of mother-infant mutual absorption. Hoarding money may be a manifestation of a more general tendency to cling to objects based on insecure attachment patterns in childhood. In the contemporary Kleinian model, negotiating of the Oedipal situation depends on the capacity to cope with separation, and to view the parental couple from the outside with relative equanimity. Perhaps the beginnings of the capacity to understand algebra and therefore to exchange money productively starts here, since the child may identify with one or other parent, and begin to sense how family positions are interchangeable.

Some patients insist on paying, usually in cash, at the end of every session. These are people who can never forget money. A monthly bill enables one temporarily to abandon the world of necessity and to enter the pre-Oedipal world of desire, but for some this is too dangerous. Nothing must be left owing, no trace of dependency is allowable. Not to pay immediately would mean to depend on trust, on a word that is a bond, and this must be avoided at all costs. One such man had never forgiven his mother for producing two further sons after him, when he was convinced he was all she ever wanted. How could he possibly trust his therapist not to take advantage of his dependency and to betray him too?

Other patients cannot bear to be reminded of their financial obligations to the therapist. Forgetting to pay a bill, or announcing that one cannot afford to go on with therapy, is not necessarily aggressive or retaliatory, but can arise out of a sense of overwhelming deprivation. Here the therapist is seen as the perverse one: 'all you really care about is my money'. The therapist who insists on her fee may have to tolerate powerful projections in which she contains the patient's greed, and is seen as unreasonable, callous and grasping. She has to be able to hang onto her own sense of value without guilt, to acknowledge that we do live in a deeply unfair world without resorting to martyrdom and self-deprivation.

Does this valuation of money as a potential secure base for therapists mean that Mammon now rules psychotherapy just as it does every other aspect of modern society? If we are to accept the language of cost-effectiveness, are we, as psychotherapists, betraying the essence of our discipline? Or, on the other hand, do we retreat into the private world of the consulting room as compensation for our feelings of powerlessness within society?

We know in our hearts that our skills are inseparable from who we are. A 'good therapist' is much more than someone who has spent a lot of money on training and been to the right institutes. We know that at one level Ferenczi (1952) was right when he said that 'it is the physicians's love that cures the patient', in the sense that more secure attachment is inseparable from good outcome. This is underlined by evidence from psychotherapy research which suggests that 'common' or 'non-specific factors' – reliability, non-judgementalness, consistency and warmth (i.e. the secure base) – contribute as much or more to good therapy outcomes as do specific techniques such as interpretations or cognitive interventions.

Therapists' income and status seem to depend on being able to demonstrate that psychotherapy is just another technical procedure: that people with schizophrenia need family therapy in the same way that diabetics need insulin. Yet we know that few people go into psychotherapy as an occupation purely for the money. Ultimately, psychotherapy is a labour of love, a vocation. We do it because we enjoy it and it provides its own reward – that is the privilege of our profession. Society envies the rich, but even more so artists and sportsmen, people who do what they do for its own sake, out of some inner necessity rather than external compulsion. At some level, we sense that the market is ultimately devoid of meaning and can never offer the love and understanding we crave. In the end, the pre-pecuniary world comes first.

The establishment of the National Health Service, 'free at the point of entry' in Britain, was a socialist attempt to remove money from one central arena of public life. As money increasingly infiltrates the workings of the health service, psychotherapy is a bastion of the doctor–patient relationship, of the narrative as opposed to the technological aspects of medicine. Like art, therapy represents an opposing principle of non-instrumentality, of 'being with' rather than 'doing to' the patient (Wolff 1971). As Marx suggested, the greater the emptiness of the inner world, the more the perverse search for external power and riches, a search which in turns fuels even greater feelings of emptiness. However, it is unwise for therapists to retreat to a precarious moral superiority. We must learn to live in two worlds, rendering unto Caesar as well as our own Gods. As psychotherapists we are trustees of a deeper reality and, like Kipling (1939), we must stand up for the 'God of Things as They Are':

> And no one shall work for money, and no one shall work for fame
> But each for the joy of working, and in each, in his separate star,
> Shall draw the thing as he sees it, for the God of Things as They Are.

But, to keep working for the joy of working, to celebrate things as they are as opposed to things that can be bought, to offer real therapy rather than retail therapy, money is needed.

Chapter 12

Endings in psychotherapy

In psychotherapy, timing is all. An interpretation delivered at the wrong time falls on deaf ears. A patient will only come into therapy successfully if the time is right, and this principle applies equally to ending therapy, the main focus of this final chapter. Why do some patients end 'too soon', others 'too late'? What are the conditions that determine an ending? How can we conceptualize the process of ending? Can attachment theory help understand the difference between a 'good' and a 'bad' ending? What is the nature of 'timing' in relation to ending. Why can some stop when they have 'had enough', even if they want more, while others greedily go on for ever, even when satiated (feeding metaphors are inescapable). These are the themes to be explored in this chapter.

Poised between past and future, every ending encompasses both hope and regret, accomplishment and disappointment, loss and gain. The inherent ambivalence of endings tests our capacity as therapists to tolerate ambiguity, to cope with both optimism and sadness in the face of loss, and to hold onto a realistic appraisal of our strengths and shortcomings. The central argument of this chapter is that the 'fit' between the attachment style of the therapist and that of the patient is a crucial determinant of what type of ending emerges.

I start by a discussion of endings in literature, moving on to discuss Freud's views on termination; then some empirical findings are surveyed; finally, the discussion moves to an attachment-based model of countertransference in relation to the length of therapy.

Endings in literature

It seems likely that writers have as much trouble with endings as psychotherapists. The statement that poems are never completed, only abandoned, could be applied equally to analysis – and the more obsessional one is, the more one may equate a parting with an abandonment. The writer has to be able to let go of his characters and to help the reader with the inevitable feelings of sadness and loss as one comes to the end of a novel. There are, of course, various ways round the problem. One is to write an interminable novel – this surely was the enormously obsessional Proust's solution. Another way round the problem of ending is to embrace it from the start – to write short stories, which, like brief therapies, trade ambition for a more economical but inevitably circumscribed set of aims.

Philip Roth's contemporary classic *Portnoy's Complaint* (1969) ends with the voice of the analyst: 'So [said the doctor]. Now vee may perhaps begin. Yes?' As I suggested at the end of Chapter 7, to end as you began emphasizes the way in which art provides a temporary escape from time's linear arrow – ultimately from the reality of death and finitude. For Freud, the unconscious was outside time, shielded from the reality principle. Perhaps in a Jungian sense we can reify 'the unconscious', seeing it as wiser than the conscious mind and so in touch with the cyclical nature of things, knowing that out of death comes new life. Alongside the sadness about the ending of therapy, there is also often a sense of *relief* for both patient and therapist. The patient can get on with life, free at last to invest her time and money where she will; the therapist can look forward to a new patient, freed from the burden of concern and partial failure that each patient represents. At the end of a good book, we feel a similar mixture of regret at having to part with the characters we have befriended and satisfaction at completion.

Another device for ending a book is just that: a technique that will remind the reader that they have been immersed in what is only a story – a device – and that they are about to be returned to reality. One analyst, at the end of a very painful session, said gently to her patient, 'I'm going to have to hand you back to yourself in a minute or two'. At the end of each session, the patient crosses the boundary back to 'real life'; ending therapy is a final version of that process of leaving the frame. As we saw in Conrad's *Heart of Darkness*, it is Marlow the storyteller, rather than the author, who takes the reader on a horrendous journey to the African interior. At the end we are returned to the dampness of a moored vessel on the River Thames waiting for an ebb tide, while Marlow refills his pipe – after all, it was only a story.

Therapy, too, can be seen as a story within a story. By the end the patient, we hope, is more in possession of her own narrative, no longer needing the therapist, in Rycroft's (1985) words, as an 'assistant autobiographer'. She can unmoor her vessel and sail freely, becoming, in Parsons' (1986) striking metaphor, the dove that did not return and who has therefore – or is this a therapist's wish-fulfilment? – found dry land. The image of water is central to *Heart of Darkness* – the sea connecting the reader back in time to the Roman conquest of Britain, and through space to the heart of The Congo – like the unconscious, an unpunctuated continuum that transcends all man-made starts and finishes.

Erikson's (1968) model of psychotherapy was of the adolescent 'moratorium', in which a young person is allowed to wander and explore both the world and him or herself, temporarily free from the grip of social obligation.

Ending entails a return to the pleasures and duties of social and biological necessity: employment, marriage, parenthood, responsibility. The beginning of the end of a successful therapy is also often marked by the establishment of a new relationship, or the renewal of an ailing one. Some patients may feel they must wait in therapy until they find the ideal partner they are looking for, and there is often much work to be done in unravelling that fantasy. The therapist will always be wondering if, in the new relationship, the patient has found a secure base that can be a genuinely 'transformational object' (Bollas 1987) which can take over from therapy, and to what extent some aspect of the desire or disappointment that belongs to the therapy is being played out.

The nineteenth-century novel, after its customary exploration of a series of moral or emotional dilemmas, also typically ends with a shift of state ('Reader I married him'), with one of the great sociobiological punctuations of arrival and departure that structure our lives: birth, marriage and death. The ambiguity of ending is nowhere more marked than in Dickens' *Great Expectations*, with its two apparently contradictory endings, one 'happy' and the other 'sad'.

Dickens' first version ends with a fleeting meeting between the narrator-hero Pip (whose very name is, like the novel, recursive; Flint 1994) and his love, the cruel and inaccessible Estella, in the centre of London where Pip is escorting his nephew, little Pip. Estella mistakenly assumes that the boy is Pip's son, so creating a Hardy-like misunderstanding. The novel ends with the words:

> I was very glad afterwards to have had the interview; for, in her face and in her voice, and in her touch, she gave me the assurance, that suffering had been stronger than Miss Havisham's teaching, and had given her a heart to understand what my heart used to be.

This straightforward but poignant ending suggests a task accomplished: the characters have been strengthened by suffering, misunderstanding has been overcome. Pip's dependency and fixation on Estella is finally broken, as his heart becomes whole. By finding a 'heart to understand', his heart he can at last let go. He has found an internal secure base that can withstand external loss, and with it reflexive function and narrative competence that arises out of a person's internalization of their object's internalization of them. Therapy begins – and ends – with finding a therapist 'who understands how I feel'.

There is both a finality and a continuity about this first version of the ending, which is strikingly absent in Dickens' later version. Here, in a dream-like return to the past, Pip and Estella meet in the garden of their childhood, familiar to them both, though all has changed. Once again they exchange vows: 'You have always held a place in my heart', they mutually confess. Then, in the final words of the book, while Estella announces that they will 'continue friends apart', Pip takes her hand and, with the mists rising, 'sees no shadow of a parting from her'. It may be that Dickens' sentimentality and his commercial good sense got the better of him here – the public don't like an unhappy ending (any more than purchasers of health care would like to be told that the aim of psychotherapy is to transform neurosis into ordinary human misery!).

However, the key theme for this discussion is the idea that parting is only possible once both intimacy and autonomy have been achieved. If we feel truly understood – found a place in another's heart – then we can tolerate aloneness; conversely once we have achieved a sense of autonomy, we can allow ourselves to get close without fear of engulfment or being destroyed by the other. Pip is no longer afraid to be either with Estella or without her and so his choices are widened, his horizons expanded.

Analysis terminable and interminable

One of the aims of therapy might be seen as reducing the discrepancy between a person's real and ideal selves. On the one hand, unrealistic self-denigration will be reduced and self-esteem enhanced; on the other, omnipotent strivings will be more tempered with realism and the patient will have a better sense of his strengths and weaknesses and be able to accept himself as he is. This takes us back to Freud's (1937b) discussion of analytic interminability. He argued that the length of an analysis depended on three main factors – the extent to which trauma plays a part in the neurosis (the more the influence of trauma the shorter the treatment, since the personality as a whole may be unaffected), hereditary disposition and what he called 'alterations of the ego', which we would now see in terms of character defences. Here he makes a specific point related to gender which merits futher examination. He starts with Ferenczi's assertion that 'Every male patient must attain a feeling of equality in relation to the physician as a sign that he has overcome his fear of castration; every female patient . . . must have got rid of her masculinity complex and must emotionally accept without a trace of resentment her female role' (Freud 1937b: 251). Freud comments:

> I think that in this Ferenczi was asking a very great deal. At no point in one's analytic work does one suffer more from an oppressive feeling that all one's repeated efforts have been in vain and form a suspicion that one has been 'preaching to the winds', than when one is trying to persuade a woman to abandon her wish for a penis on the grounds of its being unrealisable or when one is seeking to convince a man that a passive attitude to men does not always signify castration and that it is indispensible in many relationships in life.
>
> (Freud 1937b: 252)

Thus Freud seems to suggest that rebelliousness and ingratitude in men can be traced to their fear of passivity, while chronic depression in women has as its basis the conviction that analysis is useless if it cannot provide her with the penis that she wants so badly. Freud's vein of late life pessimism concludes that 'the decisive thing is that the resistance prevents any change from taking place – everything stays as it was'.

What is striking here is Freud's extraordinary double standard, even if we translate his concrete thinking into metaphorical terms. For men the task is to see that passivity does not equate with castration – to overcome a faulty cognition as the cognitive therapists would have it. For women, however, the aim is *not* to realize that one can be both active and feminine – which would be a symmetrical task with that of men – but to come to terms with envy and loss and the unrealizability of one's fantasies. To translate this into today's therapeutic terms, one might say that men have a relatively simple cognitive job to do; women a much more difficult 'Kleinian' one. Freud suggests that underneath these unrealizable desires and, therefore, interminable analyses, lies a biological bedrock of bisexuality. It is as though for him it is a Darwin-given fact that 'women don't move'. But surely the bedrock – perhaps ceiling would be a better image – is social rather than biological. 'Bisexuality' is more a matter of habit than hormones. Today we celebrate female activeness and vitality just as much as receptiveness and, conversely, value 'feminine' qualities of gentleness as well as assertiveness in men.

Nevertheless, Freud is undoubtedly pointing to two important issues that can lead to 'interminability' in therapy. What he characterizes as fear of passivity in men is in attachment terms to do with vulnerability to attack. Only when patients, male or female, feel safe enough to give up their defences – to accept their helplessness in relation to the therapist, often symbolized by a move from sitting facing to lying on the couch – can they begin to progress towards an ending. Equally, a therapy can become interminable if the patient cannot accept loss and let go of the past. For those who have been severely traumatized or deprived, it is asking an enormous amount to expect them to accept what has happened and that no amount of wishing it were otherwise can alter the past. This, in turn, can lead to a similar fear of losing therapy and everything good that is projected into it and the anxiety that, when it comes to an end, and the projections withdrawn, everything will once more be destroyed.

Termination and psychotherapy research

Proponents of brief therapy make much of the finding that, in publicly funded psychotherapy settings at least, while the avowed aim of a clinic may be to offer long-term therapy, in fact the average length of treatment has been shown to be around ten sessions (Garfield 1994). Many patients end 'prematurely' and consider themselves satisfied with the help they have received. Much better then, say the brief therapists, to *plan* time-limited therapy and to work towards an ending from the start, than for therapy to be cut short by patients who vote with their feet after a few sessions (like the patient who arrived at her sixth session to announce she was stopping, her hair newly cropped and in an unnervingly abbrievated mini-skirt).

This suggests a classification of termination in brief therapy into two types: *brief involuntary* ('too early') and *brief planned*. Equally long-term therapy can go according to plan or drag on in a way that makes the therapist, and perhaps the patient, feel unable to terminate. So third and fourth categories would be *long-term involuntary* ('too late') and *long-term planned*.

Most psychotherapy research is based on brief therapies and has little to say about the longer-term treatments and their termination that is the focus of this chapter. Outcomes are almost always evaluated in terms of symptom reduction, rather than the kinds of personality change that long-term therapists are workings towards with many of their patients. There are, however, several relevant findings. The first is the so-called 'dose–response curve' (Howard *et al.* 1986), which shows that the longer a therapy continues, the greater the numbers of patients who are helped by it. However, the 'curve' is not linear but negative logarithmic, so that there are diminishing returns in which there is a smaller incremental gain with each successive session. By session twenty-six, according to this model, most of the total gain has been achieved. Severity is a relevant factor too; Shapiro (1995) found in the Sheffield Psychotherapy Project that longer therapy (here comparing eight with sixteen sessions) only produced more improvement in the more severely depressed patients, and that the less ill patients were no worse off with eight than sixteen sessions.

For brief therapists, one of the worrying findings of their work is that, despite very good results in the short term, long-term follow-up shows that many patients tend to relapse. Thus, in a major study of depression treated either with drugs or one of two types of psychotherapy, while nearly 70 per cent of patients were recovered by the end of therapy and at 3 months, by 2 years only 30 per cent had not had further episodes of depression (Roth and Fonagy 1996). A further study looked at the impact of monthly 'top-up' sessions of psychotherapy and found that these did indeed have a role in forestalling relapse: 60 per cent of patients receiving them remained well compared with only 24 per cent those who did not (Elkin 1994).

There are complex research issues here waiting to be unravelled: the impact on outcome of length of therapy, frequency of therapy, severity of illness, combination or otherwise of drugs and psychotherapy, not to mention the model of psychotherapy and skilfulness of the therapist. In the meantime, clinicians will continue to terminate or continue with therapies based on experience and intuition, but it is certain that Procrustean models cannot be right, since the variety and uniqueness of experience is the essence of psychotherapy. Some patients need long-term therapy; others can be usefully helped with brief, or relatively brief interventions; some need intermittent therapy – to come for a while and then return; in some cases termination can be planned, in others it needs to emerge as a theme for months or even years before it actually happens; some people need to stop suddenly, while others do better with a gradual process of weaning. Flexible parenting is a precondition of secure base in children, and the same is true for therapists and their patients. In the next section, I look at different unconscious and conscious models of the termination process.

Ending and previous loss

An ending is perforce shaped by what comes before. Therapists and patients will approach ending with preconceptions and fantasies about what it means to be separated. For the patient, these will largely be determined by previous experiences of loss, as indeed they will in part for the therapist, who, in addition, will be guided by the models and metaphors of change which underlie her work.

Margaret

Margaret had been in therapy for 8 years when her therapist announced that he would be leaving to work in another town in 4 months time. Four years earlier – and, coincidentally, during a sabbatical break by her therapist – her husband, on whom, because of her severe depression and agoraphobia, she was enormously dependent, had died. She had coped with this by partial denial in which she felt his presence around her and saw him as a guardian angel guiding her life. His death had in fact led to major changes in her life and she had established a much less dependent relationship with a new partner. In the session following the announcement, she described how she had thought to herself that, having weathered her husband's death, this ending was nothing to be afraid of, and was in any case what she had secretly been anticipating almost from the start of therapy. Nevertheless, she felt unaccountably anxious and had been unable to sleep, and when she did sleep she had bad dreams – the previous night she dreamed that both her hands had been cut off. She saw this as an expression of her feelings of being unable to cope. She then described how she had been to her family doctor whom she had not seen for years, and how impressed he had been by the changes in her, telling her that a few years ago he had assumed that she would inevitably commit suicide. She then went on to say how amazed she herself was by how different she felt now, attributing this mainly to the positive and cheerful personality of her 9-year-old son which she felt had rubbed off on her. She then described how, when she told her son about the therapist leaving, he had said: 'Oh don't be so silly mummy, just get another doctor!' Finally, she said that she was screwing up her courage to ask if she could still come to visit her therapist from time to time in his new post, although she knew the answer would almost certainly be no.

This vignette contains many of the typical themes aroused at termination, in this case one imposed upon the patient by the therapist, which in 'third-party financed' practice is probably the most common scenario. The patient at first denies the loss, as she did with her husband's death. Then she recounts some aspects of the mourning response – anxiety and insomnia. Then she seeks out a substitute, a doctor she had not seen for years. Then she begins to review the therapy in a profit and loss accounting way. Then there is a flash of anger: 'Don't fool yourself into thinking it was your therapy that had done the trick, it's down to my son and I have still got him *and* can get myself another therapist thank you very much'. Finally, as with a bereavement, she begins to 'bargain' with the loss, hoping that it might not necessarily be irrevocable. In her dream she had lost both her 'helping hands', her first husband and her therapist.

Underlying all this are less conscious themes derived from childhood. Her mother had a severe puerperal depression and was in hospital for several months when the patient was aged 3; both her parents were refugees from Hitler's Germany and no mention of their origins or the past was permitted in the family; now Margaret had cut herself off from them almost completely and wondered if her father sexually abused her during the separation from her mother; she contrasted her son's cheerful demandingness with her own feelings of rejection and lack of entitlement. Separation is a punishment, perhaps a torture, but it is what you deserve. There is nothing you can do about it, just stay passive and endure the bleakness as best you can.

For the therapist, too, the ending will inevitably have unconscious reverberations. If in therapy he has sought out the safe intimacy he finds elusive in ordinary life, then he may cling onto the patient, 'too long'. If he has denied and projected his own weakness and vulnerability into the patient he may encourage termination in the unconscious wish that his inadequacies will be cured or expelled with the patient, and this may lead to a termination that comes 'too early'. There may be a real sadness at parting, but also the excitement and possibility of a new beginning.

Developmental models of ending

In addition to these personal counter-transferential influences, the therapist will be guided by the psychotherapeutic culture and milieu which she inhabits. Separation and loss are central themes in dynamic psychotherapy. Different schools may emphasize different aspects, but all contain a model of psychological development in which each stage represents both gain and loss. For Bion, the absent breast is a stimulus to the beginnings of thought ('no breast therefore imagine a breast'). For Klein, coping with rage and envy at the mother's capacity to come and go – and to wean – as she pleases is the first step towards maturation and the depressive position.

An attachment perspective allows 'timing' to be theorized, since good – or bad – timing depends on the intersection of two or more inner worlds, each with its own rhythms. Bowlby and Winnicott saw in different ways the central paradox that one can only be securely separate if one feels attached in the first place. For Winnicott (1958), the infant develops the capacity for solitude if he has been allowed to 'be alone in the presence of the mother'. Bowlby's mother provides the secure base from which the child can go out and explore the world. For Mahler, the child has in the 'rapprochement subphase' to be able to rush back to mother when her love affair with the world becomes too overwhelming.

For Freud, as interpreted by contemporary Kleinians (Britton *et al.* 1989), resolution of the Oedipus complex depends on the capacity to tolerate separation and loss, to adopt a 'third position' of contemplation which can allow parental intercourse without being compelled to either infiltrate or destroy it. As mentioned in Chapter 5, Money-Kyrle (1971) believed that analysis can come to a successful completion when the patient can see the breast as supremely beautiful, parental intercourse as supremely creative, and accept the inevitability of death. These can be translated as: being able to love without ambivalence, overcome envy and be able to mourn. In his Oedipal model, Freud saw identification with the same-sex parent as a vital part of grieving the loss of exclusive possession of the mother, and this idea reappears in the Freud–Klein model of mourning in which identification with the lost object and its 'reinstatement' in the inner world is a central aspect of coping with loss.

All these themes appear in the contemporary literature on ending. Pedder (1988) dislikes the term 'termination' with its overtones of abortion and finality. He is critical of the uncompromising view of the ending of therapy as an absolute break, akin to a death, which the 'successfully analysed' patient must be expected to undergo. He compares the ending of therapy with an adolescent leaving home who may need to come and go several times before independence is finally achieved, and argues that the therapist should be tolerant of these fluctuations of involvement and disengagement as therapy draws to a close.

One of the hardest therapeutic tasks is to differentiate these premature 'trials of termination', in which the patient appears to be experimenting with leaving but is not really ready, from the finality of irretrievable separation. Like any loss, ending therapy produces a period of psychological instability in which the patient is both drawn forward by the prospect of autonomy and freedom, but held back by anxiety at the loss of the intimacy and security which the therapy represents. He may try to distance himself from his feelings of abandonment by belittling the therapy, failing to turn up, or arranging to be away at times of sessions. Alternatively, he may regress, with a recurrence of old symptoms and anxieties, implying that he is damned if he will not leave until he has had his money's worth. He may immerse himself in a new relationship as a substitute for therapy now that it can no longer be relied upon to be there indefinitely. There may be an obvious 'identification with the lost object', if the patient decides to train in psychotherapy or counselling. At the same time, there will be a taking stock, reviewing the progress of therapy, of satisfaction at what has been achieved and disappointment at what remains undone.

The therapist meanwhile will need to be able to accept attack without justification or retaliation, to hold onto a sense of what has been positive in the therapy without denying faults and limitations. She will need to resist the temptation to impose an idealized view of therapy, which may subtly suggest that the patient has failed, or that he needs to continue indefinitely so as to protect herself from disappointment and narcissistic wound. The therapist may well feel envious of the patient's creativity and new-found sexual energy, and must resist the temptation to undermine or intrude upon them.

Attachment and loss

From an attachment perspective, the aim – or 'end' – of-psychotherapy is to help create a secure base, both in reality and as an internal representation within the patient. A secure base arises partly out of the responsiveness and attunement provided by the therapist, partly from her capacity to accept and metabolize protest and anger directed towards her. From the former arises the rudiments of intimacy, from the latter the capacity for autonomy.

A 'good ending' is possible once a secure base has been established. In less disturbed patients, this may simply mean the repair of one which is temporarily damaged, often by trauma, and therefore the process can be relatively brief. In borderline patients, there may never have been the experience of security and so the base has to be built up from scratch. This inevitably takes time.

Therapeutic strategy must be matched to attachment style. Non-intrusive responsiveness, whether from care-giver or therapist, allows for the development of an inner world, a self that can recognize the existence of other selves, and this strategy is particularily important in avoidant patterns of attachment. Conversely, ambivalent individuals need a firm and consistent therapeutic frame if they are to feel safe enough to express the anger and protest that can lead to a sense of autonomy. Autonomy is possible on the basis of a secure inner world – we can go out on a limb, stand our ground, make our own choices and tolerate separation if we can be sure that intimacy is available when needed. Intimacy is possible if the loved one can be allowed to be separate: we can allow ourselves to get close if we feel autonomous enough not to fear engulfment or attack, and also know that separation does not mean that our loved one is lost forever.

How is this relevant to ending? Ending can either be imposed from without, as in time-limited therapy, or can arise spontaneously out of the patient's wishes. This distinction can apply to any length of therapy. Some patients only want to come for a few sessions to resolve some outstanding issue, often, as Freud (1937b) suggested, an unworked-through loss or trauma, and make this clear from the start. In others, as long-term therapy progresses, it becomes gradually clear that an ending is on the horizon and by tacit or explicit mutual agreement therapist and patient begin to work towards it. In these situations, the therapist is always following the patient's lead, attuning herself, working at the 'zone of proximal development' (Vygotsky 1962), helping the patient to work with the issue that is not so easy that he can grasp it unaided, nor so difficult as to be out of reach. In other cases, the therapist will offer the patient a time-limited contract from the start, or in longer therapies set a date for ending. Which strategy is used will depend ideally on the needs of the individual patient. As we saw in Chapter 4, the avoidant patient needs an attuned, 'following' strategy; the ambivalent individual needs consistency, firm structure and well-marked boundaries.

But therapists as well as patients have 'personality styles'. Some will be good at attunement, less so at boundaries, and vice versa. At any given moment in therapy there will be a balance struck between attunement and limit-setting that reflects the transferential/counter-transferential matrix between therapist and patient (Gabbard 1995). The 'too early–too late' dilemma can be understood in terms of this matrix and the interaction of patient and therapist attachment patterns. Racker (1968) distinguishes between (a) 'complementary' counter-transference where there is an unhealthy 'fit' between therapist and patient, in which the former is shaped to enact some aspects of the patient's pathology, and (b) 'concordant' counter-transference in which the therapist resonates more empathically with the patient's unconscious needs.

Ending therapy is an *action*, not an interpretation – albeit one that is an important subject for reflection and interpretation. It is an action that may be initiated unilaterally by patient or therapist, or preferably as a collaborative decision. The analyst must be able to determine whether or not ending is a transferential/counter-transferential enactment. The patient may decide to leave because of this own unconscious conflict, or, via projective identification, as an enactment of the therapist's unconscious conflicts. To complicate matters further, the therapist may unconsciously enact some aspect of the patient's unconscious, 'picked up' by projective identification, which is then reintrojected by the patient.

Using Racker's (1968) complementary/concordant distinction, we can imagine a four-way matrix in which the timing of an ending can be con-

THERAPIST

		STRUCTURE	ATTUNEMENT
PATIENT	AMBIVALENT	concordant	'too late'
	AVOIDANT	'too early'	concordant

Figure 12.1 Endings in therapy by security of attachment

sidered (Fig. 12.1). Thus an avoidant patient with a therapist who over-emphasizes structure at the expense of attunement may end 'too early', while an ambivalent patient with a therapist who is able to empathize but is weak on structure may end 'too late'. Psychotherapy research (Roth and Fonagy 1996) suggests that good outcome with difficult patients depends on therapists who can combine firm rootedness within their particular model of therapy (and it does not seem to matter too much which sort of therapy it is), with flexibility in the face of the particular patient's needs (i.e. a combination of structure and attunement). Different therapies may tempt therapists in one direction or the other: analytic and cognitive therapies (strange bedfellows!) may over-emphasize structure; humanistic ones might tend to produce an excess of empathy. This can be related to Dozier and co-workers' (1994) finding, noted earlier, that insecure clinicians tend to reinforce their clients' insecure attachment patterns, while secure ones counterbalance them. Racker's hypothesized concordance means empathizing but not over-identifiying with the client, while in complementarity the therapist acts out the client's difficulties often in unhelpful ways, just as Dozier found through clinical research.

In supervision, particular moments in therapy can be analysed using this matrix to help the therapist separate those aspects of the interaction that arise from his own pathology and those which arise in response to the patient, both of which may be reintrojected by the patient.

Real people do not fit neatly into pre-determined categories and many, especially those suffering from borderline personality disorder, show features of both avoidance and ambivalence at different times. I end with a clinical example, illustrating the possible use of the matrix in understanding the theme of ending in psychoanalytic psychotherapy.

Mary
Mary, a solicitor in her mid-thirties, came into therapy saying that she wanted to come to terms with the fact that she would never marry or

have children. It was typical of her that she had prejudged the outcome –
the ending – before she had even begun. She had grown up in a claustro-
phobic family with an alcoholic but loving father, and a depressed and
highly controlling mother, whom Mary had learned to placate from an
early age, and continued to do so. She was close to her older sister, but
felt guilty about having done 'better' and earning more than her. At 18,
while travelling, she had been trapped in a fallen building during a
minor earthquake. She had never spoken about it in any depth before
coming into therapy.

Her narrative style was typically avoidant, starting each session with
a rather unelaborated catalogue of the week's events, and finding it very
hard to describe or show emotions. She controlled the session with great
precision both with her eyes, which she could not take off the therapist,
and by vigilantly consulting her watch throughout, always making sure
she brought the sessions to an end, usually leaving one or two minutes
early, explaining that 'I know how irritating it is when clients overrun
their time'. Time and 'watchfulness' became the central themes of therapy. She described the seemingly endless feeling of being trapped during
the earthquake, and how *not* being in control of the sessions was both
what she wanted more than anything and what she feared most of all.

Seeing her as avoidant, the therapist at the start made little comment
on this and simply concentrated on affective attunement and
responsiveness – on the mutuality of good timing, as opposed to the
clock time by which she ran her life. But as she became more engaged
and dependent on therapy, so it became safe to talk about her need to
control the ending and her fear of what would happen if she didn't. The
therapist no longer had to be a rescuer and could challenge her without
it seeming like an eruption or quake. Gradually she began to leave her
watch off, dared – at the therapist's invitation – to lie on the couch, and
asked to come twice a week. The atmosphere of therapy became more
lively and real. After a while, Mary began to say how she felt she had
had 'enough' therapy and should stop. By now her dependency was
much more apparent (she had moved beyond the avoidant position),
and so the therapist was able to interpret it in terms of her guilt about
having more than she deserved, about lustily asking for 'more'. Had she
stopped at that point it would undoubtedly have been 'too early'. At the
same time, she began for the first time to express anger towards the
therapist, especially as he appeared to her to be unsympathetic when her
beloved dog became ill.

After another 18 months of therapy and several transferential false
starts in relationships, she met and began to love a suitable and available
man, and began to talk again about ending, this time as though she
meant it. As the end approached, she began to have doubts about leaving and, as is so often the case, many of her old insecurities resurfaced,

but feeling that it was important to affirm her new-found autonomy and her capacity to understand her own needs, the therapist accepted her plan. To have done otherwise would have run the risk of ending 'too late'. She suggested a follow-up session a few months later, which duly went smoothly, if uneventfully. Later still she wrote to say how well things were going and to announce that she was pregnant.

We often say that patients come into therapy with 'unfinished business' – a cliché perhaps, but it suggests that people seek therapy when they have been unable to make an ending – a trauma or loss that has not been mourned, or a dependency that cannot be resolved. Before patients can leave therapy they have first to find their object, then to attack the object and their need for it and, finally, to let go. Secure attachment means being in touch with and able to deal with aggression and destructiveness in one's self and others. Before therapy Mary had not dealt with the traumatic episode in which she was trapped; she had not extricated herself from her hostile dependency on her mother; she had not faced the ambivalent sexuality of her relationship with her father. As these themes emerged and were at least partially dealt with in therapy, so ending became possible.

There is a constant dialectic in psychotherapy, as in life, between closeness and separation, attunement and challenge, attachment and loss. Ending is ever-present, long before the final separation, casting its shadow on therapy from the start and, when it comes, is a culmination of all the countless little endings that have prefigured it. In Rilke's (1964) words 'So we live, forever taking leave'.

Appendix

'BABI' – brief attachment-based therapy, a treatment modality based on attachment theory

A variety of integrative 'brand-name' brief therapies now exist (Holmes and Bateman 2000). These include brief dynamic therapy, interpersonal therapy, psychodynamic-interpersonal therapy, dialectical behaviour therapy and cognitive analytic therapy. Most comprise a mixture of Rogerian, psycho-analytic, cognitive, systemic and behavioural elements. These therapies have several features which make them advantageous when compared with their parent modalities:

- they are highly structured and so easy for beginner therapists to grasp and apply, and
- therefore they lend themselves to teaching;
- they can be manualized and so be used in psychotherapy research;
- most are time-limited and so are attractive to funding agencies;
- some are disorder-specific; for example, psychodynamic-interpersonal therapy is designed for therapy with depressed patients and dialectical behaviour therapy for people suffering from borderline disorders.

Brief attachment-based therapy (BABI) has much in common with these brand-name cousins. It is a time-limited therapy; it places strong emphasis on formulation; it is collaborative; it uses handouts for clients who are expected to carry out homework between sessions; it is integrative in that it uses Rogerian, dynamic and cognitive-behavioural techniques.

The underlying reason for developing BABI arises from the increasing emphasis on evidence-based therapies, coupled with the fact that there is to date no explicit therapy for adults based on attachment therapy. When compared with other brand-named therapies, BABI has several unique features. Perhaps the most important of these is that BABI has arisen out of a research base rather than vice versa. The child development studies and attachment categorization which inform BABI are the result of several decades of intense research. BABI practitioners, and its funders, can be confident that their approach is evidence-based rather than ideological.

A second unique feature of BABI is that it has clear models of both normal and abnormal functioning. There is powerful evidence that secure attachment, the capacity for exploration and companionable interaction, for healthy protest when the secure base is threatened, for appropriate mourning and for self-reflexiveness, are associated with behaviours in children and adults which would be generally considered marks of psychological health. Securely attached children are more outgoing, more popular at school, more able to ask for help when needed and, as adults, less likely to have problematic relationships or psychiatric diagnoses. The links between childhood and adult security are beginning to be robustly established. Conversely, insecure attachment, suppression of protest, being unable to regulate emotion, abnormal grief and deficient reflexive capacity are all vulnerability factors for psychological disturbance.

As a consequence of its research rather than ideological origins, BABI provides an integrative framework within which different therapeutic modalities can comfortably co-exist. Exploration of secure base and enhancing reflexive function are essentially psychodynamic exercises; working on healthy protest involves using assertiveness training that comes from the behavioural tradition; and affect regulation methods have been devised as part of dialectical behavioural therapy; helping the patient with guided grief is both psychodynamic and cognitive; understanding internal working models draws on cognitive behavioural methods.

In general, BABI is supportive for therapists as well as patients. It enables therapists to use techniques with which they are familiar within an overall framework that has a clear rationale and outcome objectives.

BABI in practice

General points

The therapist is in weekly or bi-weekly supervision and will already have had training in counselling or psychotherapy.

The key component of training lies in learning to combine prescriptive and expressive elements. Although there are many features that are specific to BABI, which appears at times to be highly structured and prescriptive, there is also a parallel aspect of therapy which allows for spontaneity and following the client's lead. Therapy sessions contain both BABI elements and more conventional therapeutic interactions that would be apparent in any Rogerian or dynamic therapy sessions. The therapist will follow the client – responsiveness is a feature of secure base.

The first 15 minutes or so of the session allow the client to describe her week and for themes spontaneously to arise. The therapist then moves to the agreed focus – assertiveness or dealing with loss, for example – for the next 15 minutes or so, using role play, written material or photographs as appropriate. The last third of the session will attempt to bring these two elements together, picking up on metaphors from the client's spontaneous themes, trying to link them with the current focus, and moving towards a homework assignment.

Step 1: contract and engagement

The client is given an appointment according to normal clinic practice. At the start, a contract is agreed for ten 45-minute sessions. The therapist explains the overall structure of BABI. The client tells his or her story in the usual way, the therapist using basic Rogerian skills of active listening and reflexion. Emphasis is placed on delineating the presenting problem and what the client would like to be different as a result of therapy:

> Tell me in your own words what has brought you for help.
> How would you like to be different in your life?
> If therapy were successful, what would have changed for you as a result, and how would you and those close to you know?

Step 2: eliciting secure base material

The usual psychotherapeutic history is taken, but informed by the questioning style devised for the Adult Attachment Interview. The client is asked to give about five adjectives to describe each parent or relevant care-giver and then to describe an anecdote or incident illustrative of each (tests narrative style). The client is asked about significant losses and separations in childhood. The client is asked about feelings of threat from parents as a child (relevant to disorganized attachment). The client is asked whether he or she thinks childhood experiences, especially with parents, have influenced or affected him or her as an adult. The client is asked why he or she thinks parents behaved towards him or her as they did (tests reflexive function).

The therapist notes how clients behave *vis-à-vis* himself and the clinic generally. Any phone calls before the appointment? Was the client on time? Did she come accompanied? How did she enter the room? How warm and open or resistant and closed is she when giving her history? The therapist uses counter-transference to classify client closeness/distance: how protective does she feel, how much sympathy does she feel, how kept at a distance?

Step 3: formulation

Stages 1 and 2 will occupy most of the first two sessions. At the end of the first session, the client is given the secure base handout and asked to bring it to the next session. In the meantime, with help from the supervisor and supervisory group, a preliminary hypothesis is being developed about the client's attachment style, and an attempt to formulate the presenting problem in attachment terms is made. For example, target problems such as binge eating, deliberate self-harm or angry outbursts will be seen in attachment terms, for example in terms of self-soothing and protection. Relationship difficulties will similarly be construed. For example, for a patient who arrived at her session with a baby in a pram, who had constant rows with her husband, it was suggested:

> Your rows are your way of ensuring that you are not abandoned, while at the same time acting as a barrier to intimacy which you find frightening. As a child you depended on your father who looked after you while your mother worked. He then sexually abused you. When you revealed this to your mother, the family split up and after that you saw very little of him. You want to be close to your husband and feel anxious when he comes home late, but at the same time, because you were sexually abused, closeness is very threatening to you. You see a lot of your mother but can't really open up to her for fear she will criticize or reject you. This, too, plays a part in your relationship with your husband and may also influence your attitude towards therapy. By bringing your baby to sessions you ensure that you have some sort of secure base – but keep your therapist at a distance.

Step 4: trawling the domains

By now the therapist and client will have some idea about which of the six domains need particular attention. Domains 1, 5 and 6 – secure base, internal working models and reflexive capacity – are the most important and will be relevant to all clients. It is less threatening, however, if particular skill-based topics are tackled first. For example, the client above had difficulty with angry outbursts. This provides an opportunity to work on assertiveness, using basic assertiveness techniques, which include informing the client about the triad of rage, submission and appropriate assertiveness; to think about relevant incidents; role-play alternative outcomes with the therapist; try to put learned skills into practice in the intervening week. Similarly, unresolved losses may be explored using a guided grief model. If the client seems to have difficulty with fun and enjoyment, then a self-esteem oriented model can be used and she can be helped to visualize pleasant activities and try them out.

Step 5: modifying attachment styles

Varying attachment styles will require different therapeutic techniques. This is a crucial area for attachment research and subtle practice. 'Role responsiveness' puts pressure on therapists to reinforce pre-existing attachment patterns (Dozier *et al.* 1994). Secure therapists counterbalance clients' attachment patterns, insecure therapists reinforce them. Most clients do not fit neatly into one or other of the research categories, although some do. More often there is a mixture of different facets, representing, for example, different attachment relationships with different care-givers – mother, father, grandparents.

- Clients with a predominantly avoidant/dismissive style will need to be helped to get in touch with emotions and to elaborate their narratives, searching their memory for detail and for less black-and-white accounts of their life. Empathic responsiveness on the part of the therapist is a key technique, with sensitivity to client expectations of rejection or aggression. Working on emotional reactions to breaks is particularly important here.
- Clients with ambivalent/preoccupied styles will need to be helped to achieve some distance from their emotions. Here a cognitive approach is required that fosters 'thinking about feeling' and learning that emotions can be modified by thoughts. Here the therapist may be induced into the unreliability the client has come to expect from care-givers. The therapist introduces structure and sticks firmly to boundaries.
- A 'dialectical' (Linehan 1993) approach to emotional regulation may be helpful for clients where attachment appears disorganized. Learning to trust the therapist is a key achievement. Self-injurious behaviours can be understood and positively connoted in terms of the search for a secure base. These clients in particular may require post-BABI therapy, often in group analysis format.

Step 6: identifying Internal Working Models

Internal working models are accessed via cognitions. This aspect of BABI uses standard techniques derived from cognitive therapy. The handout (see below) explains basic cognitive therapy techniques in accessible form. The client will begin to be aware of trigger points at which emotional difficulty may arise, based on past experience and set off by contemporary stimuli.

The focus is always on (a) threats to security, (b) the emotional response that accompanies those perceived threats and (c) how the client deals with that response. Alternative strategies are then sought. For example, the trigger might be a partner turning up later than expected. The response might be panic and anger. The response to the response might be to withdraw (seeking internal secure base), sulk (punishing the partner and locking them in as attachment figure), or engage in some sort of tit-for-tat (using projective identification to get the partner to understand how it feels to be abandoned, another aspect of secure base). Beginning to understand these processes acts as an internal secure base, which can aid emotional regulation.

As therapy progresses, the client will accumulate a collection of 'buttons' which they will identify as underlying their presenting problem. Physically making a 'button' with an outside face that says 'husband returns late' and an inward-facing one which says 'Dad abuses me and leaves me' may be helpful in some instances.

Step 7: autobiographical competence

The act of coming to therapy and talking about oneself is the start of self-reflexion. It may be helpful to use specific devices, such as getting the client to keep a mood diary, write an autobiographical account of their difficulties, bring family photographs and talk around them, use of drawings, videos or music to express feelings. All of these can foster the capacity to represent the self in relation to others and to be aware of that representation – both features of secure attachment.

Step 8: ending

In common with many brief therapies, BABI places great emphasis on nego-tiating the ending of therapy. From session 6 the therapist begins to 'count down' to the final session. Ending provides an opportunity to look at how the client handles loss and separation. The idea of the internal secure base is introduced and the client is encouraged to think about how she will cope once therapy comes to an end.

Handouts for 'BABI' clients

'BABI' – brief attachment-based intervention

Almost everyone feels anxious or depressed at some point in their lives. There are many reasons for this: stress, separation from or loss of someone or something that is dear to us, loneliness, difficulties in our close relationships, worry about the future. The way we react to difficulties may take us back to pain or trauma in childhood. Some people have a built-in tendency to worry or to want things to be perfect or to find it hard to cope; others have had difficult or disrupted childhoods, which in itself can sometimes – but not always – predispose to vulnerability in later life.

When we are in difficulty we need *support*: we try to draw on our own inner strength, seek help from friends or family, or turn to professionals whose job it is to help. BABI is a brief therapy based on the principles of *attachment*. *Attachment theory*, which is based on some very simple and obvious ideas, was developed half a century ago by the psychoanalyst John Bowlby and has been extensively researched and extended since then. Bowlby realized that as children we feel safe and good about ourselves to the extent that we have trusted and reliable adults to whom we can turn at times of need. These *attachment figures* provide a *secure base*, which allows us to relax, have fun and feel able to explore the world. As babies the secure base is usually the mother, but as we grow the range extends to the father, grandparents, brothers and sisters, and then to friends, who provide comradeship and companionship as well as security.

Although everyone has had some protection through their childhood – and would not have survived to adulthood without it – our attachment figures have not always been reliably secure. Sometimes our parents have themselves been depressed, distracted, ill, intoxicated or unavailable. This can lead to *insecure attachment*. Here we can get some measure of security, but at a price. If we are fearful that our attachment figures will lash out at us in words or physically, we will warily keep our distance from them, and may also harbour secret feelings of resentment which we take out on others – brothers and sisters or companions at school. If we worry that our parents will forget us, we may cling to them, sacrificing our capacity to have fun, make friends, stand up for ourselves and explore the world. Sometimes everything becomes so confusing we just can't find any reliable way to feel safe, and retreat into ourselves and a world of make-believe.

Loss is another universal human experience. What is lost may be a loved pet, an intact family, the death of a close family member, a job and with it the sense of being worth something. How we cope with loss depends in part on how secure or insecure our attachments have been. People whose attachments were insecure tend either to switch off their feelings or, at the other extreme, to be overwhelmed with pain and misery.

One way in which we react to loss or to the threat of loss is with anger and protest. Again, if we have been insecurely attached we may be unable to express *appropriate anger* or to *assert* ourselves when the occasion demands it. Either we explode with rage or bottle up our emotions, turning anger in on ourselves, which sometimes ends up with feelings of depression.

As adults we don't outgrow our need for a secure base – we still need someone to turn to, talk to, to be a source of succour at times of trouble. We also need to find a secure base within ourselves – a reassuring thought, religious or political beliefs, an image or an activity to comfort us when we feel bad (eg. hot baths, warm duvets, a favourite book or piece of music, food or drink). And we need hobbies, interests, fun and pleasure too, especially if we can share them with others.

All of this is true in theory, but in practice relationships are often far from helpful. People let us down, abuse us, are neglectful and selfish, are not there when we need them, or are there when we don't. It is easy to blame others, but the curious thing is that we are in part the authors of our own problems: we seem to be unconsciously attracted to people who fit in with our previous picture of the world. Our maps of the world are based on previous navigation. If our attachment figures in childhood have been insecure-making, we will seek out similar types in adult life. If we have been rejected in the past, we will expect rejection in the future and so either avoid close relationships or cling to our loved ones in a way that may eventually drive them away. It is as though we have a series of triggers or *buttons* built up from 'outside' experience and 'inside' expectation which are just waiting to be pressed.

Finally, we vary in the extent to which we are able and inclined to talk about ourselves and our feelings. Some avoid it at all costs, others just can't stop. Yet research shows that the ability to reflect on ones' situation and to express oneself – using words, pictures or music – may make all the difference between survival and going under in the face of adversity. This is called *autobiographical competence* or *reflexive function*. In therapy, we hope to find a theme or *guiding metaphor* arising out of the clients life-story which brings together some of their difficulties in one image.

In this ten-session therapy, we will touch on all these aspects of psychological functioning and in particular the *six domains* of:

- *Secure base* – within oneself and with others.
- *Exploration* – fun, pleasure and happiness.
- *Loss* – and how we have dealt with it.
- *Assertiveness and appropriate anger* – as opposed to rage or inhibition.
- *Triggers and buttons* – what trips us into states of depression or worry?
- *Reflexive function* – the ability to stand back from difficulties and think about them.

After one or two initial assessment sessions the client will come to a *formulation* with her therapist that will probably identify two or three of these domains which are particularly relevant to her and her difficulties, and together they will begin to work on them. The overall aim of the therapy is (a) to start to understand how the overwhelming need for security and self-protection may at times be self-defeating, and expose the client to the very dangers which she is trying to avoid, and (b) to begin to strengthen her sense of secure attachment so that she will be better equipped in the future to cope with the problems with which everyday life presents us.

Secure base

As a child –

- To whom did you turn when distressed, ill, or tired?
- Who did you feel understood you best as a child?
- Adjectives and illustrative episodes for mother and father (five each).
- What was your most frightening situation or moment as a child?
- How did you get comfort when frightened?

Now –

- What do you do when you are ill, depressed, worried or tired?
- To whom do you turn when upset or troubled?
- Describe a comforting image or thought, piece of music, etc.
- What is your greatest fear?
- With whom do you feel most relaxed and at ease?
- Do you ever feel cut-off and detached from people?
- Do you ever feel so frightened of people that you avoid their company?
- Do you ever fear that those you are close to will leave you, and so cling onto them even when they find it irritating?
- Is there a basic pattern to your close relationships – you as the mediator, the conceder, the strong one, the one who copes, the one who looks after everyone, the strong silent breadwinner, etc.?
- In close relationships do you tend to comfort or be comforted, or does it happen both ways?

Exploration, fun and companionship

As a child –

- What did you find funny, exciting, amusing?
- What was your biggest adventure?
- Whom did you associate with fun and excitement?
- What were you mainly interested in doing?

Now –

- What is your idea of having a good time?
- What are your main interests?
- How do you spend your spare time?
- Who would be a good person to have an adventure with – partner, family, friends?
- What would you really like to do if money and commitments were no object, e.g. if you won the lottery, or received an unexpected inheritance?

Loss

As a child –

- Did you have any major losses, separations or bereavements?
- If so, how did you react? Did you cry? Mourn? Talk to a comforting person about your feelings? Switch off?
- Did you ever run away, or 'go off', so your parents did not know where you were?

Now –

- What have been the most difficult losses of your adult life – bereavements, marriage/partnership break-ups, friends, jobs?
- How have you coped and reacted to loss?
- What loss do you fear most and how do think you would react if it did come about?
- How easy do you find it to express your feelings when you feel disappointed, let down or bereft?

Healthy protest – anger and assertiveness

As a child –

- What happened when you felt upset or cross?
- Who took these feelings seriously and listened to you?
- Did you have temper tantrums? If so, what provoked them?
- Were you able to say 'no' to things you didn't want?
- Could you ask for what you wanted and expect at least to be listened to?

Now –

- Describe an incident or an anecdote in which you felt angry. What happened? What did you do?
- If a friend or your partner does something to upset you, how do you react? Overt anger, rage, sulking, go quiet, secret revenge, feel miserable and do nothing, etc.?
- Are you able to ask for what you want from those closest to you?
- Do you ever feel abandoned or let down? How do you handle this situation?
- Has aggression ever caused major problems for you? Broken relationship, trouble with the law, etc.?
- Do you ever feel put upon, or used or abused, by other people, especially those close to you?

Buttons and triggers (internal working models)

Most of us cope reasonably well most of the time. But equally, for many of us, there are areas of life – it might be in intimate relationships, or where we need to stick to a task, or when things go wrong, or when we meet new people – that we know are likely to be problematic. Often we find ouselves making the same 'mistake', or playing out an all-too-familiar scenario, over and over again.

These weak points, or areas of vulnerability, can be thought of as a series of 'buttons' or triggers, which, when pressed, tip us into difficulty. The 'buttons' face two ways, inwards towards our inner world and outwards to the world itself. The inner facet of the button can be thought of as having a phrase or slogan on its face that summarizes a particular problem or difficulty. The outward-facing button is triggered by ordinary everyday events.

For instance, suppose that you have a tendency to 'ambivalent' attachment styles and become very anxious when you get close to someone for fear they may abandon you. Your inner button would have a slogan like 'don't let people on whom you depend out of your sight' or 'care-givers are inconsistent'. The outer button might read 'partner goes away'. When for some quite everyday reason you are separated from your partner, your 'button' is automatically pressed and you start to feel desperate and anxious.

The idea behind BABI is that these inner 'slogans' or assumptions were built up from experiences in childhood, and that they may no longer be appropriate to your adult life or may even be self-fulfilling prophesies. If you can't let you partner out of your sight, eventually he or she may get fed up and start actually to be the very inconsistent person you accuse him or her of being. Not only that, but these inner slogans or 'internal working models' lead us to seek out situations that are familiar to us, so we may end up choosing partners and friends whose behaviour is familiar to us from the past or, more likely, based on the inner face of our buttons, whom we *see* as letting us down, irrespective of their actual behaviour.

As a child –

- Describe two or three key memories of episodes that stick out for you as typical of yourself and your family – a family holiday, your first day at school, Christmas.

Now –

- Describe a situation or situations that typify your current difficulty. Make sure you include how you behave, how others behave towards you and how you react to those reactions.
- Draw a typical 'button' for yourself and try to think of a slogan that would fit on the inner and outer sides.

Reflexive function and autobiographical competence

As a child –

- How would you have drawn a picture of or described you and your family? Draw a picture as you would have seen them aged 5 and 10.
- How would you have described a family event such as a holiday or Christmas, a birthday or a funeral?
- Who was (is) your favourite famous person (pop star, sportsman, historical figure, etc.)? What do/did you find special about them?

Now –

- Describe a happy and an unhappy memory from childhood.
- Bring some photographs of yourself and your family and talk about them.
- Bring some favourite music to your session and explain what it means to you.
- Talk about your hopes for the future for yourself and your family.
- Describe a typical day now. What do you find interesting and amusing? What do you find boring, depressing or worrying?
- Think about your style of thinking about yourself. Are you the sort of person who 'would rather not think about it', or are you someone who 'can't leave things alone'?
- If therapy is successful, how would you like things to be different in your life? Describe a hoped-for typical day or week or event.

Aims and methods of BABI

BABI is an integrative therapy that draws on many psychotherapeutic traditions and techniques. The aims of BABI can be summarized as follows:

- To learn to feel more at ease in situations of intimacy and closeness.
- To learn to tolerate being alone more easily.
- To be more able, when you need it, to call on the security and safety which those close to you can provide.
- To find inner strength which you can draw on when you need it.
- To learn to ask for what you want and to refuse what you do not want.
- To let other people know about your feelings, especially difficult ones like anger and disappointment.
- To be able to enjoy yourself in the company of trusted friends or family.
- To be able to feel appropriately sad about the losses and disappointments of your life.
- For you to know yourself better, especially your vulnerabilities.
- To find alternative ways of coping when these vulnerabilities are triggered by the ups and downs of daily life.
- To have a sense of what is your typical 'attachment style' – avoidant, ambivalent or disorganized.
- To learn to talk about yourself and your life in a way that makes sense, does justice to your achievements and setbacks, and takes account of the ways in which you have been let down or harmed by others, and in which you yourself have let down or harmed others.
- Coming to accept that there is a 'baby' part of yourself that needs security and nurture if you are to have fun and to grow.

The methods of BABI include:

- Looking in detail at the six different areas which contribute to a secure sense of self.
- Doing the 'homework' involved in the different areas, e.g. finding family photographs and bringing them to sessions, drawing pictures of yourself and your 'buttons', or grieving past losses.
- Coming regularly to sessions and letting your therapist know if you are unable to make one.
- Looking in detail at the different incidents and anecdotes which come up in the course of therapy and trying to understand how the search for security has influenced your reactions and those of others.
- Thinking about yourself in relationship to your therapist, and how the feelings and behaviours which being in therapy stirs up may be illustrative of how you react in other intimate situations.

References

Adams, D. (1978) *Hitchhiker's Guide to the Galaxy*. London: Viking.

Ainsworth, M. (1989) Attachments beyond infancy. *American Psychologist*, 44, 706–716.

Alvarez, A. (1992) *Live Company*. London: Routledge.

Auden, W. H. (1962) Spain, in *Collected Poems*. London: Faber.

Balint, M. (1979) *The Basic Fault*. London: Routledge.

Bateman, A. (1998) On 'thin' and 'thick-skinned' narcissism. *International Journal of Psychoanalysis*, 79, 13–28

Bateman, A. and Holmes, J. (1995) *Introduction to Psychoanalysis: Contemporary Theory and Practice*. London: Routledge.

Beebe, B. and Lachman, F. (1988) Mother–infant mutual influence and precursors of psychic structure. In A. Godbnerg (ed.) *Frontiers in Self-Psychology*. Hillsdale, NJ: Analytic Press.

Bell, D. (1992) Hysteria – a contemporary Kleinian perspective. *British Journal of Psychotherapy*, 9, 169–80.

Belsky, J. (1993) Etiology of child maltreatment: a developmental-ecological analysis. *Psychological Bulletin*, 114, 413–34.

Bion, W. (1962) *Learning from Experience*. London: Routledge.

Blatt, S. and Behrens, R. (1987) Internalisation, separation-individuation, and the nature of therapeutic action. *International Journal of Psychoanalysis*, 68, 279–97.

Bloom, A. (1997) *The Anxiety of Influence*. Oxford: Oxford University Press.

Bollas, C. (1987) *The Shadow of the Object*. London: Free Association Books

Bollas, C. (1992) *Being a Character*. London: Routledge.

Bollas, C. (1995) *Cracking Up*. London: Routledge.

Bowlby, J. (1988) *A Secure Base: Clinical Applications of Attachment Theory*. London: Routledge.

Bottomore, T. and Reubel, M. (1963) *Karl Marx: Selected Writings*. London: Penguin.

Brennan, K., Clark, C. and Shaver, P. (1998) Self-report measures of adult attachment: an integrative overview. In J. Simpson and S. Rholes (eds) *Attachment Theory and Close Relationships*. New York: Guilford Press.

Bretherton, I. (1999) Updating the 'internal working model' construct: some reflections. *Attachment and Human Development*, 3, 343–54.

Britton, R. (1998) *Belief and Imagination*. London: Routledge.

Britton, R. (1999) Getting in on the act: the hysterical solution. *International Journal of Psychoanalysis*, 80, 1–14.

Britton, R., Feldman, M. and O'Shaunessy, E. (1989) *The Oedipus Complex Today*. London: Karnac Books.

Brockmeier, J. (1997) Autobiography, narrative, and the Freudian conception of life history. *Philosophy, Psychiatry, Psychology*, 4, 189–201.

Bruner, J. (1986) *Actual Minds, Possible Worlds*. Cambridge, MA: Harvard University Press.

Byng-Hall, J. (1995) *Rewriting Family Scripts*. London: Guilford Press.

Campling, P. and Haigh, R. (eds) (1999) *Therapeutic Communities*. London: Sage.

Caper, R. (1999) *A Mind of One's Own*. London: Routledge.

Casement, P. (1985) *On Learning from the Patient*. London: Tavistock.

Cassidy, J. and Shaver, P. (1999) *Handbook of Attachment: Theory, Research and Clinical Applications*. New York: Guilford Press.

Chisholm, J. (1996) The evolutionary ecology of attachment organisation. *Human Nature*, 7, 1–38.

Chomsky, N. (1972) *Language and Mind*. New York: Harcourt Brace.

Conrad, J. (1912/1994) *The Heart of Darkness*. London: Penguin.

Crits-Christoph, P., Cooper, A., and Luborsky, L. (1988) The accuracy of therapists' interpretations and the outcome of dynamic psychotherapy. *Journal of Counselling and Clinical Psychology*, 56, 490–95.

Dawkins, R. (1976) *The Selfish Gene*. Oxford: Oxford University Press.

De Zulueta, F. (1993) *From Pain to Violence*. London: Whurr.

Dickens, C. (1861/1994) *Great Expectations* (edited by M. Cardwell). Oxford: Oxford University Press.

Dismacio, D. (1994) *Descartes Error*. New York: Basic Books.

Dolan, B., Warren, F., Menzies, D. and Norton, K. (1996) Cost-offset following specialised treatment of severe personality disorders. *Psychiatric Bulletin*, 20, 413–17.

Dozier, M., Cue, K and Barnett, L. (1994) Clinicians as caregivers: role of attachment organisation in treatment. *Journal of Consulting and Clinical Psychology*, 62, 793–800.

Eliot, T.S. (1952) *Four Quartets*. London: Faber.

Elkin, I. (1994) The NIMH treatment of depression collaborative research program: where we began and where we are. In S. Gaffield and A. Bergin (eds) *Handbook of Psychotherapy and Behaviour Change*, 4th edn. Chichester: Wiley.

Erikson, E. (1968) *Identity, Youth and Crisis*. New York: Norton.

Fairbairn, W. (1952) *Psychoanalytic Studies of the Personality*. London: Hogarth Press.

Fenichel, O. (1946) *The Psychoanalytic Theory of Neurosis*. London: Routledge.

Ferenczi, S. (1952) *First Contributions to the Theory and Technique of Psycho-analysis*. London: Hogarth Press.

Flint, K. (1994) Introduction. In C. Dickens, *Great Expectations*. London: Penguin.

Fisher-Mamblona, H. (2000) On the evolution of attachment-disordered behaviour. *Attachment and Human Development*, 2, 8–21.

Fitzgerald, F.S. (1926/2000) *The Great Gatsby*. London: Abacus.

Fonagy, P. (1991) Thinking about thinking: some clinical and theoretical considerations in the treatment of a borderline patient. *International Journal of Psychoanalysis*, 72, 639–56.

Fonagy, P. (1997) An attachment theory approach to the treatment of the difficult patient. *Bulletin of the Menninger Clinic*, 62, 147–69.

Fonagy, P (1999a) Psychoanalytic theory from the viewpoint of attachment theory and research. In J. Cassidy and P. Shaver (eds) *Handbook of Attachment*. New York, Guilford Press.

Fonagy, P. (1999b) *An Open Door Review of Outcome Studies in Psychoanalysis*. London: International Psychoanalytic Association.

Fonagy, P. (2001) *Psychoanalysis and Attachment Theory*. London: Karnac.

Fonagy, P., Steele, M., Steele, H., Leigh, T. et al. (1995) Attachment the reflective self, and borderline states: the predictive specificity of the adult attachment interview and pathological emotional development. In S. Goldberg, R. Muir and J. Kerr (eds) *Attachment Theory: Social, Developmental and Clinical Significance*. Hillsdale, NJ: Analytic Press.

Fonagy, P. and Target, M. (1996) Playing with reality. *International Journal of Psychoanalysis*, 77, 217–34.

Fonagy, P. and Target, M. (2000) Playing with reality 11: the persistence of dual psychic reality in borderline personality disorder. *International Journal of Psychoanalysis*, 81, 853–74.

Fraiberg, S., Adelson, E. and Shapiro, V. (1975) Ghosts in the nursery: a psychoanalytic approach to impaired infant–mother relationships. *Journal of the American Academy of Child Psychology*, 14, 387–422.

Freud, A. (1936) *The Ego and the Mechanisms of Defence*. London: Hogarth Press.

Freud, S. (1896) The aetiology of hysteria. In *Standard Edition*, Vol. 3. London: Hogarth Press.

Freud, S. (1911) Formulations on the two principles of mental functioning. In *Standard Edition*, Vol. 12. London: Hogarth Press.

Freud, S. (1913) On beginning the treatment. In *Standard Edition*, Vol. 9. London: Hogarth Press.

Freud, S. (1917) Mourning and melancholia. In *Standard Edition*, Vol. 14. London: Hogarth Press.

Freud, S. (1923) The Ego and the Id. In *Standard Edition*, Vol. 19. London: Hogarth Press.

Freud, S. (1928) Dostoyevsky and Parricide. In *Standard Edition*, Vol. 21. London: Hogarth Press.

Freud, S. (1937b) Constructions in analysis. In *Standard Edition*, Vol. 23. London: Hogarth Press.

Gabbard, G. (1995) Countertransference: the emerging common ground. *International Journal of Psychoanalysis*, 76, 475–86.

Garfield, S. (1994) Research on client variables in psychotherapy. In S. Garfield and A. Bergin (eds) *Handbook of Psychotherapy and Behaviour Change*, 4th edn. Chichester: Wiley.

Garland, C. (ed.) (1998) *Understanding Trauma: A Psychoanalytic Perspective*. London: Butterworth.

Gergely, G. and Watson, J. (1996) The social biofeedback theory of parental affect-mirroring. *International Journal of Psychoanalysis*, 77, 181–212.

Gilbert, P. (1997) The evolution of social attractiveness and its role in shame, humili-ation, guilt and therapy. *British Journal of Medical Psychology*, 70, 113–47.

Greenberg, J. and Mitchell, S. (1983) *Object Relations in Psychoanalytic Theory*. Cambridge, MA: Harvard University Press.

Greene, G. (1955) *The Quiet American*. London: Penguin.

Gunderson, J, and Sabo, A. (1993) The phenomenological and conceptual interface between borderline personality disorder and PTSD. *American Journal of Psych-iatry*, 150, 19–27.

Haynes J, and Wiener, J. (1996) The analyst in the counting house: money as symbol and reality in analysis. *British Journal of Psychotherapy, 13, 14–25*.

Heard, D. and Lake, B. (1986) The attachment dynamic in adult life. *British Journal of Medical Psychology*, 149, 430–38.

Heard, D. and Lake, B. (1997) *The Challenge of Attachment for Care-Giving*. London: Routledge.

Herman, J., Perry, C. and Kolk, B. (1989) Childhood trauma in borderline personal-ity disorder. *American Journal of Psychiatry*, 146, 490–95.

Hesse, E. (1999) The Adult Attachment Interview: historical and current perspec-tives. In J. Cassidy and P. Shaver (eds) *Handbook of Attachment*. London: Guilford Press.

Hobson, P. (1993) *Autism and the Development of Mind*. Hillsdale, NJ: Lawrence Erlbaum Associates Inc.

Hobson, P. and Patrick, M. (1998) Objectivity in psychoanalytic judgement. *British Journal of Psychiatry*, 173, 172–7.

Hofer, M. (1995) Hidden regulators: implications for a new understanding of attachment, separation and loss. In S. Goldberg, R. Muir and J. Kerr (eds) *Attachment Theory: Social, Developmental and Clinical Perspectives. Hillsdale, NJ: Analytic Press*.

Holmes, J. (1992) *Between Art and Science: Essays in Psychiatry and Psychotherapy*. London: Routledge.

Holmes, J. (1993) *John Bowlby and Attachment Theory*. London: Routledge.

Holmes, J. (1996) *Attachment, Intimacy, Autonomy: Using Attachment Theory in Adult Psychotherapy*. Northville, NJ: Jason Aronson.

Holmes, J. (2001) *Narcissism*. London: Icon Books.

Holmes, J. and Lindley, R. (1998) *The Values of Psychotherapy*, 2nd edn. London: Karnac.

Horowitz, M., Marmar, C., Weiss D. (1984) Brief psychotherapy of bereavement reactions: the relation of process to outcome. *Archives of General Psychiatry*, 41, 438–48.

Horvath, A. and Symonds, D. (1991) Relationship between working alliance and outcome in psychotherapy: a meta-anaylsis. *Journal of Counselling Psychology*, 38, 139–49.

Howard, G. (1991) Culture tales: a narrative approach to thinking, cross-cultural psychology and psychotherapy. *American Psychologist*, 46, 187–97.

Howard, K., Kopta, S., Krause, M. and Orlinsky, D. (1986) The dose–effect relationship in psychotherapy. *American Journal of Psychiatry*, 146, 775–8.

Humphrey, N. (1984) *Consciousness Regained*. Oxford: Oxford University Press.

Insel, T. (1997) A neurobiological basis of social attachment. *American Journal of Psychiatry*, 154, 726–35.

James, H. (1890) *Principles of Psychology*. New York: Holt.

Jones, E. (1916) *Papers in Psychoanalysis*. London: Hogarth.

Joyce, A. (1992) Assessing the correspondence of interpretation with the therapist's initial formulation. Paper presented at the *Annual Meeting of the Society for Psychotherapy Research*, Berkeley, CA.

Kipling, R. (1939) *Sixty Poems*. London: Hodder & Stoughton.

Klein, M. (1986) In J. Mitchell (ed.) *The Selected Melanie Klein*. London: Penguin.

Kohon, G. (1986) *The British School of Psychoanalysis: The Independent Tradition*. London: Free Association Books.

Kris, E. (1956) On some vicissitudes of insight in psychoanalysis. *International Journal of Psychoanalysis*, 37, 445–55.

Lacan, J. (1977) *The Four Fundamental Concepts of Psychoanalysis* (translated by A. Sheridon). London: Hogarth.

Lear, J. (1998) *Open Minded: Working Out the Logic of the Soul*. Cambridge, MA. Harvard University Press.

Leavis, F.R. (1975) *The Living Principle*. London: Chatto.

Leiman, M. (1995) Early development. In A. Ryle (ed.) *Cognitive Analytic Therapy: Developments in Theory and Practice*. Chichester: Wiley.

Lindsay, D. and Read, J. (1994) Psychotherapy and memories of childlhood sexual abuse: a cognitive perspective. *Applied Cognitive Psychology*, 8, 281–338.

Lineham, M., Head, H. and Armstrong, H. (1993) Naturalistic follow-up of a behavioural treatment for chronically suicidal borderline patients. *Archives of General Psychiatry*, 50, 971–4.

Llewellyn, S. (1988) Psychological therapy as viewed by clients and therapists. *British Journal of Clinical Psychology*, 27, 223–37.

Loftus, E. (1993) The reality of repressed memories. *American Psychologist*, 48, 518–37.

Luborsky, L. (1984) *Principles of Psychoanalytic Psychotherapy*. New York: Basic Books.

Mahler, M., Pine, F. and Bergman, A. (1975) *The Psychological Birth of the Human Infant*. London: Hutchinson.

Main, M. (1995) Recent studies in attachment: overview with selected implications for clinical work. In S. Goldberg, R. Muir and J. Kerr (eds) *Attachment Theory: Social, Developmental and Clinical Perspectives*. Hillsdale, NJ: Analytic Press.

Main, M. and Goldwyn, S. (1995) Interview based adult attachment classification: related to infant–mother and infant–father attachment. *Developmental Psychology*, 19, 227–39.

Malan, D. (1976) *The Frontier of Brief Psychotherapy*. New York: Plenum Press.

Mallinckrodt, B. (2000) Attachment, social competencies, social support, and interpersonal process in psychotherapy. *Psychotherapy Research*, 10, 239–66.

Margison, F. (2001) Psychodynamic-interpersonal therapy. In J. Holmes and A. Bateman (eds) *Integration in Psychotherapy*. Oxford: Oxford University Press.

Meares, R. (1993) *The Metaphor of Play*. Northville, NJ: Jason Aronson.

Meins, E. (1999) Sensitivity, security and internal working models: bridging the transmission gap.*Attachment and Human Development*, 3, 325–42.

Merten, J. (1996) Emotional experience and facial behaviour during the psychotherapeutic process and its relation to treatment outcome: a pilot study. *Psychotherapy Research*, 6, 198–212.

Mitchell, S. (1998) Attachment theory and the psychoanalytic tradition: reflections on human relationality. *British Journal of Psychotherapy*, 15, 177–93.

Money-Kyrle, R. (1971) The aim of psychoanalysis. In *Collected Papers of Roger Money-Kyrle* (edited by D. Meltzer). Srath Tay, Perthshire: Clunie Press.

Mullen, P., Romans-Clarkson, S., Walton, V. and Herbison, P. (1993) Impact of sexual and physical abuse on women's mental health. *Lancet*, 344, 841–5.

Nesse, R. (1990) The evolutonary functions of repression and the ego defenses. *Journal of the American Academy of Psychoanalysis*, 18, 260–85.

Ogden, T. (1997) *Reverie and Interpretation*. Northville, NJ: Jason Aronson.

Orlinsky, D., Grawe, K. and Parks, B. (1994) Process and outcome in psychotherapy – noch einmal. In A. Bergin and S. Garfield (eds) *Handbook of Psychotherapy and Behaviour Change*. Chichester: Wiley.

Parsons, M. (1986) Suddenly finding it really matters: the paradox of the analyst's non-attachment. *International Journal of Psychoanalysis*, 76, 475–88.

Pedder, J. (1982) Failure to mourn and melancholia. *British Journal of Psychiatry*, 41, 327–37.

Pedder, J. (1988) Termination reconsidered. *International Journal of Psychoanalysis*, 69, 495–505.

Piaget, J. (1954) *The Construction of Reality in the Child*. New York: Basic Books.

Poole, D., Lindsay, D., Memon, A. and Bull, R. (1995) Psychotherapy and the recovery of memories of childhood sexual abuse: US and British practitioners' opinions, practices and experiences. *Journal of Counselling and Clinical Psychology*, 63, 42–57.

Racker, H. (1968) *Transference and Countertransference*. London: Karnac (reprint).

Reik, T. (1922) *The Inner Eye of a Psychoanalyst*. London: Allen & Unwin.

Rilke, R. (1994) Selected Poems. London: Penguin.

Roberts, G. and Holmes, J. (1998) *Healing Stories: Narrative in Psychiatry and Psychotherapy*. Oxford: Oxford University Press.

Rosenblum, P. (1994) Adverse early experiences affect noradrenergic and serotonergic functioning in adult primates. *Biological Psychiatry*, 3, 221–7.

Roth, A. and Fonagy, P. (1996) *What Works for Whom?* London: Guilford Press.

Roth, P. (1969) *Portnoy's Complaint*. London: Cape.

Rycroft, C. (1985) *Psychoanalysis and Beyond*. London: Chatto.

Ryle, A. (1995) *Cognitive Analytic Therapy: Developments in Theory and Practice*. Chichester: Wiley.

Sandler, J. and Sandler A.-M. (1994) The past unconscious, the present unconscious, and interpretations of the transference. *Psychoanalytic Inquiry*, 4, 367–99.

Schacter, D. (1992) Understanding implicit memory: a cognitive neuroscience approach. *American Psychologist*, 47, 559–69.

Schafer, R. (1992) *Retelling a Life: Narration and Dialogue in Psychoanalysis*. New York: Basic Books.

Schank, R. (1982) *Dynamic Memory: A Theory of Reminding and Learning in Computers and People*. Cambridge: Cambridge University Press.

Schore, A. (1997) Neurobiology and psychoanalysis. In M. Moscowitz (ed.) *The Neurobiological and Developmental Basis of Psychotherapeutic Intervention*. Northville, NJ: Jason Aronson.

Segal, H. (1991) *Dream, Phantasy, Art*. London: Routledge.

Shapiro, D. (1995) Finding out how psychotherapies help people change. *Psychotherapy Research*, 5, 1–21.

Slade, A. (1999) Attachment theory and research: implications for the theory and practice of psychotherapy with adults. In J. Cassidy and P. Shaver (eds) *Handbook Of Attachment*. London: Guilford Press.

Slavin, B. and Kriegman, M. (1992) *The Adaptive Design of the Human Psyche*. New York: Academic Press.

Spence, D. (1982) *Narrative Truth and Historical Truth: Meaning and Interpretation in Psychoanalysis*. New York: Norton.

Steiner, J. (1989) The aim of psychoanalysis. *Psychoanalytic Psychotherapy*, 4, 109–20.

Stern, D. (1985) *The Interpersonal World of the Infant*. New York: Basic Books.

Stiles, W., Elliott, R., Llewelyn, S. (1990) Assimilation of problematic experiences by clients in psychotherapy. *Psychotherapy*, 27, 411–20.

Strupp, H. (1993) The Vanderbilt studies: a synopsis. *Journal of Clinical and Counselling Psychology*, 61, 431–3.

Styron, T. and Janoff-Bulman, R. (1997) Childhood attachment and abuse: long-term effects on adult attachment, depression and conflict resolution. *Child Abuse and Neglect*, 21, 1015–23.

Symington, N. and Symington, J. (1996) *The Clinical Thinking of Wilfred Bion*. London: Routledge.

Teasdale, J. (1999) Functional MRI study of the cognitive generation of affect. *American Journal of Psychiatry*, 156, 209–15.

Teasdale, J., Segal. Z., and Williams, M. (1995) How does cognitive therapy prevent depressive relapse and why should attentional control (mindfulness) training help? *Behavioural Research and Therapy*, 33, 25–39.

Trevarthen, C. (1984). Emotions in infancy. In K. Scherer and P. Ekman (eds) *Approaches to Emotion*. Hillsdale NJ: Lawrence Erlbaum Associates Inc.

Tulving, E. (1985) How many memory systems are there? *American Psychologist*, 40, 385–98.

Valliant, G. (1993) *The Wisdom of the Ego*. Cambridge, MA: Harvard University Press.

Van de Kolk, B. and Fisler, R. (1996) Dissociation and the fragmentary nature of traumatic memories: overview. *British Journal of Psychotherapy*, 12, 352–61.

Van Ijzendoorm, M. and Sagi, A. (1999) Cross-cultural patterns of attachment: universal and contextual dimensions. In J. Cassidy and P. Shaver (eds) *Handbook of Attachment*. London: Guilford Press.

Viinnamaki, H. (1998) Change in monoamine transported density related to clinical recovery. *Nordic Journal of Psychiatry*, 52, 39–44.

Vygostsky, L. (1962) *Thought and Language*. Cambridge, MA: MIT Press.

Vygostky, L. (1978) *Mind in Society: The Development of Higher Psychological Processes*. Cambridge, MA: Harvard University Press.

Wallerstein, R. (1986) *Forty-two Lives in Treatment: A Study of Psychoanalysis and Psychotherapy*. New York: Guilford Press.

Wallerstein, R. (1992) *The Common Ground of Psychoanalysis*. Northville, NJ: Jason Aronson.

White, M. and Epston D. (1990) *Narrative Means to Therapeutic Ends*. New York: Norton.

Williams, M. and Wadell, M. (1991) *The Chamber of Maiden Thought*. London: Routledge.

Winnicott, D. (1958) The capacity to be alone. *International Journal of Psychoanalysis*, 39, 416–20.

Winnicott, D. (1965) *The Maturational Processes and the Facilitating Environment*. London: Hogarth Press.

Winnicott, D. (1967) Mirror-role of mother and family in child development. In P. Lomas (ed.) *The Predicament of the Family*. London: Hogarth Press.

Winnicott, D. (1971) *Playing and Reality*. London: Penguin.

Wolff, H. (1971) The therapeutic and developmental functions of psychotherapy. *British Journal of Medical Psychology*, 44, 117–30.

Index